Brian McGrath

DIGITAL MODELLING

FOR URBAN DESIGN

A John Wiley and Sons, Ltd, Publication

Published in Great Britain in 2008 by John Wiley & Sons Ltd

Copyright © 2008
John Wiley & Sons Ltd, The Atrium, Southern Gate, Chichester,
West Sussex PO19 8SQ, England
Telephone +44 (0)1243 779777

Email (for orders and customer service enquiries): cs-books@wiley.co.uk
Visit our Home Page on www.wiley.com

Other Wiley Editorial Offices

John Wiley & Sons Inc., 111 River Street, Hoboken, NJ 07030, USA

Jossey-Bass, 989 Market Street, San Francisco, CA 94103-1741, USA

Wiley-VCH Verlag GmbH, Boschstr. 12, D-69469 Weinheim, Germany

John Wiley & Sons Australia Ltd, 42 McDougall Street, Milton, Queensland
4064, Australia

John Wiley & Sons (Asia) Pte Ltd, 2 Clementi Loop #02-01, Jin Xing
Distripark, Singapore 129809

John Wiley & Sons Canada Ltd, 5353 Dundas Street West, Suite 400,
Etobicoke, Ontario M9B 6H8, Canada

Wiley also publishes its books in a variety of electronic formats. Some
content that appears in print may not be available in electronic books.

Executive Commissioning Editor: Helen Castle
Project Editor: Miriam Swift
Publishing Assistant: Calver Lezama

ISBN   978-0-470-03477-4 (hb)
        978-0-470-03478-1 (pb)

Cover design and layouts by Artmedia Press Ltd, UK

Printed and bound by Printer Trento, Italy

For John and Theresa McGrath: your stability provided the centre of gravity for my urban circumambulations.

Digital Modelling for Urban Design

With all the comforts of a shopping mall, escalators glide visitors up to the top floor of the Beijing Planning Exhibition Hall along a huge, wall-hung cast bronze model of Old Beijing. The Ming Dynasty Imperial City was substantially intact in the model shown, which depicts the city in 1949, the year the People's Republic of China was founded. On the third floor of the museum you can walk over a giant bottom-lit satellite photograph of the present-day city – as if you could pass through your computer screen and walk on the surface of Google Earth. Physical models represent the city's Master Plan for the Olympic City south to the Forbidden City and east to the Central Business District and Chaoyang Park. The model gives visitors a taste of the modern architectural and urban design spectacle that Beijing has broadcast to the world for the 2008 Olympics. Arriving at the top floor, visitors are ushered into a small theatre, where they are given special 3-D vision glasses and strap themselves into moving seats. The lights dim and the audience begins a simulation fly-through of the city of the future. Moving seats sway during the computer-generated animation above an ascendant future Beijing, reclaiming its position as the centre of the world.

National September 11 Museum Pavilion exterior with salvaged World Trade Center tridents. Image created by Squared Design Lab, provided by National September 11 Memorial & Museum.

12   The latest in digital imaging and 3-D modelling technology is likewise on display for anyone browsing the fundraising website of the National September 11 Memorial and Museum.[1] Sunlight dapples through a forest canopy. The oak leaves in the foreground dissolve to reveal the corner of a two-tiered square waterfall cascading first into a reflecting pool before disappearing below the ground. The camera tilts down then dissolves into an aerial view of the site, a forest grove with two giant pools of water. It spins around before focusing on a tracking close-up at ground level which points towards a glass building through the forest grove. Another dissolve, and the virtual camera ascends from within the glass pavilion while looking down along two tall structural columns from Minoru Yamasaki's destroyed towers. The camera flips its perspective and now spins, looking up the remnant artefacts. Two structural columns – elements from Yamasaki's destroyed towers – can be seen through the glass walls of the Museum entry pavilion. Another dissolve and suddenly it is September again and the trees have turned shades of russet, orange and yellow. The camera glides along the tree tops in the plaza scored with grassy strips. Another dissolve, the trees are green again as we zoom out and up away from one of the signature reflecting pools.

14 Spectacular digitally animated fly-throughs tied to websites or physical experiences are the common currency of 21st-century globalisation and urbanisation. Any development from Dubai to São Paulo requires the virtual magic-carpet ride – one that never quite rests or touches ground in the city. Instead of communicating the city as the site of contest and struggles for social justice and difference, urban design and its projective representations is currently a regime of high-cost, fast-moving, complex opaque simulations of a glittery, seamless modern world. It seems that no physical design project can exist without a complementary digital representation, instructing people on how to experience it. Meanwhile, these spectacular representations mask the dirty digital sweatshop work of urban design practice. Digital designers must contend with layers and layers of existing geotechnical, utility, infrastructural and legal information as well as files from environmental, engineering, parking, structural, mechanical, marketing, landscape and architectural consultants. All these layers of spatial data are compiled on Computer Aided Design (CAD) and Geographic Information System (GIS) files which, when superimposed, look as confusing and complex as Heinrich Schliemann's successive layers of ancient Troy.

Digital Modelling for Urban Design unmasks the spectacular surfaces of virtual reality to redirect the power of computer-generated modelling towards exploring the environmental, social and psychological complexity of urban design practice today. This book advocates a more complex, interactive, reiterative and collaborative urban informational feedback system for urban design practice aided by the use of digital technologies. The techniques introduced in this book reclaim urban design as a collective and contested enterprise, where the city is continually remade by a diverse array of urban actors and agents. Cities are dynamic assemblages of psycho-socio-natural patches and polyvocal cultural arenas. Urban design information and communication is being claimed by an increasingly diverse array of urban actors, while current modes of professional representation, both spectacular and bureaucratic, remain overly opaque and authoritative. YouTube, Google Earth, 3D Warehouse and SketchUp, utilising inferior production values than the professional simulators, engage countless digital modellers and video makers in the task of discussing and representing the world's villages, neighbourhoods, institutions, public spaces and cities. This claim on urban design practice through new popular modes of digital communication is not just the creation of public forms of information, mediation and representation, but a mobilisation of a new reflexive, responsive and resilient urban public sphere itself.

This book develops its argument through examples drawn from the rich urban design contexts of Rome, New York and Bangkok. In modelling Rome I analyse Rodolfo Lanciani and Giovanni Battista Piranesi's critical representations of the city as an arena for multiple narratives rather than a uniform representation of political authority. In modelling New York, I examine the changing role of urban design in the face of the dispersion of power among the multiple actors who form the bureaucratic capitalist city. In modelling Bangkok, I focus is on the role of popular media and consumer culture in shaping both urban space and the contemporary imagination in an era of globalisation. Through these examples I argue that shifts, disruptions and disjunctions between the agents producing and exerting forces to shape the city – whether over centuries in Rome, decades in New York, or in the rapid cycles of fashion in Bangkok – create rich, intricate and diverse urban forms. Digital modelling can assist in the collective engagement of a much more diverse range of actors and agents in the production of urban design experiments within circuited feedback loops is essential in confronting the pressing social and environmental issues we all face today.

Flattening Urban Design

Digital Modelling for Urban Design is directed to a wide audience of students, architects, designers, planners and citizen designers – anyone wishing to be involved in the complex decision-making processes in shaping the urban environment. This book, therefore, develops the use of digital technologies as a tool of public advocacy and the creation of collective forms of urban knowledge. Digital modelling can expand urban design practice to an informational and communication as well as a representational system. The aspects of digital modelling promoted, therefore, are not the technical aspects of software, programming or scripting, but rather the broad and accessible array of popular digital technologies. Thomas L Friedman celebrates events such as the widespread use of personal computers, the introduction of web browsers, workflow software, open-sourcing, outsourcing, offshoring, supply chaining, insourcing, informing, and a new generation of digital, mobile, personal and virtual technologies. Open-source and interconnected digital technology 'flattens the playing field' and offers the opportunity for a much wider array of actors to engage in the challenges and benefits of globalisation and urbanisation.[2]

More radically, hacker digital culture promotes 'mash-ups' – 'recombinant methods in the various forms of combining, sampling, pangender performance, bricolage, detournement, ready-mades, appropriation, plagiarism, theater of everyday life, constellation, and so on ... an ongoing task for those who hope to see the decline of authoritarian culture'.[3] The digital circulation of information, images and ideas about and for the city constitutes a virtual public realm which can continually produce new urban design models for rethinking, recreating and re-inhabiting the physical environment of cities. Feedback loops are tightened in such a networked context, enhancing the reflective and reflexive in addition to the productive aspects of design. Popular forms of digital modelling have the potential to widen access to power and knowledge in order to activate rather than pacify the public who constitute the primary audience for these new forms of representational production.

Modelling Discourse

If we are to consider digital tools in such broad terms, we must also expand our notion of urban design modelling as an activity which can assist in filtering some of the noise which the word 'feedback' also implies. Designers, scientists and policy makers all construct urban models but the definition of 'modelling' differs sharply between disciplines. Designers use the term to refer to a 3-D miniature, this year's new car, a person who shows off new clothes. A scientist's model is a quantitative demonstration of a theory of how something functions. For policy makers a model is a picture of how the environment *ought* to be made, a proscription of a 'good' form or a 'fair' process which is a prototype to follow. According to Kevin Lynch, the visualisation of urban design through models creates a mental structure, a collective philosophical and psychological image shared by city inhabitants. Lynch's primary concern is for 'good urban form' and urban design models, as public policy is of primary importance for him. Design decisions should be based on 'models' collectively understood and on normative values of good and bad.[4]

Lynch uses the Baroque city's axial network as an example of a 'good' urban design model: symbolic landmarks are located at commanding points in the terrain, connected by major streets with controlled unified facades or bordering landscapes. Strong visual effects form the groundwork for public symbolism and create a *memorable* general structure without imposing control on every part and without requiring an unattainable level of capital investment. The Baroque city *achieves sensibility* within an economy of means.[5] But the Baroque city is also a strategy for the application of centralised power in urban space. Lynch himself argues that Baroque's ideal order dominates nature, masks difference and is inflexible to dynamic change.[6] The Master Plan as an urban design practice will be traced to Baroque Rome beginning in Chapter 2.

Radial street network of
Baroque Rome situated
between the medieval city at
the bend of the Tiber River
and the scattered Christian
basilicas built over the ruins of
the ancient city. Layered ink
drawing on Mylar from
Transparent Cities, 1994.

Lynch also finds deficiencies in the stock of the urban models of his time: little is said about workplace, marginal spaces, wastelands, fringe areas, transition spaces, vacant lands, dead storage areas and underutilised places. Street traffic is prioritised, but flows, conservation and management of material and energy sources or information cannot easily be dealt with. Sensory models are not openly specified.[7] Baroque, Enlightenment and Modernist urban design models refer only to a completed form, giving no account of the process by which the form is achieved, and ignoring the reality of continuous change. They exclude media, mobility, migration, adaptation, temporary uses and transitional as well as emergent forms of social life. For Lynch, a useful model is one where the situation is stated, performance is specified and reasoning laid bare, fully open to political correction.[8] In Chapter 4, a genealogy of New York's central business districts will be traced in order to understand the emergence of urban design as a method of political correction which utilises zoning to shape real estate development.

18

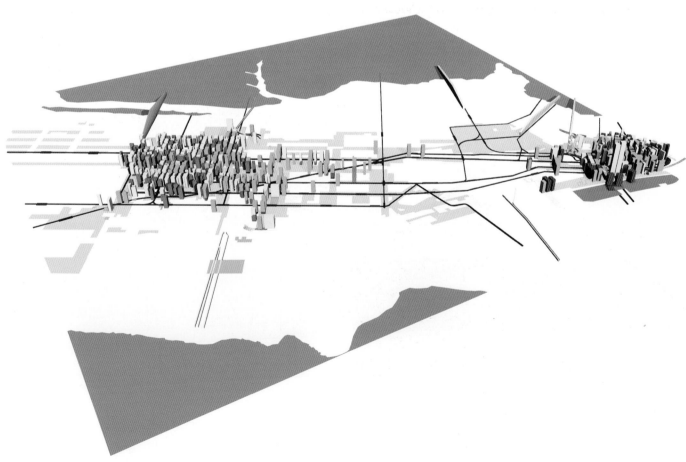

Lynch's vantage point was contained within the late-20th-century American bureaucratisation of urban design practice where computers were just beginning to have an impact on design processes.[9] Twenty-five years later, his critique is even more evident with the emergent potential and flattened world of new digital technologies. Globalisation and digitisation have greatly increased the need for dynamic, transparent, continually changing urban design models, yet modelling remains in the hands of specialist designers, scientists and policy makers. This book broadens the historical and geographical context of urban design modelling to give an expanded view of modelling for urban design. Instead of outlining normative models of how a city ought to be made by specialists, this book promotes the open-ended possibilities of a digital world of wikis, blogs, online social networks, Facebook, MySpace, Flickr, and free 3-D modelling software such as SketchUp, which are assisting the dissemination of information and technologies for re-imagining as well as remaking the global city and our place in it. The future of urban design in a context of 'lifestyle' and consumer preferences will be explored in the central shopping district of Bangkok in Chapter 6.

Detail of digital model of Bangkok's central shopping district showing the concentration of new and refurbished malls connected to the elevated Skytrain, Chulalongkorn University Faculty of Architecture, 2007.

19

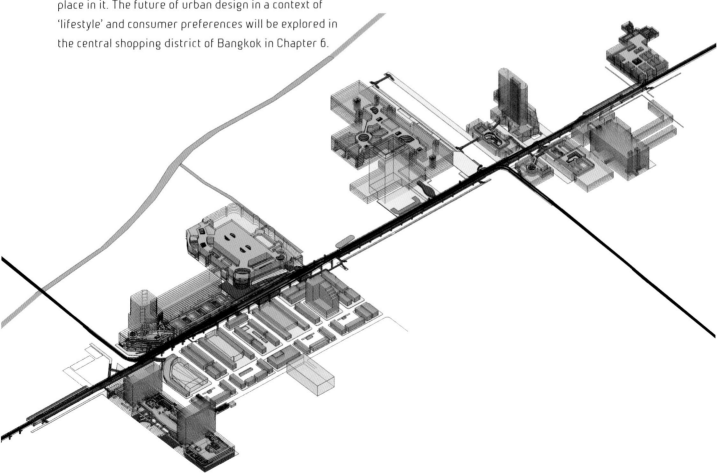

Development of the Book

Digital Modelling for Urban Design is based on over two decades of research, practice and teaching in architecture and urban design, but also draws from living and working in the three cities which comprise the examples in this book. Analytical discussions of Rome, New York and Bangkok situate historical speculation and abstract knowledge with reflections on empirical experience and real world measurement. This book, therefore, is both theoretical and practical, interspersing critical discussions linked to the writings of Michel Foucault, Gilles Deleuze, Félix Guattari, Aldo Rossi, Grahame Shane, Denise Scott Brown and Robert Venturi, with intimate knowledge of the three cities I know best. The examples, therefore, are grounded in my own bodily experience of everyday life in these three cities over time.

Living in Rome and New York between 1985 and 1995, I created an *archaeology* of urban design models by developing a comparative archive of historical information on both cities.[10] In New York and Bangkok between 1995 and 2005, I developed a *genealogy* of the transition of urban design from a bureaucratic to a marketing discipline by comparing the development of Manhattan's business districts and Bangkok's shopping centres over time. *Manhattan Timeformations*[11] is a genealogical digital model that has captured a wide international audience since it was first broadcast on a website in 2000, marking a moment of great optimism about globalisation, digital technologies and urban design. Living in both New York and Bangkok, I have been able to track the ideological and economic dynamics of globalisation, from opposite points on the planet. The digital model I developed with faculty and students at Chulalongkorn University over this time constitutes a *schizoanalysis* of four decades of the development of Bangkok's central shopping district, and comprises the last case study for the book.[12]

Arjun Appadurai has pointed out that the initial promise of globalisation to create new resources for human imagination and social practices through the twin forces of media and migration also produced new forms of hatred, ethnocide and ideocide.[13] It is, however, in Appadurai's spirit of 'grassroots globalisation': the worldwide effort of activist non-governmental organisations and movements to seize and shape the global agenda on such matters as human rights, gender, poverty, environment and disease, and to seek ways to make globalisation work for those who need it most and enjoy it least – the poor, the dispossessed, the weak, and the marginal populations of our world. The conclusion, written following two recent residencies in India and China as a research fellow with the New School's India China Institute, attempts to direct the lessons from these two decades of research in Rome, New York and Bangkok towards the urban future of India and China.[14]

Urban design, therefore, is presented here within transhistorical, transcultural and transdisciplinary contexts in order to position digital modelling as the act of creating moving, interactive, four-dimensional communication systems situated within the histories of theory, design and representation. Certainly such an expansion of the representational and informational capacities of digital modelling will result in even more spectacular urban design simulations from contact with a wider range of source material and constituencies. Two clear departures from contemporary practice – questioning who makes the city and who makes the images of the city – both call for a new public realm constituted by open and transparent forms of design and representation. The spectacle of urban design and representation can be one in which a broad array of actors advocate and participate in the making of both the city and its images rather than constituting an audience passively consuming urban simulations constructed by specialists.

Organisation of the Book

The introductory chapter of *Digital Modelling for Urban Design* presents a close analysis of the way digital modelling participated in the public debate around the redesign of Ground Zero in New York. The Innovative Design Study for rebuilding Lower Manhattan's World Trade Center was a mass media event that revealed many dilemmas and opportunities for urban design when it is *spectacularised* through digital modelling and communication technologies. Following the Introduction, the book is structured around three pairs of chapters which each present a methodological approach to digital modelling for urban design, coupled with a particular case study. Part I introduces archaeological modelling for urban design followed by a digital analysis of the Roman Forum. Part II presents genealogical modelling for urban design through the example of Manhattan's skyscraper business districts' formation over time. Finally, Part III concludes with a discussion of schizoanalytical modelling for urban design, followed by an analysis of the experience of Bangkok's central shopping district. These three sections outline a critical framework in order to question the society of the spectacle within which digital simulation for urban design is currently trapped.[15] This is not an argument against the long relationship between city life and spectacle – in fact, Rome, New York and Bangkok are among the world's most spectacular cities. Rather, it highlights the passivity of the *society of the spectacle* as only consumers rather than producers of urban design representations.

The three book sections comparatively model archaeological archives, genealogical timelines and schizoanalytical diagrams. *Archaeological Modelling for Urban Design* will lead to a discussion of historically situated urban *embeddedness*. Political, ecological and social patterns of an urban site will be examined as processes operating at various scales nested and layered within the specific terrain and events of an urban site.

Genealogical Modelling for Urban Design will question singular urban subjectivity and authorship through a process of unlocking the genetic code and links between social practices, institutions and forms over time. The study of urban morphogenesis examines the evolutionary recombination of forces which create urban form.[16] Finally, *Schizoanalytical Modelling for Urban Design* will question urban representation and identity as a singular truth in a globalising world of multiple disjunctive flows. Mediated images experienced by a mobile society suggest that the 'reality' or 'truth' of a particular locality must be continually interrogated and re-imagined through circuits of attention, memory and reflection. Digital modelling will examine the construction of recombinant urban identities as well as urban designs, where momentary constellations of fragments join to create space, events and shifting life worlds.

Archaeology and War

Chapter 1 begins with an *archaeology* of urban design in the sense the word is used by Michel Foucault,[17] exposing urban design as a discipline continually re-imagined within the ruptures in historical formations of knowledge. Urban design in Rome, New York and Bangkok will be compared through changing social discourse, visual representations and urban artefacts. *Archaeological Modelling for Urban Design* compares layered digital models of all three cities across time. Urban design modelling and representations are historical discourses and disciplines that will be situated through the comparison of the transformation of urban design practice as it moves through different places, cultures, as well as through political and economic systems. Comparative digital modelling reveals the particular ruptures in the formation of urban strata due to new paradigms, discourse and forms of representations.

Archaeological modelling unpacks urban embeddedness in three ways:

(1) Unbounding an urban site: an urban boundary establishes a closed set of relations within and outside the limits of a site. All sites are framed by physical enclosures, legal restrictions, political boundaries and property relations. We directly experience the world in small fragments and assume the accuracy of the representations of that which lies outside our field of action. Archaeology therefore is a critical act by the designer in unbounding an urban site by establishing new sets of relationships beyond normative conceptions and perceptions of site limits.

(2) Delayering: urban complexity is unpacked through a process of modelling various attributes and elements of the city as separate layers of information. This process enables the isolation and investigation of the *relationships* between urban elements and perceptions, as well as data from various disciplines – environmental, social, economic, etc. While Geographic Information System (GIS) ties urban mapping to data sets, delayering urban models is a three-dimensional operation of uncovering the disruptive practices in various strata of urban sites as materially constructed over time.

(3) Rescaling: techniques are introduced to move between various scales and levels of organisation in the design process. Digital modelling programs allow the designer to *zoom in and out* in order to engage work at several scales simultaneously: global economic and migration patterns, regional landscapes and infrastructures, district enclaves of blocks and streets, local pockets of lived spaces, and the scalelessness of the imagination.

Chapter 2, *War*, traces some of the earliest models of urban design practice and representation, focusing on how the Roman Forum was developed to display the spoils of war. Following Aldo Rossi,[18] the chapter begins with a detailed discussion of a singular urban artefact – the Roman Forum – its development over time, and how it is understood and mediated as an urban artefact through various forms of representation and experience.

This chapter examines the science of archaeology itself as a politicised urban design act, often partnered with acts of territorial aggression. Archaeology shaped the city's relation to historical knowledge, becoming an instrument of legitimising authority and power through association with Imperial Rome. The Forum, before archaeologists carved this massive void in the centre of the city, was for centuries a peaceful cow pasture on top of what became a municipal dump, after garbage collection ended with the termination of Imperial order and services. Renaissance cardinals, popes and architects essentially regenerated a 'brownfield' when one of the world's first botanical gardens and an urban 'allée' of trees were planted above and on the Forum, which today is a huge void in the centre of the city.

Genealogy and Trade

Chapter 3 turns to modelling the development of urban design as a bureaucratic discipline which develops codes and rules for shaping, hybridising and transforming urban space over time. *Genealogical Modelling for Urban Design* will diagram timelines of churches in Rome, skyscrapers in New York and shopping centres in Bangkok to understand how social actors transform neighbourhoods, institutions and public space over time. Grahame Shane's *Recombinant Urbanism* provides an urban design theory to assist in understanding the genealogy of urban design as hybridisation of urban enclaves, armatures and heterotopias.[19] Genealogical modelling can trace both the descent of top-down urban authority and legitimacy and the emergence of bottom-up forms of urban life. Genealogy is based on the premise that historical institutions and other features of social organisation evolve not smoothly and uniformly, gradually developing their potential through time, but *discontinuously*, and must be understood in terms of difference rather than continuity. New social formations appropriate and abruptly reconfigure older institutions or revive various features of extant urban models by selectively recombining them to suit their own purposes.[20]

Archaeological layered model
of Rome showing the growth
of the Forum over time, 2008.

23

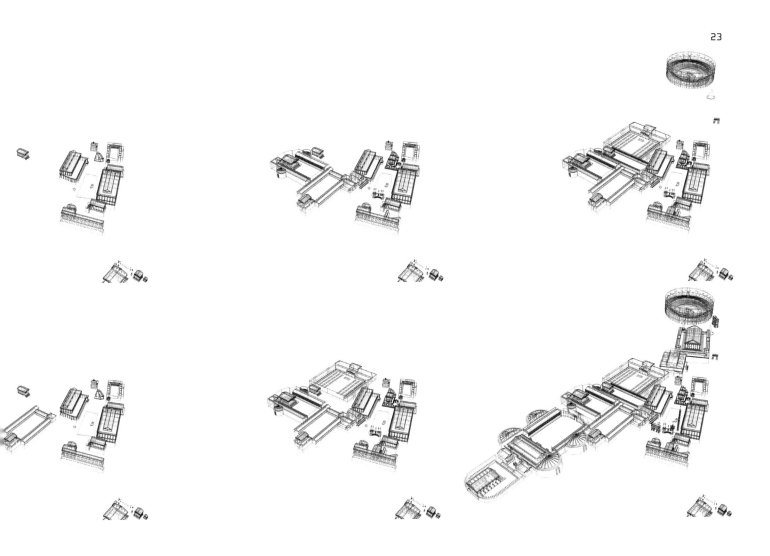

In order to explore genealogical modelling, the uniformity and singularity of urban simulation can be countered in three ways:

(1) Repositioning points of view: the standard fly-through or walk-through view is replaced by the deployment of multiple vantage points of urban data. Toggling between layered plans, multiple elevations, axonometrics and perspectives repositions the designer *within* and *without* the designed site from *various points of view*. This process considers modes of representation which can accommodate and engage various positions and interpretations rather than uniform narratives.

(2) Giving time a dimension: timelines allow for the analysis of 'family trees' of genetic descent or the creation of emergent forms through cross-fertilisation and hybridisation. The creative and destructive forces of various urban actors and agents can be traced and cross-referenced in time and space. Formal patterns and social behaviour can be diagrammed as swarms, clusters or absences in space and time.

(3) Polyvocalities: computer networking eases the integration of collaborative work. Designers work individually on local probes of larger-scale urban assemblages, which are derived through group affinities, rather than the Master Plan or a single vision. The *cut and paste* abilities of computer software allow for individual projects to be layered and juxtaposed, easing the collaborative process. Group identity is also questioned since affinities are partial and limited. Also interdisciplinary collaborations can be created by importing spatialised data from planning, preservation, real estate and the social sciences.

Chapter 4, *Trade*, describes how urban design developed the abstract coding of the city through establishing specialised business enclaves controlled through zoning incentives during the 20th century in New York – a city based on trade and finance. An online digitally modelled timeline of the development of high-rise office districts in Manhattan is presented as a genealogy of urban design in the context of the 20th-century capitalist city. Urban design was institutionalised as a modern discipline in New York after the Second World War, and the form of the city became altered by zoning codes and the creation of special districts and development incentives in concert with the changing shape of financial capitalism itself. While an archaeological approach literally digs deep down into a specific site in order to uncover the successive layers of historical strata, a genealogy, like tracing a family tree, moves in tangential lines both backward and forward in order to understand the interrelation between genetic legacy and specific features of current and future development.

Schizoanalysis and Desire

Chapter 5 utilises the methodology of *schizoanalysis* as developed by Gilles Deleuze and Félix Guattari to understand the move of urban design practice from a bureaucratic discipline to one of marketing and branding urban space in concert with consumer preferences and desires.[21] *Schizoanalytical Modelling for Urban Design* will re-examine the experience of the Forum in Rome, Ground Zero in New York and Bangkok's central shopping district as both the production of local urban artefacts and the recoding of urban imaginations and identities in a globalising world of disjunctive flows. While *archaeology* presents a methodology of layering urban models, and *genealogy* presents an analytical approach of diagramming patterns of urban processes over time, *schizoanalysis* examines the multiplicity of urban experiences in cross-sectional perspectives where one can observe simultaneously the production of symbolic space and its reception by individual sensorial perceptions. By modelling layered urban space in *moving* drawings, the urban designer is able to model not only the space of representation, the glittering surfaces of the global city, but also the representation of space, how urban space is appropriated, adapted and reformed. Much like a wall section reveals the constructional aspects of a building, the schizoanalytical urban section reveals how the global staging of the urban spectacle is constructed, perceived and imagined.

Genealogical model of
Manhattan's high-rise
business districts looking west.
The z-axis is a timeline from the
1890s to the 1990s.

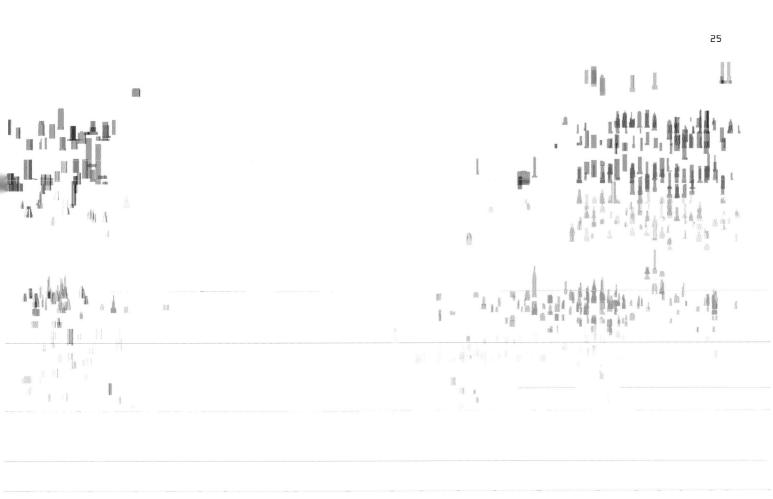

Schizoanalysis challenges singular subjectivity and truth in three ways:

(1) Seeing and saying: some urban sites and many urban relationships are imperceptible to the eye and urban experience is indescribable in both words and representations. Like the camera's expansion of the optical capacity of the human eye, the ability to render in wire-frames, transparencies and translucencies allows the designer to adjust according to new optical information: physical relationships between inside and outside, under and over. Cinema language, as described by Deleuze, can create 'thought images' through the interrelationship between movement, effect, sound, image and time.

(2) Connecting signifying areas: schizoanalysis operates in social, cultural, political, artistic and scientific contexts. It contains the spatial analysis of how demographic, economic or environmental information can be read or perceived in urban space. However, it is fundamentally a meta-modelling technique that transcends single disciplinary lenses.

(3) Aberrant movement and synchronic time: computer multimedia and modelling programs map the city in time – historically (the past), experientially (the present), and possibly (the future). Animations examine historical development, documenting and simulating street-level urban experience, and creating time-based scenarios for imagining the future of the city. New relationships will be discovered through reversals, speeding up and slowing down. Aberrant movements and non-linear time images are preferred methods rather than simulating 'natural' perception through hyper-real simulations and walk-throughs.

Chapter 6, *Desire*, looks in greater detail at the emergence of the hyper-complex shopping district surrounding a royal palace, a Buddhist monastery complex and a canal-side Muslim settlement in the heart of Bangkok. While archaeological and genealogical modelling reveals the transformation of the city over time in relation to site and programme, schizoanalytical modelling examines the human imagination in relation to the conflicting forces of localisation and globalisation. A theory of *simultopia* will be introduced to refer both to the theories of *simulation* and the *simulacra* of Jean Baudrillard,[22] but also to the *simultaneity* of forces embedded in locality and desires projected forward to experimentation, imagination and the always new. Denise Scott Brown, Robert Venturi and Steven Izenour analysed the experience of American pop culture, consumerism and the iconography of the Las Vegas strip at the different speeds and scales of the pedestrian and the car.[23] Their work will help us to look at the emergence of Bangkok's central shopping district as an urban assemblage in relation to three references: the production of the connective architecture of urban armatures, the recoding of the disjunctive architecture of enclaves and the consumption of the conjunctive architecture of heterotopias.[24]

Schizoanalytical model as a
sectional cut through
Bangkok's central shopping
district showing the
connections between
parking, interior atria and the
mezzanine of the elevated
Skytrain over Pathumwan
Intersection.

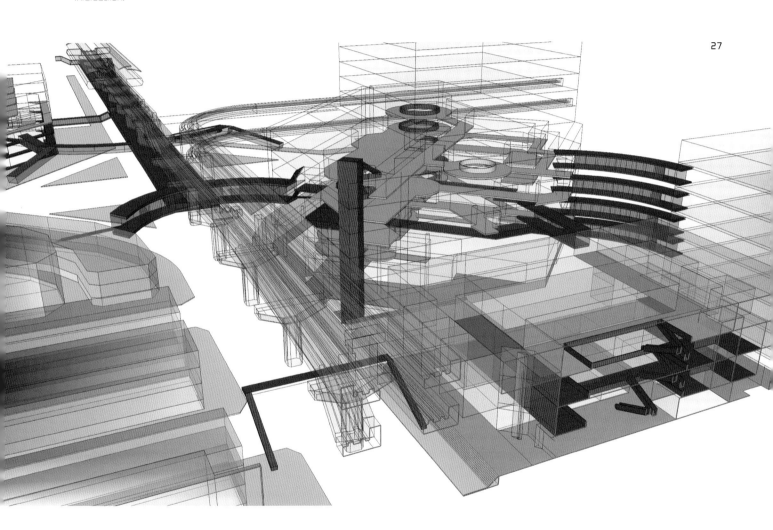

28 Possible Urban Futures

War, trade and desire encapsulate the conflicting architectures of contemporary globalisation. The identity of urban life as the production of difference is more and more challenged by recent events. In the US, discourses on 'Homeland' and the 'War on Terror' have initiated a restructuring of cities from heterogeneous places based on the production of difference: '... boundless mobility and assimilation and a national "melting pot" identity'[25] to homogenous constructions of "homeland"'.[26] At the same time, Orientalist constructions of 'foreign terror cities' are dehumanised by remote imagery and the news media. The tremendous allocation of resources to promote and conduct these two arenas of warfare has left us vulnerable and ill equipped to engage the enormous restructuring of urban space in order to address the social challenges unleashed by unparalleled circulation of media and migrations and the enormous challenges of global climate change.

New urban design practices aided by digital technologies must directly address the rhetoric and ideology behind this interlinked web of social, political and ecological problems. Digital modelling for urban design can play a crucial role in creating and providing the design tools to reverse the trend in the current imagination away from a permanent threatscape and towards a space of collective opportunities for change. Crucial in unpacking the mediated rhetoric which constitutes the current geo-political context is to question the urban fly-through simulations, GIS and surveillance technologies in order to construct counter representations of cities and environments. Reversing the homogenising project of 'Homeland' requires tools for understanding urban spatial heterogeneity and city life as difference rather than unity and order; disjunctive flows and processes rather than unifying form in an abstract sense; logics of resilience and adaptation in temporal contexts of unpredictable flux; and finally, a full engagement in a broad spectrum of social actors and agents towards facing rather than fortifying against perceived challenges and threats.

Finally, in conclusion, the book looks forward at the two radically different urban futures of India and China. These historically rich, geographically vast and rapidly urbanising countries will dominate the 21st century, and the final chapter of this book argues how digital modelling for urban design using archaeological, genealogical and schizoanalytical approaches can help us to situate the future of urban design practice globally. Here, Arjun Appadurai's concept of the cultural dimensions of globalisation as constructed within a context of disjunctive flows will frame a brief outline of my experience as part of collaborative residencies in both countries with the New School's India China Institute.[27] The transcultural and transdisciplinary collaborations in India and China and the trilateral discussion on urbanisation and globalisation between Fellows from the US, India and China provide the basis for furthering the tools developed in this book by applying them towards the production of difference rather than the homogenisation of urban space.

New construction along the
ancient Grand Canal in
Hangzhou, China.

30 **Acknowledgements**

This book would not have been possible without the continued support of Helen Castle, Commissioning Editor at John Wiley & Sons in London. The pedagogical thinking in this book was begun at Parsons, the New School of Design, Department of Architecture, initially under Susana Torre, Department Chair, but was more fully developed in a course called *Digital Modeling for Urban Design* taught both in the Masters of Science and Urban Design Program at Columbia University's Graduate School of Architecture, Planning and Preservation under the direction of Richard Plunz, and in the Masters of Urban Design Program at Chulalongkorn University in Bangkok, directed by Banasopit Mekvichai. In urban design practice I wish to thank Mark Watkins of urban-interface, LLC, and Victoria Marshall and Mateo Pintó of Till, LLC, as well as Steward Pickett and Mary Cadenasso from the Baltimore Ecosystem Study and Morgan Grove and Erika Svendsen from the US Forest Service and the National Science Foundation Long Term Ecological Research Program.

Research in Bangkok was initially supported by the Fulbright Senior Scholars Program at the US State Department. My work there has been long supported by three successive Deans at Chulalongkorn University Faculty of Architecture: Vira Sachakul, Lersom Sthapitanonda and Bundit Chulasai. I am especially grateful to Professor Naengnoi Suksri for patiently describing the physical historical development of Bangkok over the course of many weeks and for poring over old maps, and to Pinraj Khanjanusthiti who, as Deputy Dean of International Affairs, first secured access to the National Archives and Royal Army Survey offices. Former Director of Architecture, Bundit Chulasai supported the construction of the digital model of the Bangkok central shopping district illustrated here, in a course co-taught with Mark Isarangkun na Ayuthaya, Terdsak Tachakitkachorn and Kaweekrai Srihiran. The model was created by Chaiyot Jitekviroj, Kobboon Chulajarit, Krittin Vijittraitham, Nara Pongpanich, Pornsiri Saiduang, Ratchawan Panyasong and Yuttapoom Powjindom. Additionally Pirasri Povatong and Danai Thaitakoo have consistently contributed helpful insights and support in Bangkok.

The overview of the current urban development in India and China in the concluding chapter was made possible by a Faculty Research Fellowship at the New School's India China Institute (ICI). I wish to thank the Senior Advisors of ICI, Ben Lee and Arjun Appadurai, whose vision is behind this institute, as well as the support of ICI's Senior Director, Ashok Gurung, and the first cohort of Fellows from India and China, Amita Bhide, Hiren Doshi, Chakrapani Ghanta, Partha Mukhopadhyay, Aromar Revi, Wu Xiaobo, Yao Yang, Guo Yukuan, Wen Zongyong, and Yang Zuojun as well as New School faculty Jonathan Bach, Vyjayanthi Rao, and Colleen Macklin. Anita Patil-Deshmukh, ICI Senior Advisor and Representative in India, and Jianying Zha, ICI Senior Advisor and Representative in China, were wonderful hosts in each country. Victoria Marshall was an inspiring partner in difficult fieldwork in Hangzhou's urban villages.

Earlier research in this book has been assisted by many people. The basis of the cartographic and archival research work in Rome and New York was assisted by Ana Marton, John Wiggins, Sharon Haar, Jamie Malanga and Antonio Palladino, and Bangkok's shopping centres were introduced to me in 1995 by Bualong Monchaiyabhumi. Dennis Dollens published *Transparent Cities* following an introduction by Mark Robbins. Initial research was also supported by the Kaskell Fellowship for Alumni of Syracuse University School of Architecture. Publication of *Transparent Cities* was supported by the National Endowment for the Arts and the New York State Council on the Arts.

Manhattan Timeformations was commissioned by Carol Willis, Founder and Director of the Skyscraper Museum in New York, and supported by a New York State Council on the Arts Technology Initiative Grant. Lucy Lai Wong and Akiko Hattori assisted in creating the computer model of Manhattan's skyscrapers and the interface was designed and developed with Mark Watkins. This digital model was further developed as part of an artists' residency co-sponsored by the Lower Manhattan Cultural Council and the World Financial Center. John Cadenhead and Erwin Hisan were modelling assistants with the support of Peter Wheelwright, then of the Department of Architecture at Parsons. Grahame Shane, Deborah Natsios, Victoria Marshall, Joel Towers and Petia Morozov – colleagues at Columbia and Parsons – provided constant criticism and support for the work. The computer models and illustrations generated specially for this book were done with the assistance of Asis Ammarapala, Vicky Pang, Kheerti Kobla, Yuttapoom Powjindom, Stan Gray and Raymond Sih.

Endnotes 31

1 http://www.national911memorial.org
2 Thomas L Friedman, *The World is Flat: A brief history of the twenty-first century*, New York: Farrar, Straus and Giroux, 2005.
3 Critical Art Ensemble, *Digital Resistance: Explorations in Tactical Media*, Brooklyn: Autonomedia, 2001, p 85.
4 Kevin Lynch, *Good City Form*, Cambridge: MIT Press, 1984, p 277.
5 Ibid, p 281.
6 Ibid, p 283.
7 Ibid, p 285.
8 Ibid, p 280.
9 David Grahame Shane, *Recombinant Urbanism*, London: John Wiley & Sons, 2005, p 113.
10 Brian McGrath, *Transparent Cities*, New York: SITES Books, 1994.
11 www.skyscraper.org/timeformations
12 Brian McGrath, 'Bangkok CSD', *Regarding Public Space*, New York: 30/60/90, Vol 9, August 2005.
13 Arjun Appadurai, *Fear of Small Numbers*, Durham: Duke University Press, 2006.
14 Ibid.
15 Guy Debord, *The Society of the Spectacle*, translated by Donald Nicholson-Smith, New York: Zone Books, 1995.
16 Shane.
17 Michel Foucault, *Archaeology of Knowledge*, New York: Routledge, 2002.
18 Aldo Rossi, *Architecture of the City*, translated by Diane Ghirardo and Joan Ockman, Cambridge: MIT Press, 1982.
19 Shane.
20 Eugene Holland, *Deleuze and Guattari's Anti-Oedipus: Introduction to Schizoanalysis*, London: Routledge, 1999, p 58.
21 Gilles Deleuze and Félix Guattari, *Anti-Oedipus: Capitalism and Schizophrenia*, Minneapolis: University of Minnesota Press, 1983.
22 Jean Baudrillard, *Simulacra and Simulation*, Ann Arbor: University of Michigan Press, translated by Sheila Faria Glaser and Brian McGrath; 'Bangkok Simultopia', from *Embodied Utopias: gender, social change, and the modern metropolis*, edited by Amy Bingaman, Lise Sanders and Rebecca Zorach, New York: Routledge, 2002.
23 Robert Venturi, Denise Scott Brown and Steven Izenour, *Learning from Las Vegas*, Cambridge: MIT Press, 1972.
24 Félix Guattari, *The Anti-Oedipus Papers*, edited by Stéphane Nadaud, translated by Kelina Gotman, Semiotext(e) Foreign Agents Series, Cambridge: MIT Press, 2006.
25 A Kaplan, 'Homeland Insecurities: Reflections on language and space', *Radical History Review* 85, 2003, pp 82–93.
26 Stephen Graham, 'Cities and the "War on Terror"', *International Journal of Urban and Regional Research*, Vol 30.2, June 2006, pp 255–76.
27 Arjun Appadurai, *Modernity at Large: the cultural dimensions of globalization*, Minneapolis: University of Minnesota Press, 1996, http://www.newschool.edu/ici/

The *Spectacularisation* of Urban Design

During the last weeks of 2002, crowds politely lined up in the annual ritual of viewing miniature Christmas scenes populated by mechanically moving automatons in Manhattan's old department store windows. But starting on 18 December, new moving displays attracted huge crowds away from the shopping district along Fifth Avenue, to the recently reopened Winter Garden at the World Financial Center in Lower Manhattan. Here, in the apsidal space under the Winter Garden's monumental marble veneer stairs, giant plasma screens displayed digital animations of the recently unveiled 'innovative design proposals' for the rebuilding of the 16-acre World Trade Center site. The crowds were drawn and dazzled by a media-hyped, graphic-intensive assault of both digital and physical models of the various design proposals for Ground Zero. Similar to the grand panoramas in 19th-century exhibitions, not only were new technologies displayed for popular consumption, but new ways of seeing were introduced to a mass public audience – in this case the first prominent use of digital modelling for urban design.

This introductory chapter closely examines the public dissemination of urban design representations that led up to and followed the 2002 Winter Garden exhibit as evidence of a radical rupture of urban design as a form of knowledge as well as professional practice. The advent of digital modelling technologies occurred at a particular juncture in the history of urbanisation and globalisation: the optimistic moment that accompanied the arrival of the internet and the end of the Cold War. For a brief period, a previously complacent public was no longer willing to let urban design remain a bureaucratic discipline determined by designated specialists. Fed by the rapid dissemination of new images and communication technologies, a global constituency unabashedly advocated a more direct role in the redesign of the World Trade Center site. From the moment when much of the world witnessed the second aeroplane crash into the twin towers, a huge global urban design constituency began to comment on the future of Ground Zero and New York. This chapter will cover the various steps in the official design process by analysing the use of computer models, animations, interactive displays, websites, public exhibitions, opinion polls, surveys and meetings. These elements constituted a new form of public discourse emerging out of the ashes of Ground Zero which disrupted normative urban design knowledge and practice.

In his book *The Society of the Spectacle* of 1967, Guy Debord provocatively wrote: 'The whole life of those societies in which modern conditions of production prevail presents itself as an immense accumulation of *spectacles*. All that once was directly lived has become mere representation.'[1] Urban design practice joined Debord's society of the spectacle through the proliferation of expensive production values to create spectacular and hyper-real digitally modelled simulations. The display of digital models at the Winter Garden obscured the World Trade Center site's complex web of social, environmental and infrastructural contexts through the proliferation of sensational surface imagery and rhetorical symbols. While the imagery often dazzled the public, they were only momentarily engaged, and the promise of a global conversation on urban design was cut short.

Grahame Shane interprets the concluding diagram of Robin Evans's *Projective Cast*[2] as a criticism of Post-Modern architecture and urban design practice. Shane argues that Evans's diagram depicts architectural projection as a self-reinforcing closed conceptual

network of mirrored reflections bouncing between the
human imagination, the scopic regime of perspective,
orthographic architectural drawing conventions and
designed objects. Shane describes Post-Modern
architectural representations as a 'self-correcting means
of stabilization and pacification of the physical, built
environment'.[3] This chapter demonstrates how digital
modelling in the design process for Ground Zero has only
deepened the crisis of architectural and urban design
representation and practice.[4]

Ground Zero

With great media fanfare, the Lower Manhattan
Development Corporation (LMDC), a joint New York State
and New York City public body, was created by Governor
George Pataki and Mayor Rudy Giuliani immediately
following the completion of the emergency relief effort in
the wake of the catastrophic collapse of the World Trade
Center towers. According to its website until 2008, LMDC,
entrusted with overseeing the Ground Zero rebuilding
process, was '... committed to an open, inclusive and
transparent planning process in which the public has a
central role in shaping the future of Lower Manhattan'.[5]
Complicating this intention to serve the public interest
were the conflicting agendas of various power brokers:
the Port Authority of New York and New Jersey owns the
site; the private developer Larry Silverstein holds a 99-
year lease on 10 million square feet of office space; and
Westfield Corporation until recently held a lease for the
vast underground World Trade Center shopping mall.
LMDC additionally had to appease three highly active and
passionate stakeholders: the September 11 families, area
business owners and the residents of Lower Manhattan.
Finally, as the design process played out, it became clear
that a wide range of highly interested design advocates –

global and local, professional and not – intended to
participate in both the discussions and the design process
for rebuilding this 16-acre site.

LMDC's website, therefore, became the agency's
principal means of communicating and archiving the
official tale of the events around the rebuilding design
process; and continues to take the form of an online
archive of press releases, constantly re-editing and
reconstructing the narrative of a cautious public agency
navigating the waves of biannual electoral cycles. The
LMDC website throughout the Pataki administration
attempted to display a smooth web face of a rational and
linear design process which included public participation.
The website retrospectively outlined five stages in this
staging and simulation of an open design process:
Preliminary Design Concepts, Innovative Design Study,
Transit Hub, Memorial Design and Freedom Tower
Design. These stages in the design process were not
preplanned, but evolved over time as LMDC reacted to
overwhelming public interest and criticism, albeit
always acutely in sync with national and statewide
election cycles.

The current website was redesigned with the
restructuring of LMDC after the election in 2006 of a new
Governor, Democrat Eliot Spitzer. The politicised process
of the previous administration has been erased, and the
website illustrates a completed Master Plan introduced
with a photorealistic video of the completed vision
provided by Silverstein Properties. The Statue of Liberty
frames the foreground, a panorama of the future skyline
of Lower Manhattan with the Freedom Tower, as well as
office buildings designed by Norman Foster, Richard
Rogers and Fumihiko Maki.

36 Preliminary Design Concepts

In 2002, a 'Request for Qualifications' (RFQ) was solicited by LMDC for preliminary design concepts for Ground Zero. The RFQ process is a bureaucratic device for crafting a selection process which legally must be open, but in this case the field of potential designers was restricted to a handful of large-scale New York design firms. The scope of work was also reduced from the comprehensive rethinking of all of Lower Manhattan to the bounded 16-acre site itself. Architects Beyer Blinder Belle were chosen from a short list of the few local firms who could qualify under the extreme criteria of the initial RFQ and were limited to the problem of squeezing 10 million square feet of Silverstein's and Westfield's leased office and commercial space on the Port Authority property, while leaving space for a memorial.

The firm's reputation, based on successfully navigating complex historical renovations such as Grand Central Terminal and Ellis Island, assured LMDC of their ability to address both the technical and symbolic complexities of the project. They dutifully limited themselves to the most abstract and pragmatic aspects of the design. Complicating this public process, Alexander Garvin, the Director of Planning at LMDC, hired the firm of Peterson/Littenberg as his consultants for the project and Silverstein privately hired SOM to design his new office buildings.[6]

A coalition of non-profit-making interests collectively called the Civic Alliance took the progressive step of convincing LMDC to organise a public review of the preliminary design concepts. A mass event called 'Listening to the City' took place in July 2002 at the Jacob K Javits Convention Center. The six proposals presented by Beyer Blinder Belle – Memorial Plaza, Memorial Square, Memorial Triangle, Memorial Garden, Memorial Park and Memorial Promenade – were all loudly rejected by the public and press. Memorial Garden was actually designed by SOM, architects to the developer Silverstein, while the last two were designed by Garvin's consultants Peterson/Littenberg.[7] No proposal lived up to the central mission of memorialising the events of September 11, or addressed the diverse range of responses and emotions elicited by the challenge of rebuilding on Ground Zero. The proposals were presented in a neutral way – flat white featureless buildings on a beige background with green open spaces – as if this were just another large-scale Manhattan commercial development project, rather than the locus of such a powerful collective memory and imagination.

Beyer Blinder Belle's professional urban design approach follows the codes, rules and practices laid down in New York City when the Urban Design Group was formed in the Department of City Planning in 1967. As Jonathan Barnett[8] has shown, the Urban Design Group was able to shape the business districts of New York through three-dimensionally modelled bulk diagrams of zoning regulations in special districts. This technocratic and bureaucratic process remains a model of urban design practice that is emulated around the world due to its ability to shape private development towards perceived public good.

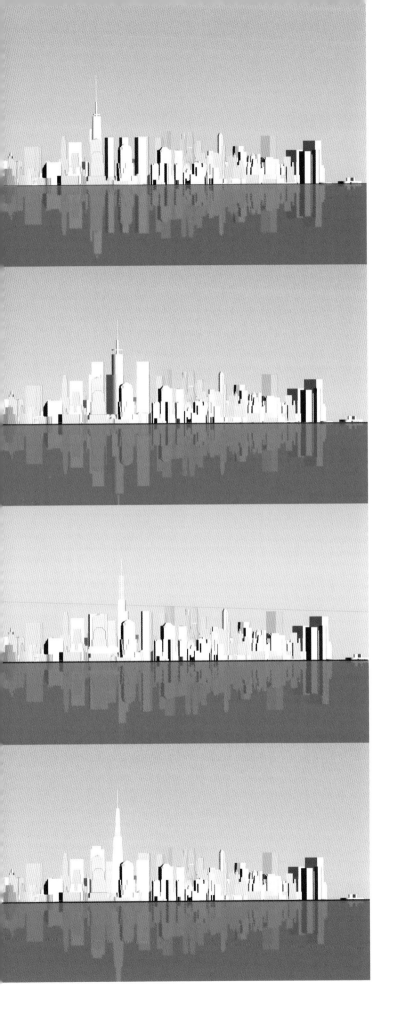

The 'Listening to the City' event also introduced new technologies for citizen interaction to New York – a place with a long, robust history of public participation. LMDC hired the company AmericaSpeaks to organise a huge public meeting at the convention centre. This non-profit company, according to Philip Nobel, '... organizes 21st Century Town Meetings TM with the aid of networked computers, trained "facilitators", corporate sponsorship, "groupware," and a handy remote control-like device that the virtually empowered citizens themselves can key to voice their assent or criticism of the agenda at hand as preselected questions and multiple-choice answers are posted on giant screens'.[9] Many participants felt this was merely a staging of democracy and felt patronised, stage-managed, manipulated and policed by private security guards.[10] Audience participants were forced to respond passively to rather than participate in this technological staging of a participatory design process as a media spectacle, bearing out Debord's insight.

Innovative Design Study

LMDC responded to the public outcry following 'Listening to the City', first, by creating an Innovative Design Study, second, by establishing an international, open design competition for the memorial, third, by adding cultural programmes for museums and performance spaces for Ground Zero, and finally by purchasing the shopping mall lease from Westfield Corporation to ease some of the commercial pressures on the site. However, Silverstein's lease continued to be important for the financial solvency of the Port Authority – $10 million a month rent continues to be charged for the control over 10 million square feet of office space which still had to be fitted onto the site – the financial issue which overshadowed everything else.

Again an RFQ took place for the Innovative Design Study, and seven teams from around the world were selected to prepare plans to be presented to the LMDC and the public. The teams included two star designer studios from Europe: Studio Daniel Libeskind and Foster + Partners; and THINK, United Architects, New York architects Richard Meier, Peter Eisenman, Charles Gwathmey and Steven Holl, SOM, and again Peterson/Littenberg. The following section examines the slide shows presented by each design team which are archived on LMDC's website as evidence of a significant shift in urban design representation from the Preliminary Design Concepts, and a new paradigm in the production of urban design knowledge. Strangely, following the excitement of the Innovative Design Study, Studio Daniel Libeskind was asked to produce a traditional Master Plan – reverting to top-down the 0process interrupted by the public outcry and to a less creative and spectacular method of urban design controls.

The Design Exhibition Spectacle

The Innovative Design exhibit was a direct response to the negative public outcry that followed the presentation of the initial planning studies. Never before have architecture and urban design been the focus of such impassioned and massive scrutiny by such a global array of different actors and stakeholders. The Winter Garden was an apt setting for the public restaging of the spectacle of modernity – the glass-roofed basilica centrepiece of Battery Park City was modelled on early-19th-century exhibition halls. Cesar Pelli's glass hothouse was designed to welcome visitors from Minoru Yamasaki's World Trade Center via a pedestrian bridge, down a grand staircase copied from Bramante's Belvedere Palace in the Vatican, leading in turn to a palm grove with river views towards a yacht marina, around which the towers of American Express, Dow Jones and Merrill Lynch clustered. The collapse of the Trade Center towers severed the pedestrian bridge and showered steel beams through both the granite facade of the office towers and the glass roof of the Winter Garden. Boats were the only means of escape from the island as the Port Authority transit lines below were cut off and flooded, and the entire World Financial Center complex – like much of Lower Manhattan – was uninhabitable for almost a year.

The wide array of visualisations prepared in this phase of the design process represents a remarkable departure from the neutral representations of the first phase and revealed the ability of digital modelling and media technologies to mobilise public passion towards design. Although the submissions are a collage of both new computer-generated techniques and traditional modes of urban design visualisation, the array of rhetorical representation and use of symbols employed in the Innovative Design Study marks a rupture in Jonathan Barnett's normative practice of modern bureaucratic urban design. This rupture runs parallel with the new technologies of public feedback gathering introduced in the Javits Center event and the new range of image making now made possible by digital modelling. After the spectacle of the Innovative Design Study for the World Trade Center site, urban design practiced as an objective and neutral bureaucratic profession has become a relic of the past.

Foster + Partners

Foster began his grand and comprehensive presentation narrative with an image of Earth from space, zooming in to an aerial view of Ground Zero directly following the collapse of the twin towers. He then showed his proposal in incremental phasing plans emerging from the ashes. His proposal includes a large garden with twin sunken memorials on the WTC tower footprints as well as a new generation of conjoined High-Tech twin towers over a new transit centre. Hand-drawn sketches take the viewer through a series of spaces beginning below ground level in the memorial before finally ascending to the top of the new towers in a cathartic journey from disaster to apotheosis. More prosaic computer-generated drawings give technical information on building systems and explain the structural engineering performance, energy efficiency and sustainable aspects of the proposal, while analytical drawings show the workings of the transport centre below ground. Technology becomes the means for New York to rise out of the ashes. The complexity of these renderings is softened by hand-drawn sketches which personalise the project through the eyes of a child visiting the site. But hyper-real computer model renderings of his proposed towers collaged into photographs of the Lower Manhattan skyline are the final signature images of the Foster presentation – the undisturbed role of New York as World Financial Capital is reclaimed through its restored skyline.

40 *Peterson/Littenberg*

Peterson/Littenberg's proposal displayed an astute
understanding of the street, block and open-space
heritage of Lower Manhattan and was stylistically the
opposite of the Foster scheme in its backward glance.
While the sensitive massing was constructed as wire-
frame base models by Steven Peterson, their project was
represented in warm 19th-century Beaux Arts
watercolours unhindered by Beyer Blinder Belle's neutral
Modernist rendering style. Replicas of Rockefeller Center
rise over the sacred ground of the tower footprints
disguised as Neo-Georgian town squares. Modern
structural and mechanical systems, so visibly on display
by Foster, are hidden beneath the brick and stone 19th-
century New York blocks. If any digital technology was
employed to create these images, it was well masked
except by the LCD projectors through which it was
presented and the website on which they can still be
viewed. Peterson/Littenberg's carefully designed
historical collage relied on nostalgia for early New York to
soothe the wound of the trauma of 9/11.

Peterson/Littenberg's
proposal displays an astute
understanding of Downtown
Manhattan's fine-grain urban
fabric. Wire-frame
construction of base drawing
by Steven K. Peterson,
watercolour rendering by
Michael McCann, 2002.

SOM

According to Philip Nobel, SOM delayed their participation in the design study due to their professional contract with the developer Silverstein to design the office buildings for the site.[11] However, they briefly secured a release from this contract and presented a schematic design. Their grey presentation was a preview of the glass towers currently under way on the site – the completed 7 World Trade Center and the Freedom Tower, under construction. Collaborating landscape architects at Field Operations provided a diagram of gardens in the sky, and again a monumental transport centre is framed as an iconic image. Here we see the site represented by corporate architectural practice in service of the needs of the developer client. Post-Second World War Manhattan, with its glass corporate architecture skilfully designed by the firm that built Lever Brothers and PepsiCo's headquarters on Park Avenue, could be recaptured here in Lower Manhattan, no less nostalgic a balm than Peterson/Littenberg's Art Deco towers.

Richard Meier, Peter Eisenman,
Charles Gwathmey and Steven Holl

The older generation of New York architecture was represented by the 'Dream Team': Richard Meier, Peter Eisenman, Charles Gwathmey and Steven Holl. Here the mix of master designers is seen with the characteristic formalism of three of the former New York Five, in contrast with Holl's signature Impressionistic watercolour renderings. Analytical 3-D diagrams are graphically very compelling, as the computer has become a great aid in design formalism. The scheme was underdeveloped, but the celebrity architects featured themselves in their slide show, working together, and they included a close-up of two hands with intertwined fingers as a sign of their collective authorship – in contrast to the famous image of Le Corbusier's authorial finger pointing at his Plan Voisin for Paris of 1925. But again the night-time skyline images, this time with the Brooklyn Bridge in the foreground, are the visualisations they hoped would win over the public. This team promised a rebuilt New York designed by the celebrated international architects who have had little opportunity to build there. It provided nostalgia for a past New York architecture that never happened.

SOM's slick glass towers are modulated by Sky Gardens proposed by landscape architects at Field Operations, 2002.

Richard Meier, Peter Eisenman, Charles Gwathmey and Steven Holl collaborated on a design of a Cartesian grid of towers. They represent an older generation of New York architects who until recently had never designed large-scale buildings in Manhattan, 2002.

42 *United Architects*

United Architects comprised a larger and diverse collaboration of computer-savvy architects. If the older generation of designers used nostalgia of New York's past, they sought to create a desire for the new. They did not seem wary of showing off their digital talents and their presentation is considerably denser and longer than the others. They included elaborate computer-generated animations showing various conceptual and technical properties of the design. United's animations were the only evidence of the use of digital modelling as a tool for generating form. However, betraying the avant-garde mythos of pure invention and the cult of the new, United surprisingly juxtaposed their designs with images of Hagia Sophia, Grand Central Terminal and an old growth forest. United Architects end their presentation with an image similar in sentiment to the Foster team's little girl – this time an image of a young boy looking at the new skyline from the Staten Island Ferry.

THINK

The THINK group was composed of an international team of architects including Shigeru Ban, Frederic Schwartz, Ken Smith and Rafael Viñoly. Again the computer renderings of the proposal on a skyline photograph comprise the signature image – this time a night-time skyline view from New Jersey reflected in the Hudson River. Towering lights evoke the popular temporary memorial of twin searchlights as virtual towers. Computer models help to visualise the conceptual aspects of the proposal which focused on cultural institutions developing over time within twin towering super trusses. Like Foster, computer-generated engineering drawings explain the structure and vertical transport. THINK group's project was the only one to sideline the commercial imperatives for rebuilding Ground Zero in order to promote arenas for new cultural production. Their idealistic proposal found a champion in Herbert Muschamp, architectural critic of the *New York Times*, who actively lobbied for this proposal in his newspaper column.[12] Their scheme allowed for stacked cultural forums to emerge over time, and they included time sequence animations in their presentation. Yet the power of THINK's concept was inadequately represented, and it was judged by most more on its skeletal form than its publicly spirited content.

The THINK group's proposal is
the most radical. Their twin
towers are composed of
cultural institutions
constructed within giant twin
trusses replacing the
volumes of the destroyed
twin towers, 2002.

Studio Daniel Libeskind's proposed skyline spirals up to the Freedom Tower's mast which mirrors the torch of the Statue of Liberty, 2002.

44 *Studio Daniel Libeskind*

Studio Daniel Libeskind's (SDL) presentation is stylistically marked by his personal handwriting: white script on black, like chalk on a blackboard, evokes both the aura of an artist's signature and the authority of a primary school teacher. His chief symbolic image, like Foster's, is a hyper-real rendered computer model of his design collaged into a photograph of the NYC skyline. But in this case SDL's proposed tower mimics the Statue of Liberty itself, with an asymmetrical beacon climbing to 1,776 feet – commemorating the year the Declaration of Independence was signed. The tower was later christened by Governor Pataki the 'Freedom Tower' as it neared time for his re-election. Libeskind's verbal presentation evoked his status as an immigrant to America himself, arousing an aura of nationalist emotion around his proposal for Ground Zero.

Libeskind's hand sketches transform into computer-generated drawings and perspectives as if by magic. Cut sectional perspectives and axonometric diagrams take apart the various programmatic layers: transport, memorial, cultural and commercial spaces. Libeskind's animation in the exhibition was remarkably simple and powerful, and different from the other entries which employ standard walk-through computer models. He showed a simple 360-degree photo collage pan from within the 'bathtub' of Ground Zero, highlighting the symbolic power of the intact concrete slurry wall holding back the Hudson River. It was a brilliant use of simple animation technique and the symbolic importance of the monumental remaining artefact from the destroyed World Trade Center – its foundation. In fact, Libeskind entitled his presentation 'Memory Foundations'. Libeskind's representations are much more controlled and consistent than the others, but it is his heroic and nationalistic rhetorical language and his use of popular symbols that probably swayed the higher political aspirations of New York's Republican Governor, if not the majority of the public.

Libeskind's design was personally selected by Governor Pataki for his highly rhetorical presentation which alluded to his view of the Statue of Liberty on his arrival in New York Harbor as a teenage immigrant, the symbolic power of the great slurry wall which remained intact, and the commemoration of the 'heroes' by marking the paths of rescue workers who died. The mass public event of the exhibition, finalist selection, and final design selection created a media sensation, skilfully navigated by Libeskind.

What distinguished this round of public presentation from the previous 'Listening to the City' event was the rich array of representational technologies and techniques employed by the participants – including the first widespread public viewing of computer-generated models and animations competing for the attention of, and emotional connection with, a mass public. This seemed to distract most people from the fact that the Libeskind proposal strongly resembles the planning logic of the first massing proposal of the initial design concepts. In spite of the initial enthusiasm for Libeskind's Master Plan, it has been slowly stripped of its initial aesthetic and rhetorical power as the transit, memorial and office building designs have progressed with other architects.

46 The Transit Hub, Memorial Design and Freedom Tower

Meanwhile, the Port Authority bypassed the emotion-laden public process that LMDC suffered through, and hired Santiago Calatrava to design the new transit hub. His sleek design and computer animations drew only praise and were accepted without controversy, until construction neared and the public cost of this monumental artefact to triumphal renewal soared to $2.5 billion. The Port Authority has numerous images and animations on its website, celebrating in elaborate pristine dove-white renderings the winged, ribbed station.[13]

The open, international memorial design competition attracted an unprecedented number of entries from professionals, students, artists and amateurs. A jury chose eight finalists which again were presented at the Winter Garden to large crowds. Furthermore, LMDC has archived all 5,201 entries online.[14] For the final selection of a memorial design, one computer animation firm created consistent visualisations of each project, assuring that the style of presentation would not overwhelm an understanding of the nature of each memorial proposal. The projects tended to read similarly, none really stirring great public attention. Eventually a collaboration was created between architect Michael Arad and landscape architect Peter Walker, and later the architectural firm of Davis Brody Bond. Arad's spare proposal consists of sunken memorials inundated by the rush of water that the concrete slurry walls of the World Trade Center's foundations held back. Notably, the initial sombre grey renderings were later softened by Walker's colourful trees and people in the final animations presented on the September 11 Memorial website.

Santiago Calatrava was
commissioned by the Port
Authority of New York and New
Jersey to design a monumental
new entry to the PATH
transportation hub, 2002.

Silverstein hired SOM to design the Freedom Tower with Libeskind as Master Plan consultant. Eventually Freedom Tower was completely redesigned as it needed to take into account city police warnings about its vulnerability to car or truck bombs. It is now designed to sit on a blast-proof armoured base. Groundbreaking took place in September 2004, just before George W Bush was re-elected president. In his 2005 inauguration address, Bush repeated the word 'freedom' 27 times in 20 minutes, continually invoking the message of Pataki's tower.[15]

Final RFQs were held for the museum and performing art centres, both for institutions to operate these cultural facilities and for architects to design them. Like the Port Authority, LMDC responded to public demand for aesthetic experimentation and chose Gehry Partners and Snøhetta to design these buildings. While Gehry's performing arts centre design has been delayed indefinitely, Snøhetta's contribution has morphed from a potentially controversial forum for art and politics, to an entry pavilion for a vast underground memorial museum now called the National September 11 Memorial and Museum – equipped with its own website for information and fund-raising purposes.[16]

While the cumulative results of all this design expertise and public participation will not be fully comprehended until the various projects are completed over the years, what is clear now is that there has emerged, for now, a public demand to reclaim urban design as an aesthetically experimental practice. The question remains, how do we learn from the Ground Zero design process? In New York, intense public scrutiny of the project to rebuild the World Trade Center led to great demands to create openness, inclusiveness and transparency. However, digital modelling for urban design often resulted in the creation of elaborate rhetorical images which concealed the complexity of the site.

50 Other Representations

Concurrent with the great high opera being played out between Silverstein, Pataki and the architects SOM, Libeskind and Arad, countless individual creative acts were performed at the various perimeters of Ground Zero. Spontaneous shrines, art projects, pro-bono design work and public gatherings appeared worldwide. Temporary memorials were created along the various red-zone perimeters: Union Square, Washington Square, Houston Street, Canal Street and the West Side Highway. Spontaneous events and temporary constructions strengthened the desire of countless visitors to commemorate and to mark Ground Zero. New models of representation of the World Trade Center and its collapse were suggested by the worlds of science and journalism.

Compelling use of digital modelling and layered imagery commissioned by journalists provided alternative ways of visualising urban information. The National Institute for Standards Testing created a digitally modelled animation to unmask the spectacle of the collapse of the towers by scientifically analysing the event through slow motion, stopping and repositioning the computer camera in order to digest and weigh all the information available. Don Foley's illustrations for the *New York Times* excavated the geology and hidden structure of the site, giving an easily understood image of the three-dimensional complexities and constraints on the site.

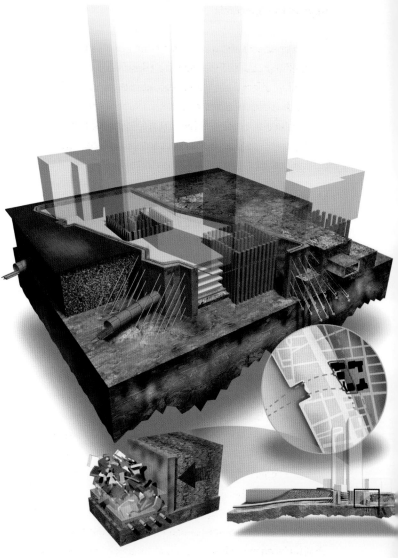

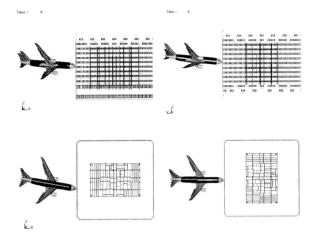

The National Institute of Standards and Technology conducted a technical investigation of the collapse of the two World Trade Center towers through computer simulations. Animations were created for broadcast on public television, 2002.

Beyond the Spectacle

> The spectacle, though it turns reality on its head, is itself a product of real activity. Likewise, lived reality suffers the material assault of the spectacle's mechanisms of contemplation, incorporating the spectacular order and lending that order positive support ... reality erupts within the spectacle, and the spectacle is real. This reciprocal alienation is the essence and underpinning of society as it exists.[17]

Digital modelling offers new possibilities in reclaiming urban design practices through the use of information visualisation and communication technologies. However, the process for the redesign of Ground Zero reveals the problems involved in its implementation in complex and controversial situations. New York government, business and design leaders underestimated, misunderstood and lacked the tools to address the unprecedented popular interest and demand in participating in the thought process of rebuilding Ground Zero. As the process of redesigning Ground Zero played out, computer-generated animations were used much more to dazzle, confuse and placate an interested public rather than to create a coherent audience of informed citizen to participate in urban design issues.

Critical urban design is dedicated to the production of difference which underlies urban life. Appadurai says that difference itself has become the underlying problem and the project of elimination by the nation-state in the era of globalisation. However, the elimination of difference is impossible in the world of 'blurred boundaries, mixed marriages, shared languages, and other deep connectivities'[18]

To develop the tools to create a critical practice of digital modelling for urban design at a time when urban life as difference itself is under attack, this book will outline a critical archaeology, genealogy and schizoanalysis of urban modelling, representation and design. In the following chapters we will go back three millennia to uncover the Roman Forum as a space created with the spoils of war, track through one century in New York's emergence as the capital of capitalism and four decades of Bangkok's struggles for national identity in the age of globalisation. Digital models of these three sites will aid us in constructing a critical understanding of urban design in contemporary society. In this way I hope to employ digital as a critical practice where urban design can be seen as the production rather than the elimination of difference.

Endnotes
1 Guy Debord, *The Society of the Spectacle*, translated by Donald Nicholson-Smith, New York: Zone Books, 1995.
2 David Grahame Shane, 'Balkanization and the Postmodern City', from Peter Lang (ed), *Mortal City*, New York: Princeton Architectural Press, 1995, pp 55–69. Robin Evans, *The Projective Cast*, Cambridge: MIT Press, 1995.
3 Shane, p 68.
4 Brian McGrath and Jean Gardner, *Cinemetrics: Architectural Drawing Today*, London: John Wiley & Sons, 2007.
5 www.renewnyc.com
6 Philip Nobel, *Sixteen Acres: Architecture and the outrageous struggle for the future of Ground Zero*, New York: Henry Holt and Company, 2005, p 114.
7 Ibid, p 115.
8 Jonathan Barnett, *An Introduction to Urban Design*, New York: Harper & Row, 1982.
9 Nobel, p 103.
10 Interview with some who attended a session and provided a first-hand account of the experience.
11 Nobel, p 147.
12 Herbert Muschamp, 'Visons for Ground Zero', *New York Times*, 19 December 2002, p B 10.
13 http://www.panynj.gov/drp
14 http://www.wtcsitememorial.org/submissions.html
15 Frank Rich, 'The Coup at Home', Op-Ed column, *New York Times*, 11 November 2007.
16 http://www.national911memorial.org
17 Debord, p 14.
18 Arjun Appadurai, *Fear of Small Numbers*, Durham: Duke University Press, 2006.

Chapter 1

Archaeology

54 The floor of the New York Stock Exchange was unusually full of activity over one weekend in 1981. Instead of the frantic shouts and rush of stock traders, brokers and their clerks and regulators that accompanies the normal weekday frenzy on the floor of the 'Big Board', this spring weekend saw a rush of movers and construction workers. The old wooden desks, counters and cabinets that filled George B Post's 14,000-square-foot neoclassical trading room were hurriedly dismantled and dumped outside, along with the litter of left-over paper trails. Suddenly from above, circular UFO-like objects with bright lights underneath were lowered from the 72-foot-high ceiling, like a scene from the movie *Close Encounters of the Third Kind*.

When the stock traders left work on Friday, they conducted their last trades by paper. When they next arrived on Monday morning they began to trade within a computer network called the Intermarket Trading System (ITS) that linked several major US stock exchanges for the first time in 1978. Post's 1903 building was designated a National Historic Landmark two months later. By the end of 2006, the New York Stock Exchange had significantly reduced its space for physical trading of stocks and introduced its Hybrid Market for expanded electronic trading traders could now fly through a virtual trading floor, observing trading activity and monitoring the markets in a 3-D modelling environment. The New York Stock Exchange Advanced Trading Floor was designed in 2001 by Asymptote (Hani Rashid and Lise Anne Couture).

I was living in New York in 1981, unaware that the gritty post-industrial city suffering from a severe financial downturn was about to reorganise itself as a global financial hub with the advent of financial deregulation and new computer technologies. ITS ushered in a revolution in global business, and the first years of my professional practice in the early 1980s were dominated by the renovations of corporate interiors to accommodate the computerisation of the workplace. The abandoned industrial places and decaying blue-collar neighbourhoods in Manhattan, such as the waterfront piers, SoHo, the East Village and Chelsea, became a frontier for artists and a new species called 'yuppies'. Novelist Tom Wolfe's *The Bonfire of the Vanities* and Oliver Stone's film *Wall Street*, both from 1987, appeared as morality tales of a decade in New York where the deadly sin of greed was hailed as good.

Between 1981 and 1985 I worked in New York with Polshek Partnership on many projects fuelled by the massive transformation due to digitalisation of the workplace. However, it was only when I founded my own professional practice, between 1985 and 1990, that I began my own archaeology of urban design . During these five years I lived and worked in both Rome and New York and was able to document and map the massive transformation under way in New York City as part of a larger historical cycle of urban change evident in Rome. I travelled between these two cities at a moment of rupture in the history of globalisation marked by the widespread introduction of personal computers and the demolition of the Berlin Wall. Travelling in China and Eastern Europe too, during this period, instilled in me a great hope for the future. It was an era of great optimism with the end of the Cold War and the promise of new communication technologies. It is in this historical context that I began to assemble an archive of maps, city views and on-the-ground perceptions of Rome and New York which culminated in the publication of *Transparent Cities* by SITES Books in 1994.[1]

New York's early–20th-century industrial landscape was in a state of ruins in the 1980s as the city changed from an industrial to an informational economy. Detail Hudson River piers drawing, pencil on Canson paper, 1988.

Transparent Cities is a boxed archive of acetate plates of maps of Rome and New York which can be overlain in thousands of combinations, SITES Books, 1994.

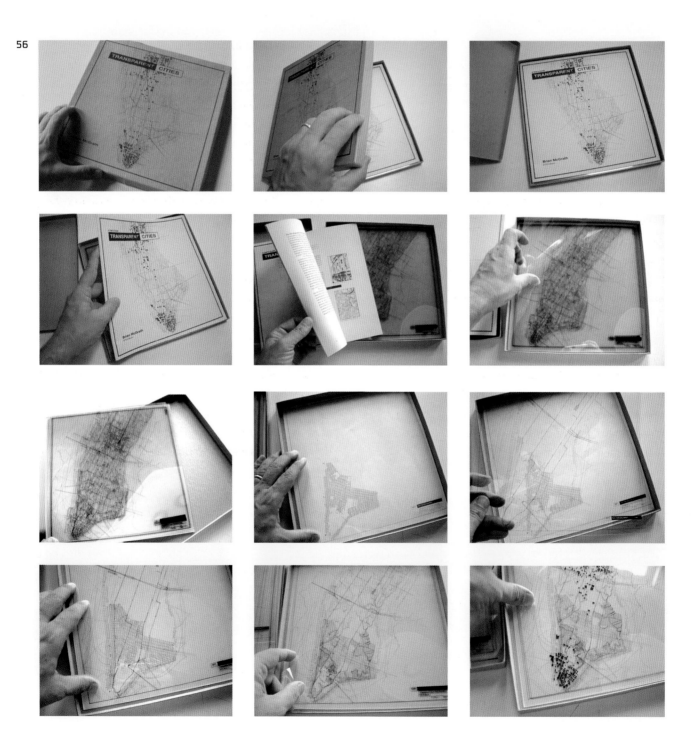

1985–95: *Transparent Cities*

The 24 transparent plates of *Transparent Cities* record instances of the fluctuations and changes in the spatial and political structure of the urban landscapes of Rome over two millennia and New York over three and a half centuries. Selected information from historical and contemporary maps of both Rome and New York was redrawn at the same scale and reproduced on transparent plates, which can be examined individually or as overlays in any combination or sequence the viewer desires. The project was inspired by Cubist painting and the seminal essay by Robert Slutsky and Colin Rowe on literal and phenomenal transparency in art and architecture.[2] The two cities can be studied diachronically or synchronically, individually or analogously. By manipulating the plates in literally hundreds of possible combinations, the reader may recombine past and present, existing and demolished, seen and hidden. The overlays show plans at street level as well as under and above ground, exploring the city in cross section and in three dimensions. Manipulating the plates introduces the fourth dimension of time.

Transparent Cities offers an alternative way of seeing and imagining the city, one that reflects rather than suppresses the dynamic and heterogeneous space Kevin Lynch found missing in contemporary city models and which was so evident in my observations of the changing urban landscape around me. Modelling the city as transparent does not fix one layer or interpretation over another. By not preferring any authoritative map, moment in time or urban idea, the transparencies reveal the coexistence of a multiplicity of spatial ideas within cities. By depicting cities in the process of becoming, rather than in a static, final or fixed state of completion, transparent modelling can be used for understanding and designing the emerging city. It is a tool and methodology that reflects the contemporary city's impermanence and diversity.

The plates of *Transparent Cities* contain fragmentary and partial tracings from selected archival maps from the rich cartographic histories of Rome and New York. While the plates are literally transparent – reproduced on acetate – transparency is explored more in the sense of Gregory Kepes's idea of overlapping Cubist space.

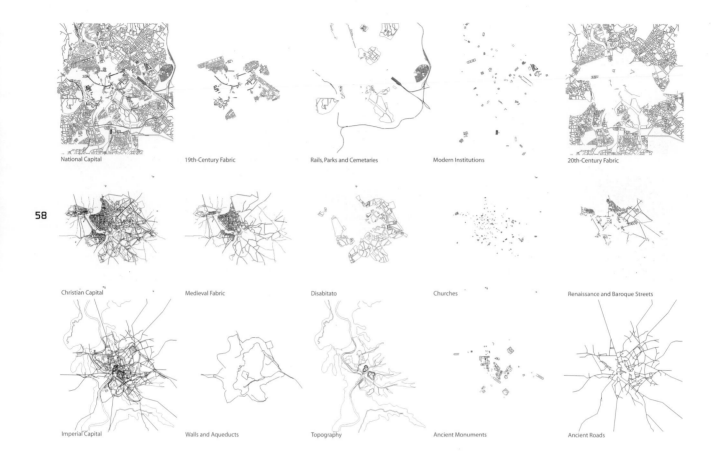

National Capital   19th-Century Fabric   Rails, Parks and Cemetaries   Modern Institutions   20th-Century Fabric

Christian Capital   Medieval Fabric   Disabitato   Churches   Renaissance and Baroque Streets

Imperial Capital   Walls and Aqueducts   Topography   Ancient Monuments   Ancient Roads

If one sees two or more figures partly overlapping one another, and each of them claims for itself the common, overlapped part, then one is confronted with a contradiction of spatial dimensions. To resolve this contradiction, one must assume the presence of a new optical quality. The figures are endowed with transparency: that is, they are able to interpenetrate without an optical destruction of each other. Transparency, however, implies more than an optical characteristic; it implies a broader spatial order. Transparency means a simultaneous perception of different spatial locations. Space not only recedes but fluctuates in a continuous activity.[3]

Matrix of the digital archive and archaeological analysis of Rome's urban design elements from top to bottom: Imperial, Christian and the National Capital. All maps are oriented with north to the top, 1996.

Matrix of the digital archive and archaeological analysis of New York's urban design elements from top to bottom: Financial, Industrial and Mercantile Capitalism, 1996.

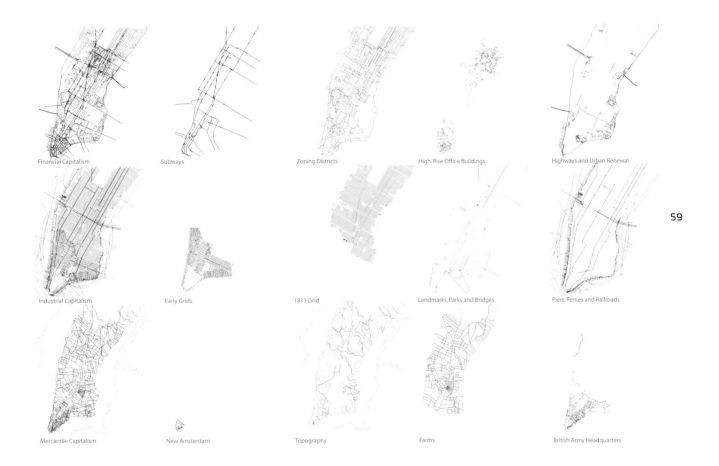

Financial Capitalism

Subways

Zoning Districts

High-Rise Office Buildings

Highways and Urban Renewal

Industrial Capitalism

Early Grids

1811 Grid

Landmarks, Parks and Bridges

Piers, Ferries and Railroads

Mercantile Capitalism

New Amsterdam

Topography

Farms

British Army Headquarters

By overlaying transparent maps of Rome, the ruptures and discontinuities in the landscapes, institutions and spatial practices of the Imperial, Christian and National Capitals can be mapped as marked by different regimes of power in different ways during different eras. In New York, the city is not a political capital, and its space is more the result of the 'creative' destruction of capitalist development and fuelled by ideas of progress and modernity. According to Marshall Berman, capitalism and modernity are always marked by the search for continuity in a landscape of constant upheaval.[4] An overlay of maps reveals the transformation to the logics of Mercantile, Industrial and Financial Capital. New York City's economic cycles of boom and bust demonstrate the creative destruction of capitalism as notions of progress and modernity continually push spatial transformations according to new social, political and technological conditions.

In 1985 I also started to teach architecture at New Jersey Institute of Technology in Newark. Students accompanied me to Rome during the summer, sketching in the field, and working on urban architectural design projects in the New York area. We worked with the organisation Architects/Designers/Planners for Social Responsibility in the spring semester of 1990, on an urban design project for resolving the conflict between housing and community garden advocates in the Lower East Side of Manhattan. The studio used the transparent modelling method, the lessons of the spatial palimpsest of Rome and a collaborative working technique to develop a project where a rapidly changing New York neighbourhood could have both houses and gardens.[5]

1995–2005: An Archaeology of Globalisation

By 1995, the computer had revolutionised not just stock trading and financial transactions on Wall Street, but architecture and urban design practice as well. Teaching digital architectural drawing and design studios first at Parsons, the New School for Design, and later urban design studios at Columbia University, I found the transparent archaeological modelling technique took on a new creative power through digitalisation. Working on studios in Washington Heights, the South Bronx, East Harlem and Lower Manhattan with Grahame Shane, we furthered the techniques developed in the Lower East Side of Manhattan, by working with community groups and public agencies to develop alternative models for the gentrifying city of the 1990s.

The last decade of the 20th century also brought a much more diverse student body to New York's architectural schools, and it became clear to me that a deeper understanding of Asian urbanism was necessary. Between 1995 and 2005, I spent each spring semester in Thailand, teaching in a new Masters of Urban Design Program at Chulalongkorn University in Bangkok. During this decade I was able to develop the same course – Digital Modelling for Urban Design – at both Columbia and Chulalongkorn, which resulted in new digital archives of both cities as well as multiple exchanges between students and faculty over the years. In my trips to Bangkok, I collected an archive to prepare a third archaeology: Bangkok's transformation from a water-based Dhamma kingdom, to the hybrid modern landscape created by the modernising King Rama V, and finally the global city which emerged at the turn of the 21st century.

Archaeological modelling is necessary in order to analytically cut through the layered rhetoric of globalisation discourse and to map the speed, volume and diversity of urbanisation today. Consider Rem Koolhaas's recent description of the contemporary city:

One of the peculiar beauties of the twentieth-century context is that it is no longer the result of one or more architectural doctrines evolving almost imperceptibly, but which represent the simultaneous formation of distinct archaeological layers: they result from a perpetual pendulum movement where each architectural doctrine contradicts and undoes the essence of the previous one as surely as day follows night. The resulting landscape needs the combined interpretive ability of Champollion, Schliemann, Darwin and Freud.[6]

In the years since Koolhaas made these observations, the urban context has become even more complex, layered and difficult to decipher. Arjun Appadurai has highlighted the cultural dimensions of the present era of globalisation as marked by the disjunctive flows of people, technologies, ideas, money and media operating at different scales and speeds.[7] An archaeology of the urban design present must examine today's simultaneous formation of urban strata triggered by the heightened pace of contemporary globalisation and urbanisation which outpaces both human and environmental capacities to adapt.

Appadurai has described the difference between the **globalisation of knowledge**, where the disciplines of Western Enlightenment have dominated research about urbanisation and modernity, and **knowledge of globalisation**, the ability to understand the many aspects and dimensions of the rapid changes unleashed in the recent past. Discussions on globalisation are currently dominated by global media, financial capital, nation-states and the international agencies formed to manage the world after the Second World War – such as the UN, World Bank and the IMF. Appadurai instead argues for a democratisation of research about globalisation – a crucial task for urban designers today as countless people around the globe attempt to shape their own space in the world.[8] How can the digital archives of archaeological modelling be both an instrument of inquiry into the disruptions unleashed by globalisation and a democratisation of knowledge about urban design?

60

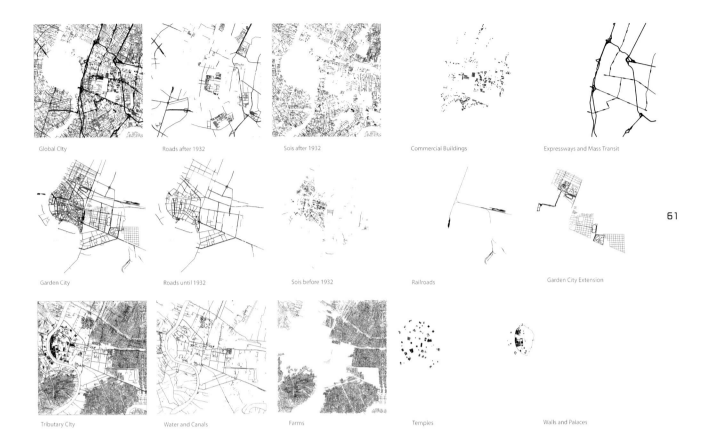

Global City

Roads after 1932

Sois after 1932

Commercial Buildings

Expressways and Mass Transit

Garden City

Roads until 1932

Sois before 1932

Railroads

Garden City Extension

Tributary City

Water and Canals

Farms

Temples

Walls and Palaces

61

Matrix of the digital archive
and archaeological analysis
of Bangkok's urban design
elements. Top to bottom:
Global, Garden and Tributary
City, 2008.

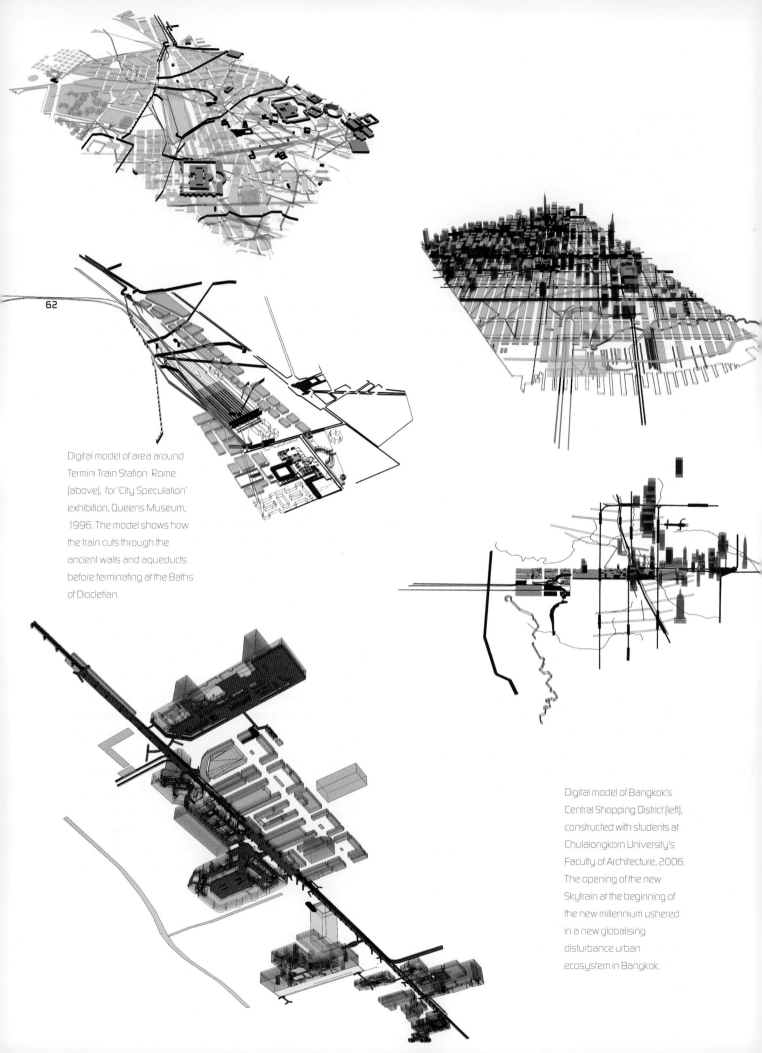

62

Digital model of area around Termini Train Station, Rome (above), for 'City Speculation' exhibition, Queens Museum, 1996. The model shows how the train cuts through the ancient walls and aqueducts before terminating at the Baths of Diocletian.

Digital model of Bangkok's Central Shopping District (left), constructed with students at Chulalongkorn University's Faculty of Architecture, 2006. The opening of the new Skytrain at the beginning of the new millennium ushered in a new globalising disturbance urban ecosystem in Bangkok.

From Transparent Cities to Archaeological Modelling

In 1996, I was invited to participate in a large exhibition at the Queens Museum. I assembled a huge matrix of left-over acetate reproductions from *Transparent Cities*, while a video monitor displayed a looping video of 3-D digital models constructed from my cartographic research of Rome and New York. This was my first opportunity to test archaeological modelling in a digital environment. The animations cross-reference journeys in both cities: travelling by train through the ancient aqueducts and walls of Rome, before entering the city through Termini station and arriving at the 19th-century Piazza Nazionale constructed among the ruins of the Baths of Diocletian. New York was approached through the Lincoln Tunnel before spiralling up the ramps of the Port Authority Bus Terminal. Passing through the subway interchange at Times Square, the animation ends at the neoclassical New York Public Library sitting within the skyscrapers of Midtown Manhattan. These models began to examine archaeological modelling as a way of exploring the historical ruptures embedded in urban space.

Michel Foucault's early research forms an **archaeology** of the formative period of Western Enlightenment from the 17th to the 19th century. *The Order of Things: An Archaeology of the Human Sciences*, *The Archaeology of Knowledge*, and *The Birth of the Clinic: An Archaeology of the Gaze*, all examine how words, institutions and space are historical forms of knowledge stratified over time.[9] Foucault's archaeology distinguishes between the formation of statements and the 'non-discursive' formation of environments in order to uncover the relationship between words and environments unique to every era.[10] This chapter employs archaeological modelling not to narrate a continuous history of urban design, but to analyse the formation of urban design as a disruptive discipline and practice.

Archaeological modelling is therefore a method in analysing **ruptures** in physical urban strata as a way of uncovering what Foucault refers to as the stratification of knowledge. The method uncovers the formation of new discursive, institutional and spatial practices unique to a place and time.[11] In the following three sections, the activities of archaeological mapping and archival collecting in Rome, New York and Bangkok are shown as searches for new urban design models within the ruptures of a rapidly modernising world at the beginning and end of the 20th century. Through mapping and archiving these disruptive spatial practices at the beginning of the 20th century, we will be able to identify urban form itself as evidence of new knowledge made visible, tangible and visceral at our present disjunctive moment at the beginning of the 21st century.

In addition to considering urban design as historical ruptures, we can also consider archaeological modelling as a first step in conceiving urban ecologies not in equilibrium or balance, but in a constant state of chaos or flux. **Disturbance** ecology looks at ecosystems – including urban ecosystems – as landscapes in flux. Any semblance of rationality or order achieved in a fragment or through urban design will cause a disturbance outside its boundaries. Archaeological modelling for urban design requires a multi-scaled as well as a multi-layered approach which can be applied to a critical analysis of the disjunctive flows of contemporary globalisation described by Arjun Appadurai. In the chapter 6, we will look at Bangkok's Skytrain as an agent in creating a globalising disturbance model in the city at the beginning of the 21st century.

1893–1901: *Forma Urbis Romae*

Rodolfo Lanciani (1845–1929) was the chief archaeologist of Rome, who excavated many monuments of the Forum, including the House of Vestals. His monumental atlas, *Forma Urbis Romae* (1893–1901) mapped four million square metres of the unearthed ancient city, previously unknown, on 46 plates at 1:1000 scale.[12] Not just a resource for the study of the ancient city, it was meant to be used as a basis for the organisation of modern development and a blueprint for new construction. The vast amount of new knowledge and physical remains of antiquity uncovered in the wake of rapid redevelopment and modernisation of the city prompted Lanciani to promote his atlas as an archaeological urban design model for the new Rome.

Lanciani's atlas distinguishes ruptures or moments of epochal change in the history of the city with three colours: the Imperial City until the fall of the empire is in black, the papal city until the 1870 liberation of Rome in red, and the expansion and redevelopment schemes of Lanciani's own time – the emerging National Capital in blue. For us we will refer to the three disjunctive periods in Rome's history as the **Imperial Capital**, **Christian Capital** and **National Capital**. However, Rome's Definitive Regulatory Plan of June 1871 called for two new boulevards: Via Nazionale near the new train terminal and Via Cavour near the Vatican which disregarded Lanciani's discoveries and recommendations. Developers from northern Italy, England, Germany and Austria quickly constructed new neighbourhoods in these areas. The design competition for the nationalist monument to Vittorio Emanuele II which now towers over and turning its back on the Imperial Fora was held in 1884.

Between 1870 and 1885 – the first 15 years Rome served as national capital – 1150 acres were developed, 140 kilometres of new roads were constructed, new neighbourhoods containing 95,000 new rooms in 3000 new buildings were built, and 81 million cubic metres of dirt excavated. As a consequence many antiquities and much new scholarship came to light along with four square kilometres of the ancient city. Lanciani conceived of his map as a guide to builders who needed to record the superimposition of previous buildings to act like a geological map – the soil of Rome is the soil of archaeology.[13]

For Lanciani, nothing was more banal and disharmonious than the new quarters that replaced the ancient villas of the *disabitato* as the population doubled in 15 years due to frenzied real-estate speculation. Lanciani blames Rome's aristocracy for selling the old estates: 'To our great names our misfortune ... a disgraced race discovered they could make a little of what their ancestors had built and maintained.'[14] Everyone joined a race to destroy the quickest. The atlas, intended to be used as instrument of conscience for democratic dialogue, failed, for 'ignorance is great ally of controlling power and land owners'.[15]

Digital model of Baroque over
Imperial Rome showing the
shift of the centre of the city
from the twin peaks of the
Capitoline Hill seen in the
centre of the map to the trident
of Piazza del Popolo to the
north and the Vatican enclave
to the north-east.

Model of the new
neighbourhoods which
developed after 1871
beyond the medieval city, yet
mostly within the 3rd-century
Aurelian Walls.

Model of 20th-century
developments over the Imperial
City no longer contained by the
Aurelian Walls.

1915–28: The Iconography of Manhattan Island
American architect Isaac Newton Phelps-Stokes
(1867–1944) assembled in his lifetime a vast collection of
maps, views and historical documents of New York which
today is archived in the New York Public Library. His
archive is reproduced in six volumes published between
1915 and 1928, *The Iconography of Manhattan Island*.[16]
New York City – like Rome at the same time – was a vast
construction site during the period that Phelps-Stokes
assembled his archive. The city was excavated for the
construction of grand rail stations, subways and
skyscrapers rather than to uncover ruins. The 'Imperial
City of the New World' was emerging at the turn of the
20th century, based on financial rather than military
conquests. Instead of surveying ruins, Phelps-Stokes
frequented auctions and antiquarian shops collecting
records, views and maps of the city. Like Lanciani, he
divided his documents into distinct time periods.

> The *Iconography* divides itself, chronologically as
> well as topographically, into two main parts. The
> first begins with the second voyage of Vespucius,
> in 1498, on which, probably for the first time, the
> precincts of Manhattan Island were approached by
> Europeans, and ends with the report and plan of
> the Commission of 1807, which sound the death
> knell of the old city. The second begins with the
> development of the new city in accordance with
> the Commissioner's plan, and ends with the
> Hudson-Fulton Celebration of 1909.[17]

A third period was emerging while Phelps-Stokes's head
was buried in his archive – the modern skyscraper city
which was being constructed during the first three
decades of the 20th century.

> What I could not guess was that this little low-
> studded rectangular New York, cursed with its
> universal chocolate-coloured coating of the most
> hideous stone ever quarried, this cramped
> horizontal gridiron of a town without towers,
> porticoes, fountains or perspectives, hidebound in
> its dreary uniformity of mean ugliness, would fifty
> years later be as much a vanished city as Atlantis
> or the lower layer of Schliemann's Troy.[18]

In 1933, Edith Wharton describes centuries of
archaeological change collapsed within her own lifetime.
Sixty years later, Rem Koolhaas again used the same
analogy of Schliemann's Troy as an argument for
architects to develop new tools to decipher the
contemporary city.

Contemporary New York's present financial service-
led economy consists of 'high-tech marvels that have
been superimposed over a low-to-medium tech
infrastructure – essentially a layering of late 20th (and
now 21st) century over the 19th century city'.[19] The
logistical intricacy of this superimposition depends upon
data archives and the layered maps of centuries of
infrastructure to unravel the complexity of constructing
in what is at once an aging as well as highly
technologically advanced landscape. Our digital archive of
New York, like that of Rome, consists of four maps of
various urban elements from three disjunctive eras: the
colonial **mercantile city**, the **industrial city**, and the
informational city.

Model of industrial New York, dominated by the grid legislated by the New York State Commission in 1811 over the British mercantile city at the end of colonial rule in 1783.

The informational New York
consists of a delicate digital
infrastructure superimposed
over the gridded industrial
city and its subways.

Map of informational New York
showing the two high-rise
business districts
superimposed over the rocky
narrow island of Manhattan.

1890–1932: The Geo-body of Bangkok

Simultaneously with Lanciani's and Phelps-Stokes's efforts, King Chulalongkorn (1853–1910) of Siam – present-day Thailand – instituted a systematic survey and cartographic project of Bangkok. His detailed maps were part of a national modernisation project in the face of encroaching European colonialisation – the French in Indo-China, the British in Burma and Malaya and the Dutch in Java. The individual plates of his Royal Survey maps – eventually distributed in various archives around the city, as newer mapping bureaucracies and techniques were created following the founding of the constitutional monarchy of Thailand in 1932 – are only now being reassembled by the Faculty of Architecture at Chulalongkorn University.[20]

Thongchai Winichakul, following Foucault's archaeology of Western Enlightenment, has described how cartography created a rupture in the Siamese conception of their 'geo-body'. Modern cartography, borrowed from the West, transformed an indigenous spatial imagination based on a tributary culture of unbounded centres and peripheries to one based on the bordered nation-state.[21] The cultural dimensions of disjunctive local and global flows can be traced in Chulalongkorn's first maps of Bangkok. Siam and Thailand were never colonised, but developed modern discourses, institutions and spatial practices according to Western norms due to the influence and pressures of European powers in the neighbouring colonies. Modernisation in Siam was a top-down, royally sponsored process, 'which probably constitutes one of the most comprehensive, elite-directed reform movements in modern history'.[22]

King Rama V's Garden City
expansions to the north and
east of the walled enclave
Rattanakosin Island city.

Land surveying and mapping was an important part of this imported technology in recasting Siam as a modern nation-state. Although the Royal Survey plates only begin in 1890, over 100 years after Bangkok was founded by the present Chakri dynasty, they give us a clear indication of the formation of Bangkok over time. The plates are highly detailed and are colour coded according to building construction. This colour separation allows us to read the recent masonry shop houses and monumental European-style structures of the modernising city, as a layer superimposed on the still vibrant, canal-based, older fabric of wood houses and irrigated agricultural fields. The maps extend far into the countryside, so they are also evidence of the agricultural basis of the urban morphology of the modern city which emerged in the absence of Master Planning after 1932. These historical maps hold the key to unlock the formation of the complexity of Bangkok's fragmented urban fabric today.

Chulalongkorn's original maps have been recently assembled, digitally copied, and analysed by a team of scholars at the Faculty of Architecture at Chulalongkorn University. Bundit Chulasai, Terdsak Tachakitkachorn and Pirasri Povatong have compiled, reproduced and created a database for three historic maps of Bangkok. The 1887 *Plan of Bangkok* was created by the Royal Survey Department during the early part of King Chulalongkorn's reign. According to the researchers' report, the city of Bangkok was surveyed for the first time during the year 1886, and a map was printed in Britain the following year, showing the entire city east of the Chao Phraya River at a scale of 1:4000. They also included a cadastral map at the scale of 1:1000 – the same scale as Lanciani's atlas – that the Royal Survey Department made in 1907, when it was under the Ministry of Agriculture, and finally the last Royal Survey Department map of 1932, when it was under the Ministry of Defence.[23]

Global Bangkok's many
commercial districts sprawl
east of the historic city, with
the most exclusive
developments situated in
garden-like settings of the
19th-century expansion.

The Royal Survey maps had been scattered in various archives and collections following the democratic coup of 1932, when the modern state of Thailand was formed. The research team found three sets of the 1887 *Plan*, 190 sheets of the 1907 maps and 34 sheets of the 1932 maps from various map repositories and archives in Bangkok, including the Land Department, the Royal Thai Survey Department, the National Library and the National Archives of Thailand. After an initial inventory, each set of maps was subsequently digitised and studied. A new cartographical framework was created by combining the maps' coordinate system, which will form the basis for urban design research in the future.

Marc Askew has argued that 'historically, Thais have not been really interested in comprehensively documenting their principal city'.[24] The work of the Chulalongkorn research team has disproved such faulty assumptions about Thai urbanism both historically and in the present. Our digital archive of Bangkok again assembles four maps of urban elements from three distinct historical periods which constitute the contemporary city: the canal-based **tributary city** before Europeanisation, the **garden city** which was created as a first wave of modernisation modelled on European colonial discipline, and the **global city**, marked by the disjunctive flows of today's mediated world (see illustration on page 59).

Roma Urbis Romae, *The Iconography of Manhattan Island* and *The Royal Survey Maps* all prefigured the introduction of computer technology based on Geographic Information System (GIS) mapping and 3-D modelling programs which store, layer, archive, retrieve, display, map and model urban information selectively. Data and space can now be cross-referenced, so the formulation of new knowledge of cities is more and more based on what these databases hold, and how the data can be represented. However, *Transparent Cities* introduced the idea of de-layering urban strata as a critical act in undermining the authority of the single map and uncovering the ruptures in the creation of new forms of urban space and knowledge. Computer technology has yet to be embraced as an archaeological critique of knowledge and power structures in the making of urban space. The digitisation of *Transparent Cities* as archaeological modelling for urban design forms the basis for a deeper understanding of the disruptive practices, and formation, of urban design knowledge across time and space.

Bangkok's new mass-transit
system glides over and
under its still extant canal
network.

18th-c. key in Italian

8th-c. inscription in Latin

8th-c. figures carved in stone

16th-c. figures atop Farnese Villa gate

18th-c. figures drawn by Piranesi

18th-c. figures etched in copper

Piranesi's etchings of the Roman Forum (1760). Fragments of ancient ruins are juxtaposed with Renaissance landmarks and scenes from everyday life. The triumphal Arch of Titus is in the foreground to the right, while the grand entry to the Farnese Orchards can be seen to the left. Alessandro Farnese, Pope Paul III (1468–1549) built the gardens on top of the Palatine Hill to legitimise his authority and the Church's through its collateral relation to the monuments of the Forum. Compare this view with Piranesi's second etching of the Arch analysed in Chapter 5. Renaissance and Baroque construction exerted collateral damage as well; the Forum became a marble quarry for the new landmarks of the city.

Assembling New Urban Design Models

Deleuze outlines three different spatial realms which encircle any archaeological statement in Foucault's writing. In digital modelling for urban design, these imply different ways in which urban design is practised through the interaction of actors in specific environments involved in what Arjun Appadurai has called 'the social production of locality'.[25] Locus does not just emanate from the 'genus' of a place, as suggested by Christian Norberg-Schulz and Aldo Rossi (see the following chapter), but from the continuous work of social actors. Similarly, mapping is not the literal act of colonial surveying that Thongchai has critiqued in Thailand, but is much more strategic. There must be a careful analysis and critical positioning of urban design practice within different kinds of spatial and representational production.

We will conclude this chapter on archaeology by considering three types of space which can be generated from the ruptures in our digital archives. Rather than through the seduction of walk-through simulation discussed in the Introduction, archaeological digital modelling can result in more critical urban design practices. New forms of archaeological modelling can focus on the disruptive nature of urban design as a tool to locate interventions within and between the disjunctive global flows which mark the contemporary city. The three kinds of space that can be generated between the layers of digital archaeological models are **collateral**, **correlative** and **complementary** space.

Collateral Space

Collateral space is 'an associate or adjacent domain formed from other statements that are part of the same group'.[26] Grahame Shane has called such spatial formation the creation of urban enclaves, bounded areas which comprise special districts based on a common collective imagination of a civic body or group of urban citizens.[27] Collateral space defines the group and the group defines the space and must necessarily exclude others outside the boundary of the enclave. Ordering and coding through spatial position, time and significance is important in the collateral space of enclaves. This is how urban design becomes a statement of the power of a certain group's discourse – it moves from description of a cultural norm to the prescription of a bounded spatial logic. This book will compare models of the collateral space created in three specific urban localities: the Roman Forum (Chapter 2), Manhattan's skyscraper business districts (Chapter 4), and Bangkok'sCentral Shopping District (Chapter 6). For digital modelling for urban design, collateral space introduces the construction of digital archives to carefully analyse new construction in relation to existing built or natural conditions, in order to examine what in war is called collateral damage – the unintended consequences of military action.

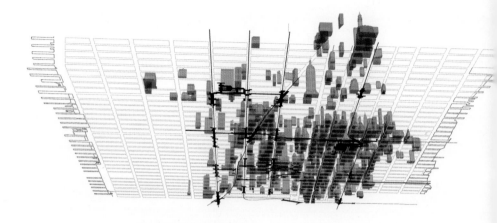

The correlative space of the
high-rise business districts of
Lower and Midtown
Manhattan developed over
time according to various
legislative restrictions and
incentives. (See discussion of
genealogy in Chapter 4.)

80 Correlative Space

Correlative space consists of naturally and reciprocally
related linkages between non-adjacent subjects, objects
and concepts.[28] Shane has described the linear,
connective movement systems in urban design as urban
armatures.[29] Correlative space is created by movement
systems which bring together different groups, urban
elements and ideas about the city. Leaving the situated
collateral space of urban enclaves, the correlative space
of urban armatures will be explored from Chapter 3,
Genealogy. Pope Sixtus V of Rome developed a system of
urban armatures which linked the dispersed Christian
churches of the city into one network. In New York, the
subway system and suburban commuter train lines
allowed for the concentration of new business districts in
both Lower and Midtown Manhattan (Chapter 4), while
the new Skytrain in Bangkok has created a multi-level
urban armature which interconnects formerly distinct
urban shopping enclaves (Chapter 6). While
archaeological analysis of collateral space considers the
consequences of urban design in situated space,
genealogical analysis (Chapter 3) will consider the
relationship between urban design interventions in
time, experientially, sequentially or as phased
incremental development.

Complementary Space

Complementary space is used to describe the creation of
non-discursive statements.[30] Urban design speaks to the
multitude through spatial relations and symbols rather
than words. Shane refers to heterotopias as spaces
outside normative city models, where deviance is hidden
or isolated, and sites of experimentation and illusions are
created.[31] They are the change elements of the city and
often act on the unconscious. Complementary space will
be explored in the transformation of the triumphal march
in Rome to the Christian pilgrimage, and finally the use of
archaeology to legitimise modern regimes of power. In
New York we will examine the space of capitalism as it
moved from a direct relationship to trade and the port of
Lower Manhattan, to the creation of consumer capitalism
after the Second World War in Midtown, connected
through the corporate offices on Park Avenue, the
advertising firms on Madison Avenue and the television
broadcasting studios along Sixth Avenue. American-style
global consumerism was introduced in Bangkok through
shopping as a primary social activity. These retail spaces
evolved in relation to mediated models of lifestyle from
Tokyo, Hong Kong, and most recently, Seoul. A method
called Schizoanalysis, introduced in Chapter 5, will be our
primary tool in digitally modelling the complementary
space of heterotopias. Urban design modellers have
always had to consider the inner worlds of city
inhabitants as well as the outer realm of city space.
Schizoanalytical modelling in the digital age must
consider the psychological dimensions of a mediated
globalised world in relation to the design of physical and
material space.

Multiplicities and Seriality

Digitally archiving the formation of urban space as the stratification of knowledge is not to serve as the basis of constructing a historical narrative. Instead, our digital archives of Rome, New York and Bangkok are used to construct multiple and diverse serial analyses of cities in the service of originating new practices of urban design. Deleuze points to a way out of the problem of historical narratives. 'One must pursue the different series, travel along the different levels, and cross all thresholds; instead of simply displaying phenomena or statements in their vertical or horizontal dimensions, one must form a transversal or mobile diagonal line along which the archaeological-archivist must move. [Foucault] created a new dimension, which we might call diagonal dimension, a sort of distribution of points, groups or figures that no longer act simply as an abstract framework but actually exist in space.'[32]

Urban complexity can be unpacked through such a serial process of modelling urban design as a multiplicity rather than a unifying singularity. Modelling various attributes and elements of the city as separate layers of information taken from Geographic Information Systems, historical maps, land cover, land use and remote sensing, all are used in contemporary urban design practice, but the tools of transversal analysis are lacking in contemporary urban discourse. This book establishes the critical processes which enable one to isolate and investigate the *relationships* between discourse, urban elements and perceptions, mined from data from various disciplines – environmental, social and economic.

Deleuze calls Foucault both the *New Archivist* and the *New Cartographer*, as his archaeological method departs from standard categorical and mapping techniques. Foucault does not classify history into formal categories based on authoritative interpretation; rather his methodology is to 'assemble an archive of detailed descriptions of micro-processes which constituted the creative forces of new statements and visibilities, which only later become formalized into institutions and space'.[33] Ultimately, the archaeologist's goal is to uncover the micro-forces which break through historical strata. Foucault's archaeology suggests a radically different practice for urban design.

Hidden processes that underlie shifts in urban design thinking – such as the introduction of electronic trading in the New York Stock Exchange – can be located by situating contemporary urban discourse and representations in historical contexts and events. The archaeological method provides a key tool in countering the 'spectacular' problem of urban design today by locating meaning not in the simulation of surface representation of things, but within the space of historical ruptures. Archaeological modelling for urban design can be used to compare relations between multiple contested perceptions and systems of meanings. It is through the engagement of new ways of relational and comparative thinking through digital modelling that new criteria for urban design can be defined beyond the limits and problems of its *Spectacularisation*. The archaeological method allows one to model and design within the disjunctive flows that comprise the collateral, correlative and complementary spaces of the contemporary city.

82   Endnotes

1 Brian McGrath, *Transparent Cities*, New York: SITES Books, 1994.

2 Colin Rowe and Robert Slutsky, 'Transparency: Literal and Phenomenal', from Colin Rowe, *The Mathematics of the Ideal Villa and Other Essays*, Cambridge: MIT Press, 1976, pp 159–76.

3 Gregory Kepes, *The Language of Vision*, Chicago: Theobald, 1944, p 77.

4 Marshall Berman, *All that is Solid Melts into Air*, New York: Viking Press, 1982.

5 Frank X Arvan, *Houses and Gardens on the Lower East Side: Can we have both?*, New York: ADPSR, 1991.

6 Rem Koolhaas, *The Terrifying Beauty of the 20th Century: OMA*, New York: Princeton Architectural Press, 1991, p 154.

7 Arjun Appadurai, *Modernity at Large*, Minneapolis: University of Minnesota Press, 1996.

8 Arjun Appadurai, 'Grassroots Globalization and the Research Imagination', *Public Culture*, 12(1), Durham: Duke University Press, 2000, pp 1–19.

9 Michel Foucault, *The Order of Things*, London: Tavistock, 1970, translation of *Les Mots et les choses*, Paris: Gallimard, 1966; *The Archaeology of Knowledge*, London: Tavistock, 1972, translation of *L'archéologie du savoir*, Paris: Gallimard, 1969; *Birth of the Clinic*, London: Tavistock, 1973, translation of *Naissance de la clinique, Une archéologie du regard médical*, Paris: Gallimard, 1963.

10 Gilles Deleuze, *Foucault*, translated by Sean Hand, Minneapolis: University of Minnesota Press, 1988, p 31.

11 Deleuze, pp 48–9.

12 Reproduced by Edizioni Quasar, Rome, in 1990 at 1:2000 scale.

13 Rodolfo Lanciani, *The Destruction of Ancient Rome*, New York: Macmillan, 1901.

14 Ibid.

15 Ibid.

16 Isaac Newton Phelps-Stokes, *The Iconography of Manhattan Island*, New York: Dodd, Vol I, 1915, Vol II, 1916, Vol III, 1918 (including the Landmark Map), Vol IV, 1922, Vol V, 1926, and Vol VI, 1928.

17 Phelps-Stokes, 1909–28.

18 Edith Wharton, *A Backward Glance*, New York: Scribner's, 1933, p 55.

19 Paul Drucker, 'Information and the Future of the City', *The Wall Street Journal*, 4 April 1989, p 27.

20 Bundit Chulasai, Terdsak Tachakitkachorn, Pirasri Povatong, Chulalongkorn Faculty of Architecture Research Center (unpublished research abstract, 2006).

21 Thongchai Winichakul, *Siam Mapped: A history of the geo-body of a nation*, Honolulu: University of Hawaii Press, 1994.

22 Han ten Brummelhuis, *King of the Waters: Homan van der Heide and the origin of modern irrigation in Siam*, Chiang Mai: Silkworm Books, 2005.

23 Bundit Chulasai, Terdsak Tachakitkachorn, Pirasri Povatong, 2006.

24 Marc Askew, *Interpreting Bangkok: The Urban Question in Thai Studies*, Bangkok: Chulalongkorn University Press, 1994.

25 Appadurai, 1996.

26 Deleuze, pp 4–6.

27 David Grahame Shane, *Recombinant Urbanism*, London: John Wiley & Sons, 2005, p 176.

28 Deleuze, pp 6–9.

29 Shane, p 198.

30 Deleuze, pp 9–12.

31 Shane, p 231.

32 Deleuze, p 22.

33 Deleuze, p 2.

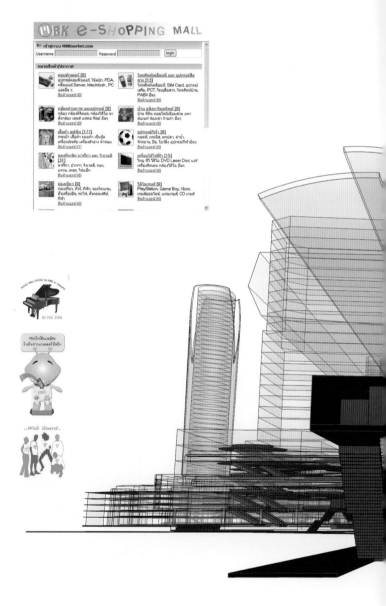

Section through the National Stadium Station in Bangkok. The physical space of Bangkok's central shopping district is complemented by the space of entertainment, advertising, media and websites which encourage membership in online social groups (see Chapter 6).

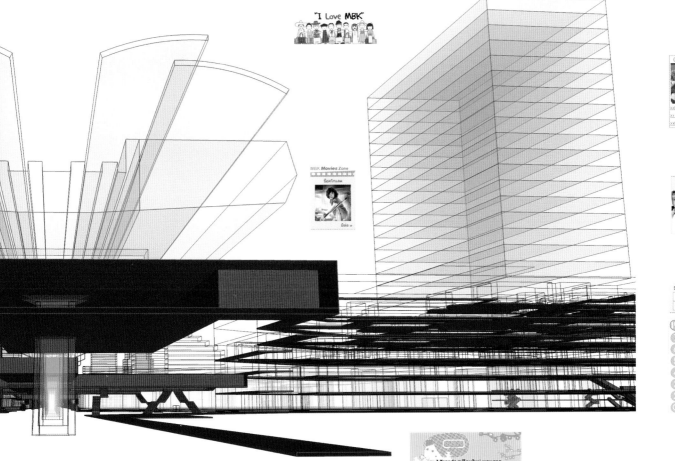

Chapter 2

War

Slowly climbing the steep ramp to Rome's Campidoglio at dusk, the confines of the narrow streets of the medieval city left behind and the jumble of rooftops left below, Michelangelo's raised piazza, bounded by facades glowing gold in the reflected sunlight, is dominated by the bronze equestrian statue of Roman Emperor Marcus Aurelius in its centre. In 1539, Pope Paul III moved the ancient statue from the porticoes of the papal Lateran Palace where it had been on display for centuries, to face the city and the sunset to the west.[1] Its position invites us to turn towards the skyline view dotted by the domes of the Baroque city; they seem to float like helium-filled balloons above the city, with Michelangelo's dome of St Peter's soaring above all. After the sun sets, a small stairway behind Rome's city hall entices you into an excavated abyss scattered with fragmented white marbles of the Roman Forum glowing under the moon rising over the Coliseum in the background. Once the central public space of ancient Rome from 627 BC to AD 394 when its temples were closed for ever, this giant excavated space is now a huge sunken void in the heart of modern Rome. Like Ground Zero in New York, its edge can only be skirted around the ruins of the monuments which celebrate the city's violent and disruptive past.

According to Aldo Rossi, the Roman Forum is of fundamental importance for a comprehensive understanding of **urban artefacts** and a demonstration of the 'intimate and protracted relationship' between urban architecture and its specific site or **locus**.[2] A discursion to the Roman Forum is necessary to understand more fully how the void of Ground Zero in New York itself acts as an urban artefact. This chapter continues the process of creating a methodology of digital modelling for contemporary urban design through an archaeological analysis of the collateral space of the Roman Forum. For Rossi, 'The Roman Forum constitutes one of the most illustrative urban artefacts that we can know: bound as it is with the origins of the city; extremely, almost unbelievably, transformed over time, but always growing upon itself; parallel to the history of Rome as it is documented in every historical stone and legend ... ultimately reaching us today through its strikingly clear and splendid signs.'[3]

Tourists climb the gently ramped Cordonata stair leading to Michelangelo's Piazza del Campidoglio, the seat of the municipal government.

Michelangelo's piazza turns its back on the Roman Forum, the centre of the Imperial city, which became a cow and sheep pasture during the Middle Ages. Instead it faces the Medieval City tucked into a bend in the Tiber River.

The piazza faces north-west towards the medieval Christian city, which shrank within the bend of the Tiber River.

It is now a sunken garden, accessible only to daytime tourist and archaeological itineraries.

The Roman Forum's displays of triumph and the spoils of Imperial conquest culminated in the construction of the monumental Trajan's Forum, built at the height of Rome's territorial conquests. Yet Trajan's Forum still remains partially buried under the street Mussolini constructed as the Via dei Imperiali. Transformations and additions to the civic realm of the Republican Forum resulted in examples of urban design practice that, like Mussolini's, were hardly intimate and protracted, but marked by sacrifice, blood and violence. The Forum is now hauntingly emptied by the practice of scientific archaeology, except for the overheated tourists vainly attempting to make sense of such a vast fragmented space, and the feral cats who prowl with the ghosts at night.

No longer the centre of the city, never mind an empire, the Roman Forum of the Middle Ages was used primarily for grazing sheep and cows. After a thousand years at the shrunken city's periphery, the Forum again became a centre of interest between the 15th and 18th centuries, as it became a reference and model first for Renaissance architects such as Alberti and Bramante, and later for the architects of the European Enlightenment's Grand Tour. Before Mussolini's excesses ended the legitimisation of modern power through Rome's classical symbols, many of the capital cities of the emerging classical and colonial worlds were born from these travellers' experiences of the Roman Forum.

This chapter excavates the Roman Forum first as an archaeological excavation of collateral space, and then as a way of understanding the relationship between power and knowledge in urban design and representation. This discussion will continue in Chapter 3 as I examine the networks of legitimacy political powers invested in them by employing Rome as an urban design model. In Chapter 5, through the engraved *Views of Rome* by Giovanni Battista Piranesi, I will complete our analysis of the Roman Forum not as a singular urban artefact, but as an unstable mediated space which hovers in experience and in the imagination between construction and destruction.

Digital model of the Forum at
the beginning of the 19th
century. The Piazza del
Campidoglio is in the
foreground, with the Roman
Forum directly behind.
Trajan's Column can be seen
to the left, indicating the buried
Imperial Fora below. The
Coliseum can be seen further
beyond the Forum.

89

1801–1803: The Emergence of Scientific Archaeology

The spiralling bas-relief that climbs Trajan's Column
depicts the Emperor's brutal conquest of Dacia between
AD 101 and 106. However, a visitor climbing the 185
stairs up to the top of the column will not find the heroic
statue of the victorious Emperor, represented as a
general with his spear and armour. But a statue of St
Peter with his keys by Giacomo della Porta, that was
placed there by Pope Sixtus V in 1588, a millennium after
the fall of Imperial Rome. This act symbolically
transferred the power of the Emperor to that of Sixtus
through the representation of the first pope of the Roman
Catholic Church.

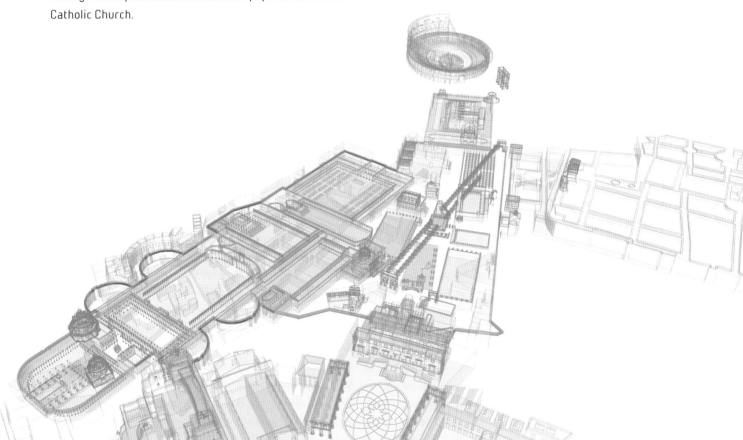

According to James Packer, the scientific discipline of archaeology in Rome grew out of the desire to consecrate contemporary power through a direct connection to history.[4] Packer acknowledges that the contemporary appearance of Rome's monuments as isolated and preserved fragments of antiquity is '... a comparatively recent phenomenon, an effect of the first tentative "scientific" excavations of the early 19th century'.[5] Just two hundred years before the rushed efforts to excavate the ruins of the remains of the World Trade Center, archaeologists began the slow, painstaking process of removing centuries of rubble, fill and debris from the Roman Forum, thereby dissecting and diluting the collapsed collateral space of Christian and Pagan Rome.

Archaeology as a scientific field of knowledge begins with the earliest efforts to clean and restore the relics of Roman antiquity in 1801, when Pope Pius VII commissioned Carlo Fea and Antonio Canova to inspect and maintain the ruins of antiquity. This new practice introduced by the papacy was later inherited by secular political figures from Italy and around Europe looking to legitimise their political authority. Shortly after Pius's first archaeological efforts, French troops invaded Rome and Napoleon annexed the city in 1809. Napoleon, eager to associate his new empire with that of Rome, allocated huge funds for the excavation and repair of antiquities in the 'free and imperial city' of Rome,[6] but much of the portable remains were looted and, together with the spoils from the Egyptian campaign of 1798–1801, embellished the 'Musée Napoléon' at the Louvre in Paris.

The first archaeological digs in the first decades of the 19th century began to uncover small areas around Trajan's Column and some monuments in the Forum such as the Arch of Septimius Severus (excavations shown in red).

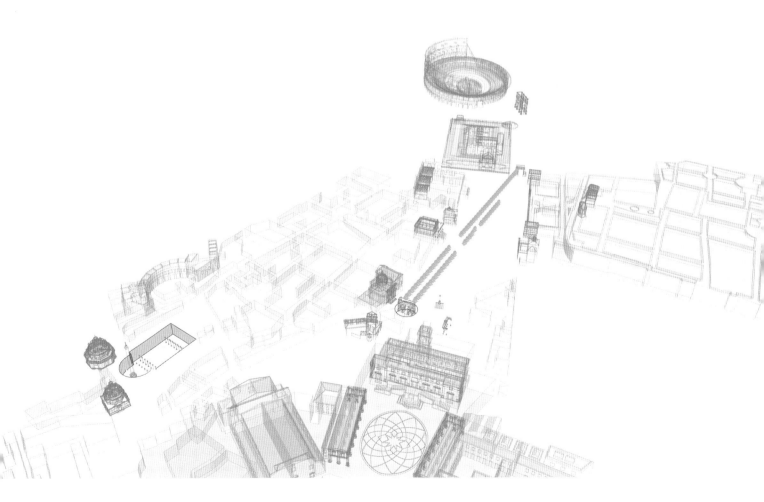

Aldo Rossi quotes the Comte De Tournon's programme for restoration work in the Roman Forum undertaken during Napoleon I's occupation. 'The restoration of these monuments consists above all in freeing them from the earth that covers their lower parts, connecting them to one another, and finally rendering access easy and pleasurable.'[7] Rossi focuses on the activity of embellishment rather than the looting of the Forum to assert the fundamental role of situated urban artefacts in creating the architecture of the city based on urban locus rather than relational context. However, Napoleon I's wartime looting and Napoleon III and Baron Haussmann's creation of triumphal monuments in Paris point to an architecture not based on the situated collateral space *locus*, but on appropriation and the correlative space of linkage – physically between modern monuments and by association with their historical antecedents, and the creation of mass urban spectacles such as grand parades and international exhibitions.

After 1814, the papacy continued excavations and restorations on their own, including the reconstruction of the Arch of Titus, the east gate to the Forum. However, Rome changed very little until 2 October 1870, when the newly formed Italian state inherited a provincial city from the popes. After that date, archaeology in Rome – the capital of the new Republic of Italy – became a politically charged urban problem tied to discourses on national identity and urban redevelopment. Archaeology became a critical political instrument as well as a physical impediment in 'the massive building campaigns which transformed Rome from a sleepy papal town into a bustling late nineteenth century metropolis'.[8]

In 1870, Rome became the
National Capital of Italy.
Archaeological excavations
went hand in hand with new
road construction and
expansion of the city. In this
view we can see the
excavations of the Republican
Forum, which uprooted the
centuries-old trees that
bisected the Forum.

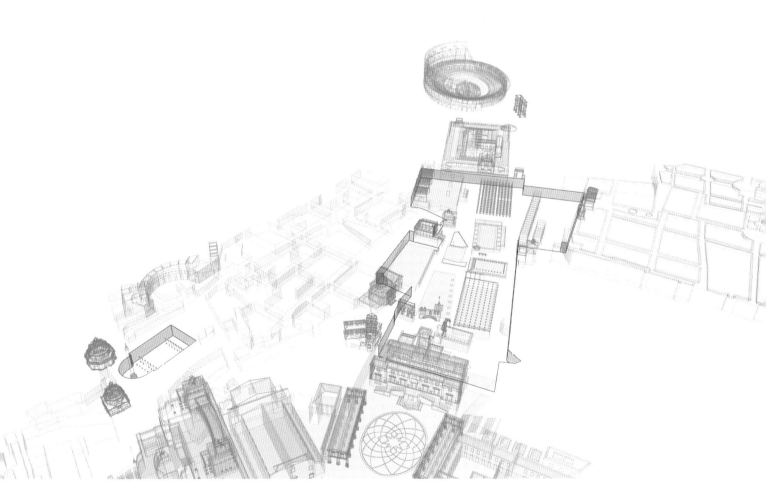

94   The re-imagination of 'Roma Capitale' was behind the vast demolitions of the Fascist regime between 1932 and 1943. On 21 April 1924, Mussolini outlined his plans to modernise the capital and to 'liberate the antiquities' from the 'unsightly' medieval fabric. In October 1932, the Via dei Imperiali, now called the Via dei Fori Imperiali, was inaugurated. By 1978 pollution and car vibrations had taken their toll even on the protected areas of the vast archaeological park in the centre of the city. A project, yet to be realised, was inaugurated to close the Via dei Fori Imperiali and remove Via Consolazione in 1980. This slow progress in reclaiming the space of archaeology from Mussolini's modern city of the car is now accompanied by the continued progress on Rome's underground metropolitan transit system.

In 1932, Mussolini inaugurated the Via dei Imperiali, connecting his headquarters at Palazzo Venezia to the Coliseum and beyond. The medieval fabric was demolished to make way for his tree-lined boulevard.

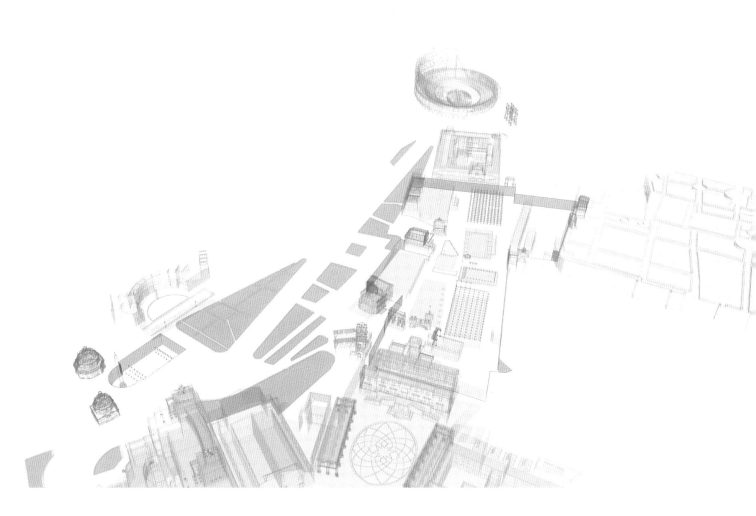

96   Packer's reading of scientific archaeology's politics is an example of Foucault's archaeology of knowledge applied to archaeological discourse itself. 'While the French between 1809 and 1814 saw antiquities as window dressing, and the late 19th century developers saw them as inconvenient obstacles, for the Fascists, only the most important monuments were worthy of saving as iconic monuments in a modern automobile based city. For contemporary urban designers, the project to cancel the fascist mark on the city is also politically motivated.'[9] The consequence of that contested discourse on the space of the Roman Forum sheds light back on to the politics surrounding Ground Zero, where the site as the locus of tragedy, disaster and environmental contamination was swept clean of all remains but a single surviving stair and the concrete bathtub foundation, and awaits reconstitution as a memorial, transit hub and business centre.

Extension of the
archaeological zone today.
Plans to close Via dei Fori
Imperiali coincide with the
construction of a new
subway linking the Coliseum
with Piazza Venezia.

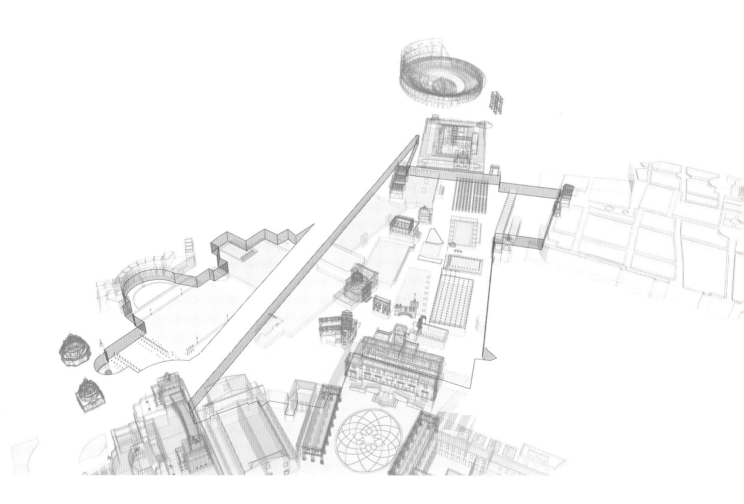

98   **50 BC – AD 203: Modelling the Spoils of War**

Rossi situates the irregular design of the Forum in relation
to Rome's origins both geographically and historically in
order to present an argument about the architecture of
the city evolving slowly in relation to formal archetypes
constructed within in a specific terrain. For example, the
Forum came to occupy a low and marshy zone between
the steep surrounding hills, each inhabited by distinct
tribes. It first became a necropolis, then a place of battles
and religious rites, but then, according to Rossi, the Forum
became the site of a new form of city life – the place
where the geographically separated tribes converged to
create a new form of urban space. Topography indicated
the way for paths and then for roads along the least steep
slopes of the surrounding hills, and separate villages
joined and strengthened in civic engagement.[10]

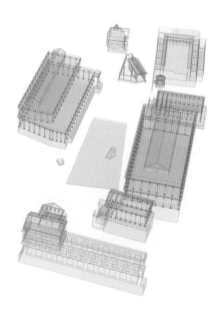
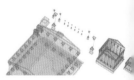

46 BC: the first Imperial Forum built in honour of Julius Caesar is constructed parallel to the old Forum, with a temple dedicated to the deified Emperor at the head.

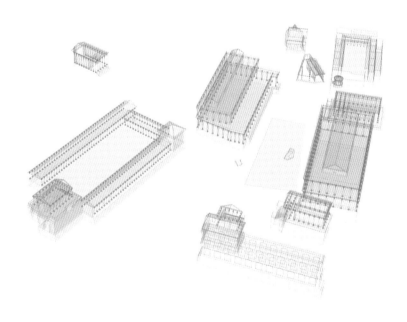

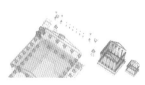

Rossi's model of urban design is articulated not as a plan created by a single designer at one moment in time, but as an evolving and adaptive structure indebted to the specificity of the terrain and inscribed by archetypal forms developed over centuries through social practice and ritual. 'Because the city is pre-eminently a collective artefact it is defined by and exists in those works that are of an essentially collective nature. Although such works arise as a means of constituting the city, they soon become an end, and this is their being and their beauty. The beauty resides both in the laws of architecture which they embody and in the collective's reasons for desiring them.'[11]

100

16 BC: the Forum of Augustus is positioned perpendicular to the Julian Forum, with the Temple to Augustus at its far end.

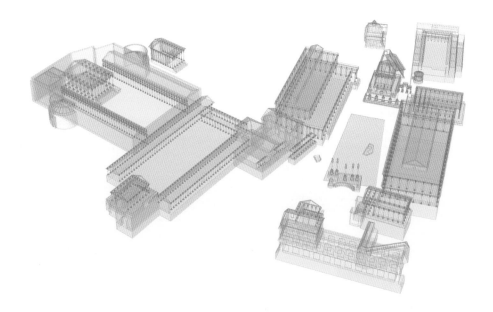

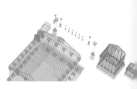

Rossi's definition of an urban artefact states that it represents both history and invention.[12] The Forum was, therefore, an urban artefact of 'extraordinary modernity' as well as a repository of history and a marker of terrain. The modernity of the Forum, for Rossi, was characterised by its central role within the city and empire. It is not its functional role as political and judicial centre which captivates Rossi's modern imagination, but the occupation of the space by masses of people idly passing time.[13] By the 5th century BC, the Forum ceased to be primarily a marketplace and became a public square in this modern sense. Crowded with statues, temples, monuments and later aggrandised by Augustus's urban renewal and enlargement, the Forum became the central meeting place of Rome, the heart of the city, and on occasion the theatre of bloody events. For Rossi, locus is not just physical context, but something much more profound tied to the magnetic attraction to the human imagination it commands.

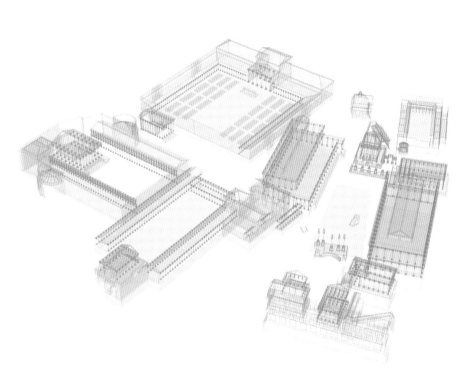

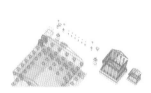

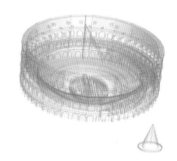

102 However closely tied to the origins of Rome, the Republican Forum formed just a small fragment of the centre of the Imperial city. The Imperial Forum complex grew over time parallel to the history of Rome's Imperial conquests, and marks a radical interruption to the continuous development Rossi narrates. The history of the Forum can be divided into three millennia: the first, from 700 BC to AD 300, comprises a model urban growth including the two centuries of the consolidation of the city of Kings (753–510 BC), and followed by five centuries of the Roman Republic (509–27 BC) that resulted in Rossi's intricate urban artefact, the Republican Forum.

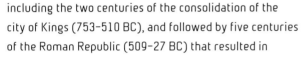

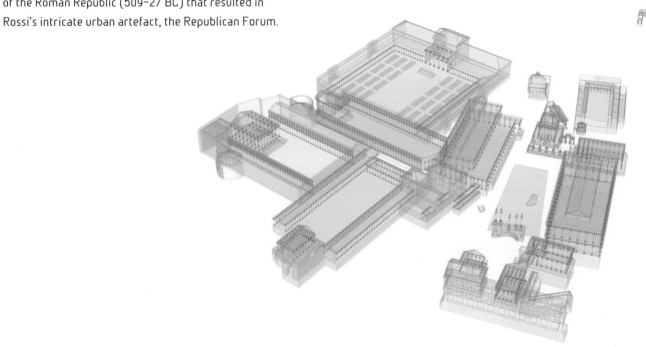

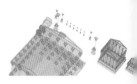

The original centre of Republican Rome occupying the valley between the Palatine and Capitoline Hills became much too limited during the Imperial era due to the population increase fed by the growth of the Empire. The original space of the Forum occupied a parallelogram focused on the rostra, or stage, with the Capitoline behind. New civic buildings – Basilica Aurelia, Forum Julium for legal business, Basilica Julia, the temple of the deified Julius Caesar – filled the former marketplace. The culminating three centuries of the Empire (27 BC – AD 330) resulted in most of the massive building programmes during the Pax Romana, an era of splendid urban embellishment before the capital moved to Constantinople.[14] The closer the Empire came to its decline, the more furiously and grandly it seemed to build.

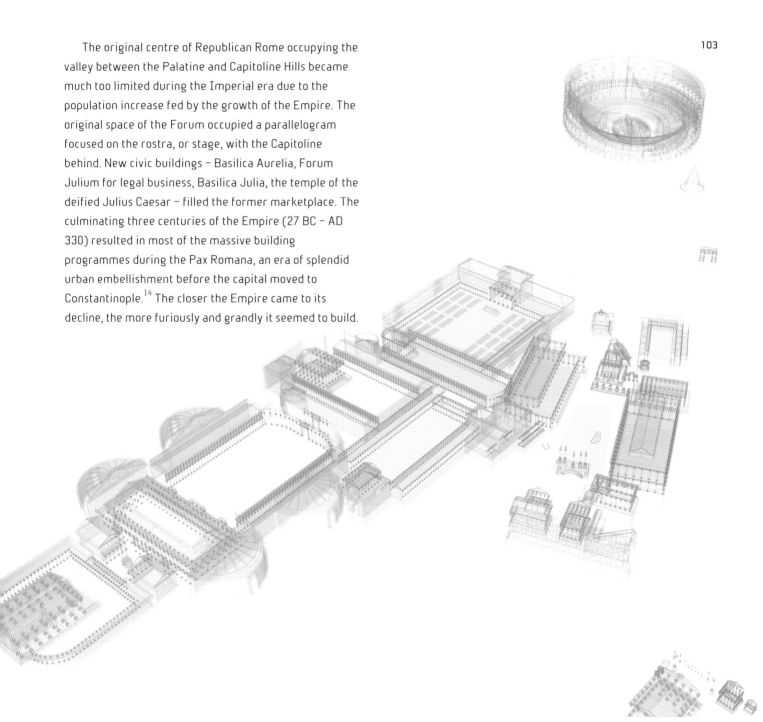

104   The original Forum could no longer grow slowly or
organically along a line to the south-east, but through a
designed sequence of linked spaces which required
massive property acquisition and alterations of the
terrain. The first Imperial Forum built was the Forum
Julium, followed by the Forum Augusta, the Forum of
Peace, the Forum of Nerva and finally Trajan's Forum –
flattening the ridge which connected the Quirinal to the
Capitoline Hill. The top of Trajan's Column marks the level
of the top of the removed hill, marking the ruptured
relation between urban design and terrain. Rossi's
process of locus and evolutionary growth is suddenly
abandoned as the Empire increases in size and power.
The maximum extent of both the Empire and the
expanded Imperial Forum complex was reached during
the reign of Trajan (AD 98–117).

The spoils of war: the growth
of the Empire and the growth
of the Forum, 50 BC – AD 113.

Urban Design as Triumphal Model

The design of the Roman Forum can be understood as a *spectacular* urban artefact in the Imperial era through Alan Plattus's analysis of the ritual of the Roman Triumph. For Plattus, the Roman triumphal march was a social drama as well as a display of political propaganda and military power as it proceeded through arches widely separated throughout the city, passing the great open theatres, arenas and circuses, before arriving at the Forum at the base of the sacred Capitoline Hill and the Temple of Jupiter. Plattus calls the triumph a sacred rite of purification. Violence, war and death brought the Roman army into intimate contact with a foreign and impure enemy. The victorious Emperor and his army were cleansed by passage through the magic portal of the triumphal arch, which removed the blood of the enemy so it would not infect the city. The spectacle of the Imperial city-state and the glory of its urban landscape were firmly established in the minds of its audience through triumphal parades. The arch acted as 'a marker and a modulator of (ritual) passage ... a real gate into an ideal or at least ritually idealized city'.[15]

Red indicates the inhabited part
of the medieval city, the *abitato*.
Churches are scattered at the
periphery over the ruins of the
Imperial city occupying sites of
former tombs and ancient
Roman houses in the
uninhabited city.

Among the hundreds of triumphs, a first-hand description survives of the same triumphal march for Vespasian and Titus:

> It is impossible adequately to describe the multitude of those spectacles and their munificence ... But nothing in the procession excited so much astonishment as the structures of the moving statues ... many of them being three or four stories high ... The war was shown by numerous representations, in separate sections, affording a very vivid picture of its episodes. Here was to be seen a prosperous country devastated, there whole battalions of the enemy slaughtered; here a party in flight, there others led into captivity; walls of surpassing compass demolished by engines, strong fortresses overpowered ... these structures now portrayed the incidents to those who had not witnessed them, as though they were happening before their eyes.
>
> The spoils in general were borne in promiscuous heaps: but conspicuous above all stood out those captured in Jerusalem. These consisted of a golden table, many talents in weight, a lamp stand, likewise made of gold ... After these, and last of all the spoils was carried a copy of the Jewish law.[16]

For Plattus, triumphal arches represent one of the single most important elements in Roman urban design, '... the stories of victory carved and monumentalized on the arches were matched by the pattern of the triumphal march itself. Thus the arches were nodes in a network which organized and gave meaning to a sprawling city. The bas-relief was unlocked into life'.[17] This network expanded with each successive conquest, as the Arch of Titus itself added another passage gate for subsequent processions.

The urban spectacle of the spoils of war and triumph that Plattus describes, however, is a far cry from the mediated one which followed the terrorist attacks on 9/11 or the wars in Afghanistan and Iraq. In the Roman triumph civic bodies were physically engaged in a collective ritualistic public event rather than passively sedated at home by numbing repetition of televisual imagery. The continuing circumambulation of thousands of visitors around the perimeter of Ground Zero, however, a few blocks from the triumphal ticker-tape route of Lower Broadway's 'Canyon of Heroes', still calls for embodied rituals around the World Trade Center site. Diller + Scofidio's viewing platform, constructed in 2002 at the end of Fulton Street, for a brief moment provided such a space. Lines of people wound up the switch-back ramps, in order to pause at a platform overlooking the giant abyss, and, at the annual anniversary commemoration of September 11, family members descend the long construction ramp down into Ground Zero itself.

300–1300: The Recycling City Model

Richard Krautheimer's portrait of medieval Rome follows the period from the collapse of the welfare and supply system at the end of the 4th century to the removal of the papal curia to Avignon in 1303 when the population may have declined to as low as 17,000.[18] Constantine's St Peter's Basilica was built over Roman tombs adjoining the Circus of Caligula and Nero in AD 312, with antique columns taken from all over the city. With 136 shafts, the basilica had no two alike, and the architraves and friezes differed from one intercolumniation to another.[19] The Roman temples were closed for ever by the end of the 4th century AD, as pagan Rome became a Christian city.

108   The great shift in the centre of Rome from the Forum to the bend of the Tiber River followed the siege of AD 537–8 when the aqueducts were cut during the Gothic War, resulting in the abandonment of the great baths, and the drying of the fountains and reservoirs. Although the Tiber periodically flooded this area, the reduced population relied on the lifeline of the river for provisions – agricultural products, floating flour mills, fish and water supply.[20]

In medieval Rome, the hills no longer counted, except where they carried outlying clusters — on the Caelian, the Esquiline, and the Aventine. The abitato moved into the unhealthy low land, the città bassa near the river, (over the ruins of) the ancient show area (the military *Campus Martius* or Field of Mars dedicated to the god of war). Ancient Rome had grown from the settlements on its hills and it remained centered on the Forum, the Capitoline, and the Palatine. Medieval Rome was anchored to the Tiber.[21]

Higher quarters of the city suffered the most; the hills were abandoned and the Campus Martius at the bend of the Tiber became the only place in the city with a ready water supply until Pope Sixtus V built the Acqua Felice aqueduct in 1587. The infrastructure to supply water for a large population was no longer adequate after the 6th century.[22]

Spreading east behind the Capitoline Hill was the *disabitato* – the vast uninhabited part of the medieval city contained within the ancient Aurelian Walls. The Forum became a threshold and crossroads between the inhabited and uninhabited areas of the city. In AD 608, the last monument was erected in the Forum – the Column of Phocas – and by the end of the 7th century, 'A worshiper raising his eyes toward the apse of the Church of SS Cosmos and Camarius could behold at the same time the great mosaic figure of the Saviour and a group of the twin founders of the city sucking the wolf'.[23] In AD 630, Pope Honorius I removed the gilt-bronze tiles from the Temple of Venus and Rome at the Forum and in AD 663 Emperor Costante II removed bronze tiles from the Pantheon for the roof of St Peter's, according to Lanciani.[24]

From the 9th century on, the east end of the Forum around the location of the Arch of Titus became a fortified suburb close to the *abitato* – the compact inhabited quarter of the city at the bend in the Tiber River. Centered on the church of S Maria Nova, built around 855 atop the ruins of the Temple of Venus and Rome, Richard Krautheimer discovers from 10th-century leases, houses and workspaces for coppersmiths, blacksmiths, wheelwrights, cobblers, masons, and many lime burners – given the abundance of marble from the Forum's ruins. There was even a 'banker's crossroads' near the Coliseum serving pilgrims on their way from the *abitato* to the Lateran.

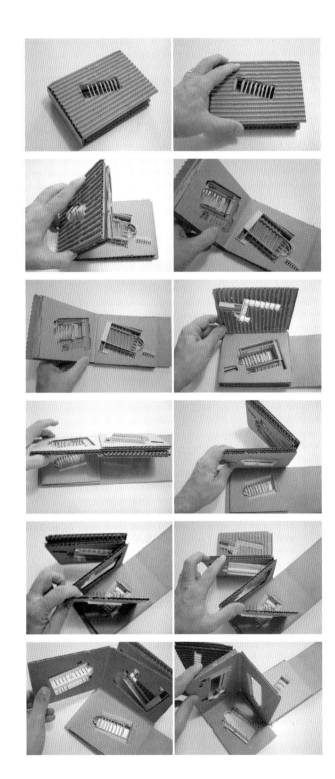

The growth and importance of the suburb at that time was probably tied to the Frangipani's occupation of the Coliseum, [sic] the slope of the Palatine, since the late eleventh century. Around the church of S. Maria Nova the cluster of housing swelled and extended both in front of the church and southward up the slope of the Palatine along a path ascending to the church of S. Maria in Pallara, now S. Sebastiano alla Polveriera. Two streets, one across the Roman Forums and another passing by the Imperial Fora, linked the area to the edge of the *abitato* along the north cliff of the Capitoline Hill and on the south stretch of the Corso.[25] Access [to this suburb] was defended by a tower built against the Arch of Titus, known as the *turris cartulari*.[26]

Krautheimer's research reveals much of the social activity of the Forum during the Middle Ages: the lime burners and craftsmen intersecting with the clerics, travellers and pilgrims at this crossroads between the inhabited and uninhabited parts of the city.

Churches: The New Urban Artefacts

Christianity was born at the periphery of the Roman Empire in the province of Judea, and slowly occupied peripheral places in the Imperial city of Rome. While Constantine (272–337), the first Christian Emperor, built large Roman-style basilicas in four opposite corners outside the city at St Peter's, Santa Maria Maggiore, St John's in the Lateran and St Paul outside the Walls, most early churches occupied ordinary houses in the city. The architecture of these churches reflects the vicissitudes endured by the city itself. A short circuit around the periphery of the Forum still reveals the character of these buildings as artefacts of the medieval city.

San Clemente is entered from the side door off the road to the Lateran. A few stairs descend into the side of a dark basilica. The proportions seem strange, but the top of a column and archway poke out of the floor of the far wall, giving an indication of something below. Fortunately a door in this wall leads to a small office where a friendly monk indicates a stair leading down. Below the floor of the church is another basilica, wider than the one above. The space is a strange amalgamation of columns from the earlier basilica and foundations for the new walls and columns above. There are two semicircular apses as well, and you can squeeze between the curving walls, like through a Richard Serra sculpture, and find yet another stair down. This subterranean level is the Roman house in which the church was first inaugurated as a titular church in the 4th century.

Towering on a hill over both San Clemente and the Coliseum is the church and convent dedicated to the four crowned saints. The complex still has the aspect of a fortified retreat outside the city. A brick tower looms over the huge doors of the front gate which leads to a square atrium. A small window on the side is open, and a nun agrees to open the next set of doors which leads to a second courtyard. The side walls of this courtyard contain a colonnade of an earlier church and a third doorway leads to the basilica itself. It is a shallow, tall space with an enormous apse. Both San Clemente and Santi Quattro Coronati were splendidly rebuilt in the 12th century within the larger ruins of 4th-century basilicas. While San Clemente shrank and reorganised five metres above the earlier church, the church of the four crowned saints shrank laterally within its older shell.

Sectional drawing showing the
layers of the Basilica of San
Clemente. The 11th-century nave
and one side aisle fit within the
width of the 8th-century nave
and the courtyard of the Roman
house (1989).

1300–1944: Urban Design as Representation and Destruction

The rusticated Renaissance retaining wall of the Orti Farnesiani leads to a suburban retreat built by Alessandro Farnese on the top of the Palatine hill within the ruins of Augustus's former palace. The first botanical orchards of the world, the Farnesiani Orchards were designed in 1535 by Jacopo Barozzi da Vignola. The 15th century brought a renewed interest in the antiquities of Rome through the activity of both aristocratic families and foreign visitors documenting its ancient artefacts and disseminating visual representations and material fragments from Rome around Europe.

112

The red tone indicates the *disabitato*, the uninhabited part of the city consisting of isolated farms, monasteries and convents, including the Papal enclave at the Lateran.

The Forum underwent a major facelift during the papacy of Alexander VII between 1655 and 1667. In its ruined state it had been mostly used as pasture land for sheep and cows, and even served as a bi-weekly cattle market.[27] Alexander moved the market, levelled the surface and planted four rows of trees serving as a wide carriageway with two shaded sidewalks. This beautification and greening programme provided the elegant travellers between city and suburbs with a shaded promenade for their coaches, and common folk on foot could take in the cool evening air. 'Thus the Forum not only regained dignity but also became a suburban public green, part of the town, yet reaching out.'[28]

Archaeological model showing the Christian churches built above the Fora over the garbage and landfill that began to accumulate following the termination of municipal services in the 4th century.

113

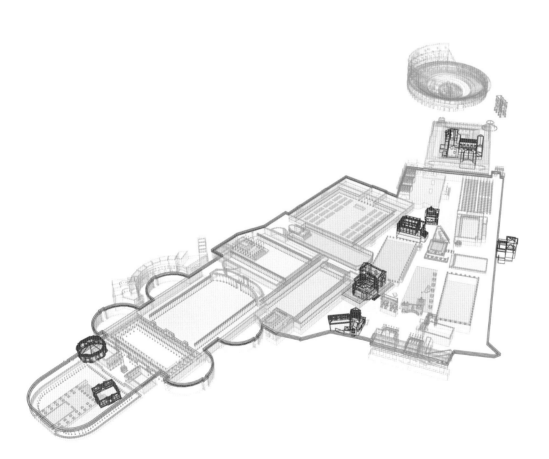

The renewal of Rome was to extend beyond the city proper; the vast enveloping area of the *disabitato* and its offshoots into the countryside the highways, were to be integrated with the built-up core and like this core architecturally articulated by the long, scenographic vistas of tree-lined avenues, green *teatri*, as it were. The zone of gardens and fields extending to the Aurelian walls and the highways beyond, like the built-up area, was an integral part of Alexander's Rome as he envisioned it.[29]

Baroque Rome's system of new streets connecting the dispersed churches rebuilt with the stone mined from the ancient monuments. Our archaeological analysis has shown that Baroque Rome consisted of recycling the Imperial city on top of landfills. It can therefore be seen as an example of 'brownfield' remediation rather than a 'master plan'.

114

The rows of trees joining the triumphal Arches of Septimius Severus and Titus are part of a stenographic green urban promenade, built on the garbage landfill removed by the scientific archaeologists of the 19th and 20th centuries, and as such can be considered, with the botanical orchards of the Farnese family on the Palatine, one of the first examples of 'brownfield reclamation' – the contemporary idea of greening post-industrial landscapes.

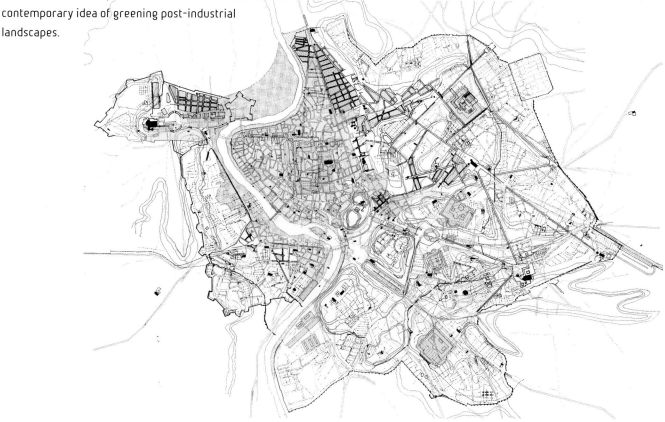

The Dispersed City Model

Discoveries during Lanciani's time, facilitated by new urban construction and archaeology, revealed incredible finds: the torso of the Farnese Hercules was uncovered in the Baths of Caracalla, the head in a well across the Tiber in Trastevere, and the legs were found 10 miles from the city.[30] This destruction and dispersal of the statue of Hercules mimics the material dispersal of the ruins of the ancient temples to new ecclesiastical construction sites across the city. Reading Lanciani, we can define a new urban design model in Rome: the shifting and recycling of the material of the city – the existing city is terrain itself to be mined, sorted, manipulated and rearranged, an analogue recombinant urban design model and a common practice in the shifting landscapes of today's post-industrial cities.

Greening the Forum: Alessandro Farnese built a botanical garden on the Palatine Hill in 1535 and Pope Alexander VII planted four rows of trees across the Forum in 1655.

115

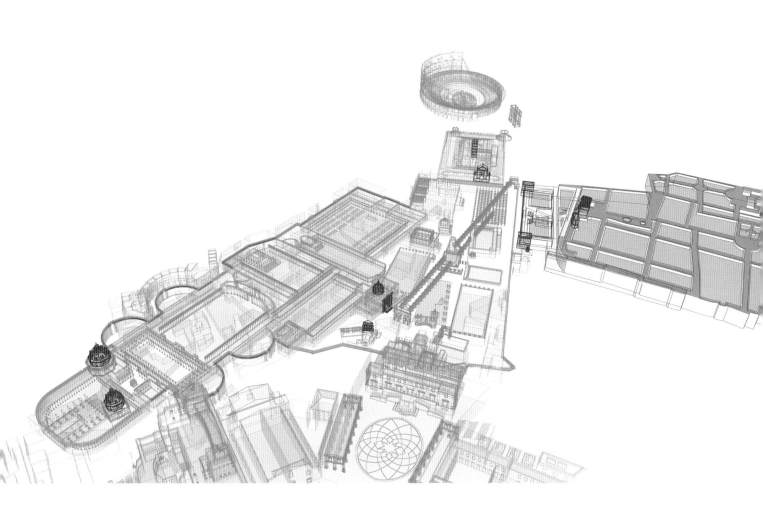

Lanciani combines archival and archaeological evidence to explain the rise in the level of the ground in Rome from the medieval to the modern period. The laws of garbage disposal were not enforced after the emperors moved to Constantinople in AD 330, and the failure to remove rubble and rubbish increased the ground level at the city wall by 10 to 15 feet in less than 100 years – a mark indicated when the walls were restored in AD 402. The Porta di San Paolo gate constructed in that year is 12 feet higher than the gate of AD 272. The 10-foot protected base of the Augustus obelisks shows the Campus Martius had risen 10 feet when it fell.[31]

The Roman Forum is, according to Rossi, an urban artefact which represents the slow growth of the architecture of the city tied to the terrain; for Plattus, the site of the ritualistic display of the spoils of Imperial triumph; and for Packer the site for archaeological appropriation of historical symbols and models to legitimise power. Lanciani and Krautheimer's portraits of the medieval city show how inhabitants actively make the city the excavation site on which to rebuild itself as a recombination of new materials with fragments of the past. This recycling of matter and memory is an act of sorting of history and building artefacts, reconfiguring the space of the city away from the structures of one regime towards the goals of another. Materially, the millennium between the 4th and 14th centuries is a sufficiency economy model where the city no longer is the receptor of wealth, water, food and material from a vast Empire through a massive network of infrastructure, but utilises what is immediately available. Medieval Rome provides evidence of the adaptive and materially recombinant model of the informal mega-city of the present (see Conclusion) and perhaps the resilient city of the future.

Destructions and Dispersals

According to Rodolfo Lanciani, however, chief archaeologist of Rome at the turn of the 20th century, the Renaissance was brutal to the ruins of the ancient city. He asks why this culturally rich period was so destructive. The slow erosion caused by rain, temperature change, as well as the ravages of earthquakes, floods and fires, all contributed to the destruction of ancient Rome, but according to Lanciani, these causes alone cannot explain the remarkable disappearance of the material remains of the ancient city. He gives the example of the Circus Maximus – 250,000 feet of marble – without a trace left. Lanciani argues that the overall destruction of Rome could have been accomplished only with the aid of human intervention, and not just by the hands of barbarian invasions, but by Romans themselves. He says 'there is no edifice in Rome dating from the fifteenth century which did not simultaneously carry with it the destruction or the mutilation of some ancient structure'.[32]

Model of the marbles
removed from the Fora which
were dispersed around the
city to construct the
Renaissance and Baroque
churches and palaces (model
view from below).

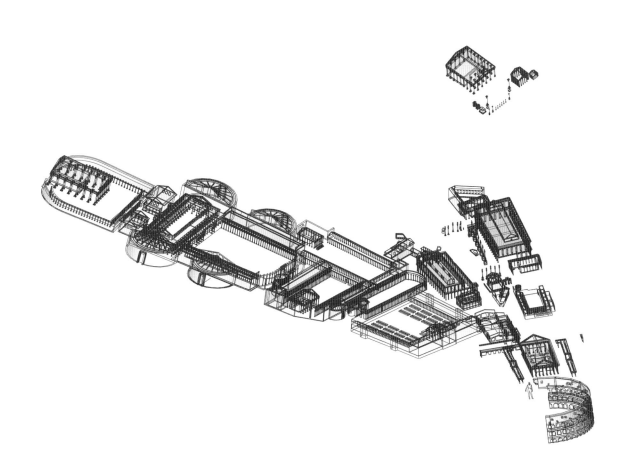

Digital model view of all layers
of the Roman Forum, built and
demolished, rendered
simultaneously. Christian
churches are in red, quarried
Imperial monuments are shown
above and archaeological
remnants below.

118   Through archival research, Lanciani uncovers the construction practices of the 15th century. Before beginning their work, Renaissance builders would secure permission to use ancient structures to quarry. In 1426 at the Basilica Julia in the Forum, the pope shared in the profits from the scavenging for building materials. The new St Peter's all came from ancient loot. In 1503, Bramante destroyed the early Christian basilica with its mosaics, sculptures and frescos. The Coliseum was used as quarry – the year 1452 alone saw 2,522 carts of travertine carried from the Coliseum to the Vatican.[33]

For Lanciani, this is an inexplicable problem in the history of art, how the masters of the Renaissance greatly advanced the practices of art, architecture and urban design, but took the ancient world apart. Lanciani devotes an entire chapter to the marble cutters and lime burners who used ancient Rome as a quarry. As Lanciani writes, no great ruin in Rome was without its own kiln for burning lime. Excavations of the House of the Vestal Virgins revealed two lime kilns and two deposits of lime and charcoal were found with marble statues nearby ready to be burned.[34]

The medieval city was much less destructive in its reuse of old buildings, reoccupied and reinterpreted like terrain itself. The materially re-sorted city remains a powerful urban model for the contemporary world as vast modern urban landscapes are restructured and built from scratch in the face of global warming, climate change and great social migrations and upheavals. As Umberto Eco has pointed out, we are 'living in a new middle ages'.

> Our own Middle Ages ... will be an age of 'permanent transition' for which new methods of adjustment will have to be employed. The problem will not so much be that of preserving the past scientifically as of developing hypotheses for the exploration of disorder, entering into the logic of conflictuality. There will be born – it is already coming into existence – a culture of constant readjustment ... The middle ages preserved in its way the heritage of its past but not through hibernation, rather through a constant retranslation and reuse, it was an immense work of bricolage, balanced among nostalgia, hope and despair.[35]

Arjun Appadurai has pointed out in *Modernity at Large* that localities are produced by social actors – an argument significantly different from Rossi's concept of a situated locus evolving slowly over time. Appadurai views locality as 'primarily relational and contextual rather than as scalar or spatial. I see it as a complex phenomenological quality, constituted by a series of links between the sense of social immediacy, the technologies of interactivity, and the relativity of context'.[36] While archaeological modelling for urban design developed a method of archiving the ruptures in collateral space, it is this correlative space of emergent linkages and relationships that necessitates a second methodology for digital modelling for urban design: genealogy.

Endnotes   119
1 Charles L Singer, *The Renaissance in Rome*, Bloomington: Indiana University Press, 1985, p 258.
2 Aldo Rossi, *Architecture of the City*, translated by Diane Ghirardo and Joan Ockman, Cambridge: MIT Press, 1982, pp 119.
3 Ibid, p 120.
4 James Packer, 'Politics, Urbanism, and Archaeology in "Roma Capitale": A Troubled Past and A Controversial Future', *American Journal of Archaeology*, Vol 93, No 1 (Jan 1989), pp 137–41.
5 Ibid, pp 137–8.
6 Ibid, p 138.
7 Rossi, pp 123–4.
8 Packer, p 138.
9 Ibid, p 139.
10 Rossi, p 119.
11 Ibid, p 126.
12 Ibid, p 123.
13 Ibid, p 120.
14 AEJ Morris, *History of Urban Form*, New York: Prentice Hall, 1994, pp 55–69.
15 Alan Plattus, 'Passages into the City: The Interpretive Function of the Roman Triumph', *The Princeton Journal*, vol 1, 1983, pp 93–115, p 100.
16 Ibid, pp 104–5.
17 Ibid, p 93.
18 Richard Krautheimer, *Rome, Profile of a City, 312–1308*, Princeton: Princeton University Press, 1980, pp 230–1.
19 Rodolfo Lanciani, *The Destruction of Ancient Rome*, New York: Macmillan, 1901, pp 31–2.
20 Krautheimer, pp 237–41.
21 Ibid, p 237.
22 http://www.iath.virginia.edu/rome/
23 Lanciani, p 118.
24 Ibid, pp 122–4.
25 Krautheimer, p 317.
26 Ibid, p 319.
27 Richard Krautheimer, *The Rome of Alexander VII 1655-1667*, Princeton: Princeton University Press, 1985, pp 109–10.
28 Ibid, p 110.
29 Ibid, p 113.
30 Lanciani, p 44.
31 Ibid, pp 53–5.
32 Ibid, p 206.
33 Ibid, pp 198–213.
34 Ibid, pp 190–7.
35 Umberto Eco, *Travels in Hyperreality*, translated by William Weaver, New York: Harcourt, Brace, Jovanovich, 1986, p 84.
36 Arjun Appadurai, *Modernity at Large: Cultural Dimensions of Globalization*, Minneapolis: University of Minnesota Press, 1996, p 178.

Chapter 3

Genealogy

The fly-through animation glides up Broadway from Lower to Midtown Manhattan. The 'canyon of heroes' of the financial district is familiar, with the Art Deco towers of Wall Street looming on the skyline. However, the buildings do not sit on the ground, but are floating in an empty void, with the ground of the island of Manhattan deep below. The on-line view travels along a temporal plane – 1950 – within a 3-D computer model where time is literally given a dimension. In the x/y/z Cartesian space of a 3-D modelling environment, time is here measured along the z-axis where one year equals 100 feet. Post-Second World War glass towers loom overhead, while the Art Deco limestone spires of Wall Street emerge from below. The fly-through not only travels through space up Broadway, but along a temporal plane within the gap in construction between the Great Depression of the 1930s and the post-war building boom which began in the 1960s.[1]

The transition from an archaeological to a genealogical modelling moves from an understanding of the discipline of urban design as a situated subject of historical knowledge, towards understanding the generation of *urban design practice* in relation to a larger discursive field within which *urban actors and agents* constitute themselves as subjects interacting in space.[2] In the last chapters of this book, *Schizoanalytical Modelling for Urban Design*, we will learn to imagine urban designs in relation to internal, psychological forces as well as outside social and environmental conditions. Schizoanalysis will help us to understand how urban subjects constitute themselves as social agents – in other words, how we see and perceive ourselves in relation to others in a mediated, urbanising and globalising world.

Graph of the number of high-rise office buildings constructed in Manhattan between 1890 and 1990. The lower line is Lower Manhattan, the middle line is Midtown Manhattan and the top line is the total number. Three economic peaks are evident – the stock market boom in the late 1920s, the post-war boom in New York as a corporate headquarters peaking in the late 1960s and the 'Bonfire of the Vanities' that followed the computerisation of the workplace in the 1980s. Two valleys of economic busts are also evident: the long lull from the Great Depression in 1929 to the end of the Second World War and the precipitous decline during the oil shock of the mid-1970s (hand drawing, 1994).

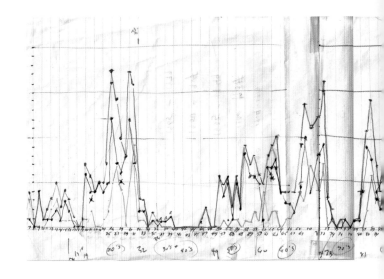

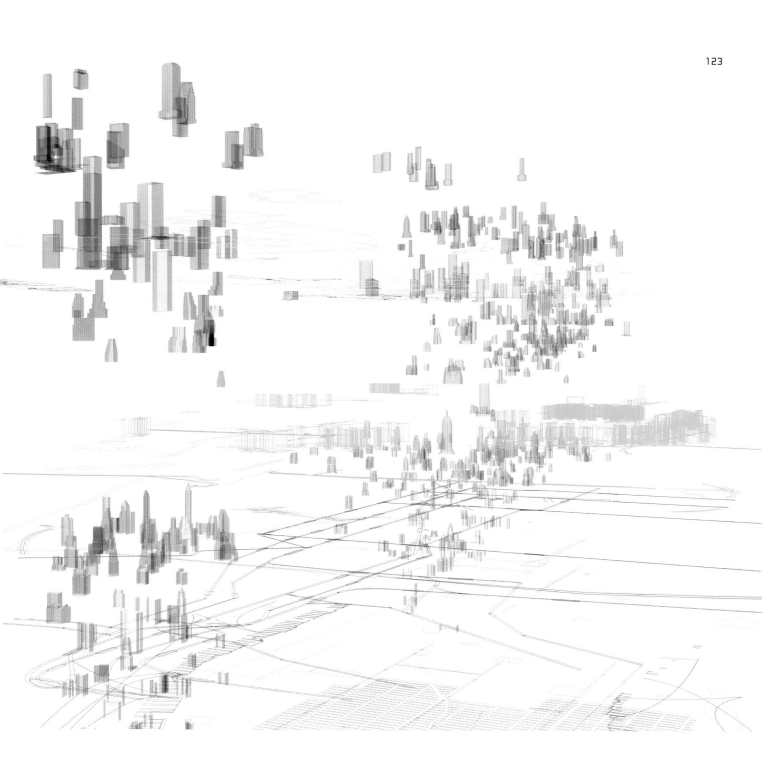

Online fly-through of
Manhattan Timeformations,
www.skyscraper.org/timefor
mations (2000).

123

The first construction boom in Midtown Manhattan was scattered along Broadway and travelled up 5th Avenue. Cross-town armatures were developing already along 42nd and 57th Streets.

124

5th Avenue

57th Street

Rockefeller Center

42nd Street

34th Street

Broadway

Foucault traces his development of a genealogical approach to Darwin's influence on Nietzsche: we must understand our place in an external world structured by chance, accident and succession.[3] *Genealogical Modelling for Urban Design* will not employ genealogy as lines of family descent, but in the sense Foucault employs – as a way to map the emergence of spatial patterns in time. The genealogical approach examines urban design deploying different models, technologies and tools **distributed in space**, **ordered in time** and **composed in space-time**. We will now examine the city as shaped by the constant exertion and resistance of force by urban actors and agents relating to linkages and relations of people, institutions and flows across space and time, which encompass global as well as local imaginations. We have seen how urban design distributes forces in space by enclosing, controlling, arranging and placing in series. Now we will examine how urban design orders time by subdividing temporal increments, programming action, and directing gestures of everyday life. Finally, in the last section we will examine urban design composition as experienced in space-time blocks.[4]

3-D models of high-rise office
buildings built before the
Second World War in
Midtown. Buildings in yellow
were built before the 1916
set-back law.

Following the end of the
Second World War, Park
Avenue, built over the rail
lines leading to Grand Central
Terminal, became the Main
Street of corporate America.
3rd and 6th Avenues
developed quickly following
the demolition of the elevated
train lines.

126

6th Avenue

Park Avenue

3rd Avenue

57th Street

42nd Street

Genealogical modelling furthers our analysis of the archaeological archives of Rome, New York and Bangkok through diagrammatic timelines of the various forces generating space. 'The history of forms, the archive, is doubled by an evolution of forces, the diagram.'[5] The genealogical diagram will be generated from the superimposition of several maps separated by planes of time. '[F]rom one diagram to the next, new maps are drawn. There is no diagram that does not also include, besides the points which it connects up, certain relatively free or unbound points, points of creativity, change and resistance – the struggles of each age.'[6]

While archaeological modelling began with the image of Schliemann's Troy, Charles Darwin's theory of evolution through natural selection underlies genealogy as a method. Genetic mapping and the science of ecology has radically altered the smooth narrative of evolutionary biology. Nature and cities are now seen as chaotic systems in which order or steady states are just moments within the dynamics of disequilibrium. Natural systems thrive not through a linear process of succession, but through the dynamics of disturbance and feedback. Events such as fire, floods and disease create new opportunities for new species to take hold and others to evolve. Genealogical modelling examines how urban design practice in various time periods became concerned primarily with the creation of fragments of order in a chaotic world. Genealogical modelling for urban design is based on a theoretical framework of disturbance rather than succession ecology, and builds resilience models based on continual renewal, adaptation and change rather than sustainability models which look for equilibrium in a nature imagined as in balance.[7]

The post-war construction
boom was concentrated in
the 20 blocks from 40th
to 60th Streets and between
3rd and 6th Avenues.

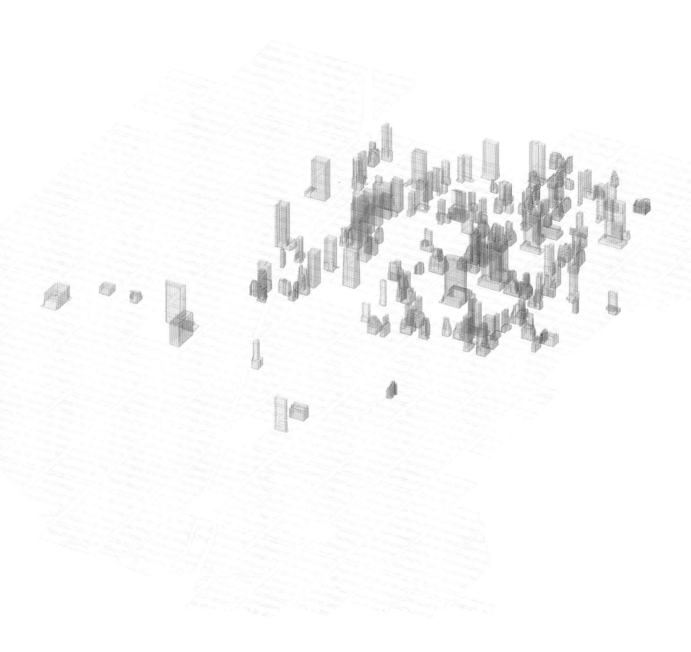

The construction boom that followed the introduction of computer technologies into the workplace resulted in an extension of Midtown west to Broadway and 8th Avenue.

128

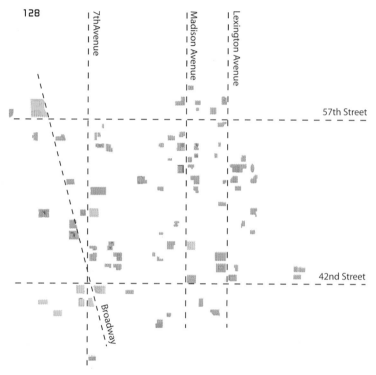

7th Avenue

Madison Avenue

Lexington Avenue

57th Street

42nd Street

Broadway

Descent and Emergence

For Foucault, genealogy is the examination of both descent and emergence. **Descent** is defined as 'the ancient affiliation to a group, sustained by the bonds of blood, tradition, or social class' – in other words the product of struggle, war and conflict.[8] In *Recombinant Urbanism*, Grahame Shane introduces the enclave – the centering device for cities – as the first element of urban design, which we referred to as collateral space in Chapter 1.[9] However, Foucault's genealogy of descent reveals the 'unstable assemblage of faults, fissures, and heterogeneous layers that threaten the fragile inheritor from within or from underneath ... The search for descent is not the erecting of foundations: on the contrary, it disturbs what was previously considered immobile; it fragments what was thought unified; it shows the heterogeneity of what was imagined consistent with itself'.[10] Any urban enclave, neighbourhood, fragment or district must exert force to maintain a fragile dominion, and genealogy will construct relational diagrams to uncover the correlative space of urban design.

New global media companies
such as Condé Nast and
AOL/Time Warner occupied
the new West Midtown
Frontier.

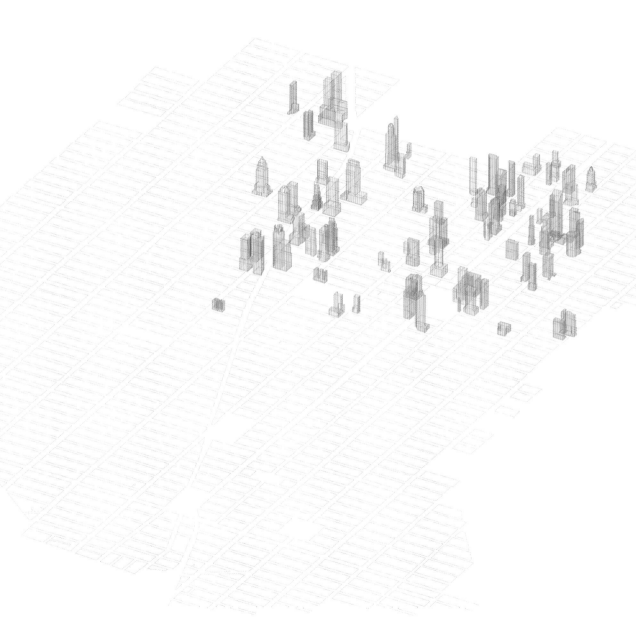

Shane's *Recombinant Urbanism* does not see enclaves as the stable urban artefacts that Rossi describes, but as dynamic elements that change over time in relation to the development of urban armatures. Urban armatures are the linking and sorting elements of the city and create correlative spaces. Armatures become the prime instruments of creating correlative space as they arrange sequences both in linear space, and through symbolically mediated associations.[11] For Foucault, genealogy must 'identify the accidents, the minute deviations – or conversely, the complete reversals – the errors, the false appraisals, and the faulty calculations that gave birth to those things that continue to exist and have value for us; it is to discover that truth or being does not lie at the root of what we know and what we are, but the exteriority of accidents.'[12] Shane describes the micro-role of urban actors in creating, altering and deviating fragmentary, self-organising, self-centering and self-regulating urban enclaves in relation to the linear movement as increments in urban growth. Together these constantly mutating elements constitute the DNA of the city.

130

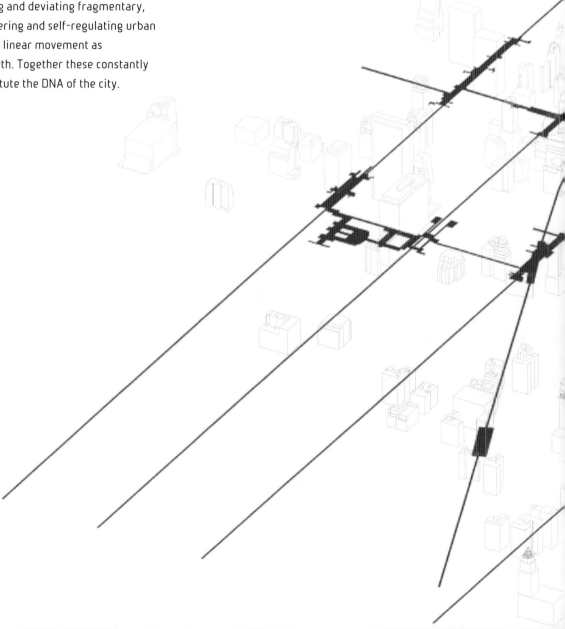

Midtown Manhattan as correlative space: corporate America had headquarters on Park Avenue, while the advertising was located on Madison Avenue and the three national broadcasters were located along 6th Avenue. Now, many global media conglomerates are located between 6th and 8th Avenues (subway lines are in red).

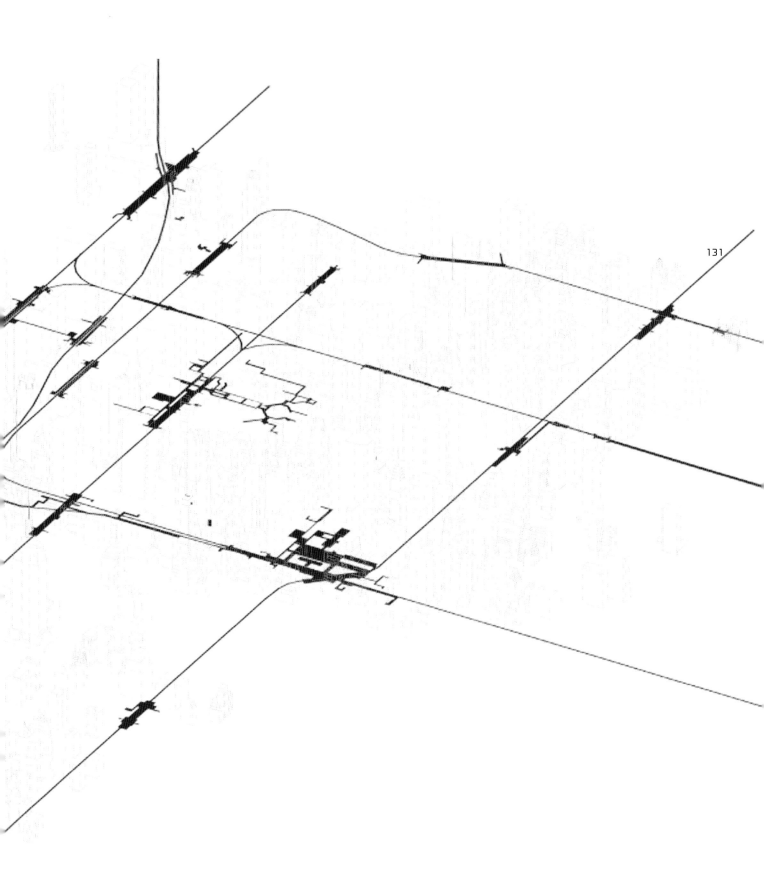

131

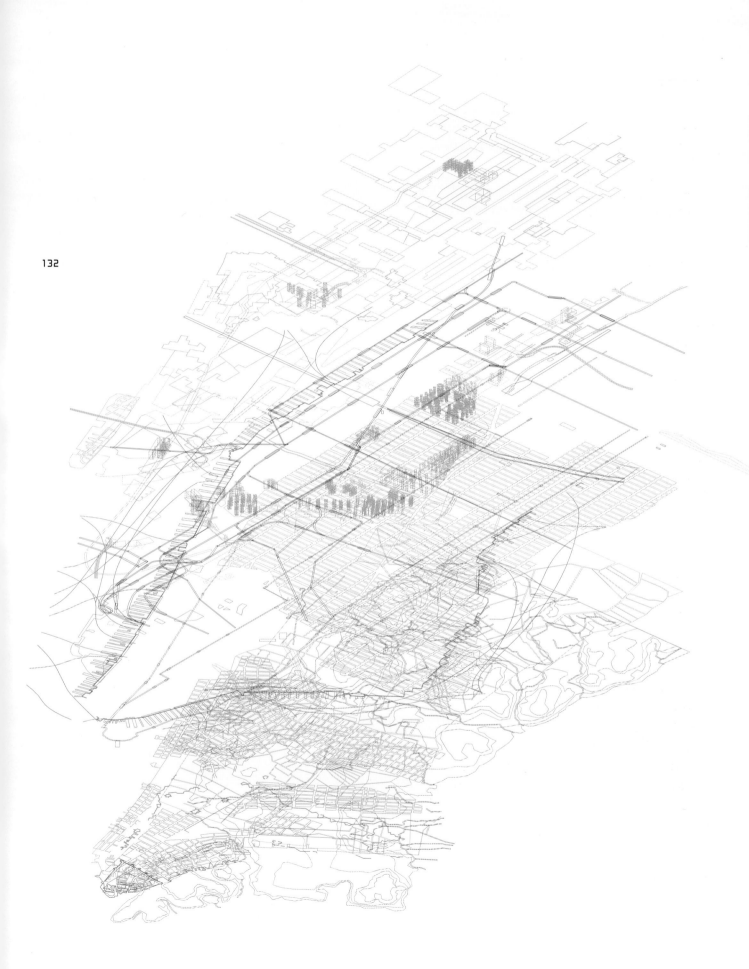

132

How have the Central
Business Districts of Lower
and Midtown Manhattan
emerged over time?
Manhattan Timeformations is
a genealogical modelling of
urban design as a
bureaucratic rather than
master planning discipline.

Emergence, for Foucault, is 'the moment of arising. It stands as the principle and the singular law of an apparition. As it is wrong to search for descent in an uninterrupted continuity, we should avoid thinking of emergence as the final term of a historical development. … Emergence is always produced through the generation of forces and the analysis of emergence "must delineate this interaction, the struggle these forces wage against each other or against adverse circumstances".[13] For Shane, heterotopias are the elements of change in the city. They house all exceptions in the dominant city model, and are therefore key triggers to the emergence of new urban design models.[14]

The aim of an analysis of emergence is to capture forces at the moment of their eruption.[15] Urban design must be analysed as a destructive as well as constructive force which radically alters environmental and social relations. Genealogical modelling will examine descent and emergence in the sometimes bloody succession of emperors and popes in Rome or kings in Siam, but also in the 'creative destruction' of the capitalist city struggling with the contesting agendas of different urban actors in participatory democracies.[16] We can also translate the emergence of new urban design models as a struggle or conflict between spatial entrenched norms and new technologies, flows and images. Emergence is analysed in relation to larger environmental forces, in localised social interactions with others and in our internalised battles with ourselves.

134 Three Urban Design Genealogies

Genealogical Modelling for Urban Design begins with an analysis of *temporal planes* in order to understand the descent and emergence of urban design practices in different places at different moments of time. Our genealogical time planes will form the basis of creating new digital models in which layered spatial and temporal information can be cross-referenced. We begin with a simple comparison of three genealogies of urban design: Rome and the Master Plan, New York and the Central Business District, and lastly Bangkok and Life-style. Eugene Holland has written: 'Genealogy is based on the premise that historical institutions and other features of social organization evolve not smoothly and continuously, gradually developing their potential through time, but *discontinuously*, and must be understood in terms of difference rather than continuity as one social formation appropriates and abruptly reconfigures older institution or revives various features of extant social organization by selectively recombining them to suit its own purposes.'[17]

The goal of the genealogical technique of constructing temporal planes, therefore, is to understand the production of urban difference over time.[18] Cities evolve through continual change. The production of difference is the result of the exertion of various external and internal forces: natural, environmental, political, social, economic and psychological. The production of difference, the result of emergent and self-organising principles, must be strategically supported, sorted and redirected rather than suppressed, separated and controlled through the practice of urban design. Digital genealogical modelling for urban design will give us a new understanding of these multiple forces and how they are continually reshaping urban environments, social space and individual psyches.

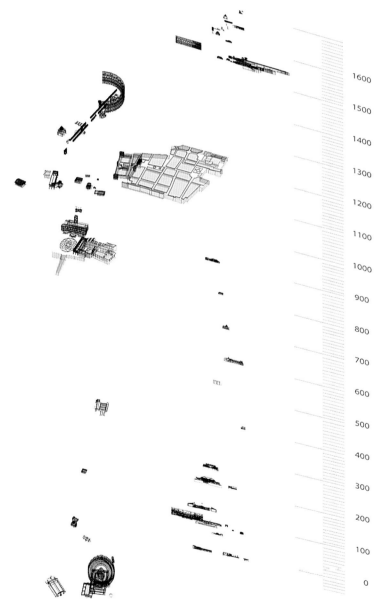

Exploding our archaeological
models of the Forum on time
planes reveals two distinct
construction periods: the
Papal and Imperial Capitals,
interrupted by a millennium of
retrenchment.

1600
1500
1400
1300
1200
1100
1000
900
800
700
600
500
400
300
200
100
0

Rome: A Genealogy of the Master Plan

According to Sigfried Giedion, Sixtus V climbed the same
streets of Rome that the pilgrims had to follow. This
bodily experience of distance and topography led, for
Giedion, not only to a physical destination but to the
conception of a plan for the city that was not drawn on
paper, but within the bones of the pope himself. In March
1588, he opened the new road by walking with his
cardinals all the way from the Coliseum to the Lateran
Palace.[19] Many modern architects and planners in
America drew inspiration from Giedion at Harvard, as a
means to heroically justify the will of a single individual in
shaping the city, and it is therefore following Sixtus V up
the hills of Rome that we can trace the birth of the Master
Plan in urban design.

In *Design of Cities* (1976) and the series of
documentary films *Understanding Cities*, Edmund Bacon
(1910–2005) makes the claim that a single powerful idea
can create an urban design. Clips from his films show his
accomplishments as Executive Director of the
Philadelphia City Planning Commission (1949–70) in
relation to the development of Rome under Sixtus V. He in
fact shows a younger avatar of himself wilfully walking
through a gushing fountain to maintain the singularity of
his destination along the central axis of Benjamin
Franklin Parkway. His book begins with a quote from
Daniel Burnham, '… a noble logical diagram once recorded
will never die; long after we are gone it will be a living
thing asserting itself with ever-growing insistency'.[20]

135

Bacon asserts that the city is an act of will – clearly for him it is a will to power and a means to achieve immortality. In creating a Master Plan for Philadelphia, Bacon connected his actions as a public official with the popes of Rome and the emperors in Beijing. Embodying Giedion's conception of the plan for Rome created by the moving body of the pope, Bacon shows a young man walking down the axis of Benjamin Franklin Parkway – climbing straight through its monumental fountains – to demonstrate his power as Master Planner. But as feminist artist Barbara Kruger famously asked in her design collaborations with the architectural firm Smith-Miller + Hawkinson, 'Guess who put the Masters in the Master Plan?'[21]

In Pope Sixtus V's plan for Rome (1485–90), Christian churches became the primary artefacts of the city, not as separate enclaves, but as part of a network of new armatures connected by the processional bodies of clerics and pilgrims. Following the decline of the Empire and the Great Schism with the Eastern Church, Rome had been in decline for centuries, and was surpassed by the more mercantile cities of the Italian peninsula, such as Venice and Genoa. The urban design of Rome ushered in a new era for the city as the centre for a reconstituted Catholic world, soon to spread around the globe with the beginning of colonial explorations.

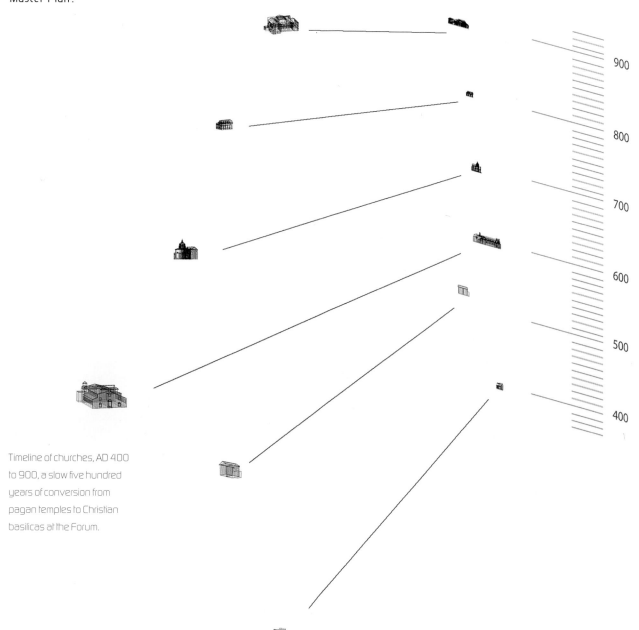

900

800

700

600

500

400

Timeline of churches, AD 400 to 900, a slow five hundred years of conversion from pagan temples to Christian basilicas at the Forum.

Charles Singer describes the ceremonial passage called the *possesso*, literally the ceremonial taking of possession of Rome by the new pope.

Papal servants, the captains of the *rioni* of Rome each with the flag of his district, representatives of the Knights of St. John and other military orders, the Roman barons, papal secretaries, the papal singer, non-Roman clergy, abbots from the city's monasteries, the cardinals, and the heads of the various papal tribunals and other members of the Curia – all had their designated places in the hierarchically arranged order of procession … The pope, coming near the end, also was borne on a white horse, and his presence … was dignified by a baldachino … in addition, the colourful garb of men and horses, the fluttering standards, the glittering gold of the processional cross and thuribles, and the dazzling jewels of the papal triple tiara – all contributed to the overall sense of splendour.[22]

Sixtus V also constructed the Acqua Felice, making the Esquiline, Quirinal and Viminal hills again habitable for a renewed city connected by his new network of armatures. Four Egyptian obelisks, salvaged from antiquity, were pulled down at the Circus Nero, the Mausoleum of Augustus and the Circus Maximus to be re-erected at key points around the city – the Lateran, Piazza del Popolo and atop the Esquiline Hill – guiding pilgrimages through a network of once scattered, but now interconnected, churches. Christianity was founded and grew at the periphery of the Empire, and became situated in the city first in houses and eventually in basilicas scattered around the fringes. Sixtus V's Baroque network realigned the space of the city around churches and squares, making what was peripheral central, and inverting the hierarchical codes of the city. Bacon marvels at how the placement of the obelisk in front of St Peter's by Sixtus in 1586 led to the completion of Bernini's elliptical colonnades 80 years later. For Bacon, the erection of a single artefact – a point in space – created order out of chaos.[23]

137

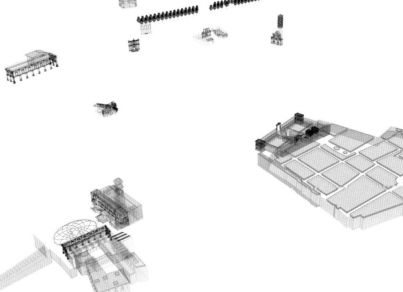

Renaissance and Baroque additions and renovations with Pope Alexander VII's allée of trees as an armature connecting the two triumphal arches at opposite ends of the Republican Forum: the Arch of Septimius Severus and the Arch of Titus.

Imperial Fora timeline: the monuments built in Rome grew increasingly larger the nearer the Empire approached its collapse.

300

200

100

0

Art historian Louis Marin captures the period of rediscovery, reinterpretation and renewal of Europe through contact with ancient Rome. In an exhibition of 16th-century drawings of the bas-reliefs from Trajan's Column, Marin describes how, in the process of transcription from spiral bas-relief to narrative exhibited drawings, everything changes. 'The triumphal ascending *spiral* that rises up around a vertical axis from the *bottom upward*, from the die and the pedestal toward its capital, from the inscriptions toward the upright statue, becomes a *horizontal band* unfolding its some fifteen meters of images *from left to right*.'[24] Marin says Trajan's Column is there *to be seen* in itself as a monument of power rather than as a historical narrative *to be read*. 'Do we really see it? Or, to put the question more carefully, is its ostentatious, triumphal, monumental visibility actually coupled with a precise, rigorous readability of the bas-reliefs with which it is covered? Between a work's visibility and its readability lay two different gazes.'[25]

The princes of Europe followed Sixtus V's example, both in the use of the Baroque model of connective armatures creating correlative urban space, but also in the historical narratives displayed in that space. Rome was an indispensable stop on the 'Grand Tours' which necessarily accompanied the education of every young aristocrat. In the 18th century, the city became an artistic centre where young sculptors, painters and architects from all parts of Europe met and learned their crafts by viewing the works of past masters and measuring the remains of ancient buildings.[26] The first known artist to draw the bas-reliefs dedicated his work to King Philip II of Spain as 'Trajan's compatriot'. This drawing was revived and corrected in 1672 and dedicated to Louis XIV, 'the Trajan of France'.

The centre of the papal city shifted from the Forum to St Peter's, and with it, the Forum and Coliseum supplied much-needed building material. In the 16th century, the Forum became a quarry. The ancient buildings dismantled for the new papal constructions are highlighted in red.

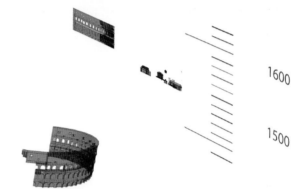

1600

1500

Three French sovereigns have desired to own a reproduction of the column: François I, Louis XIV and Napoleon III. Napoleon erected his column (1806–10) in the centre of Place Vendôme (laid out in 1702) in Paris to celebrate his victory in Austerlitz. Fischer von Erlach's Karlskirche in Vienna (1715) has twin triumphal columns with spiralling reliefs facing the Karlsplatz, which became a key node on the monumental Ringstrasse. Emperor Franz Joseph I decreed the construction of this monument marked show street at the centre of the Austrian-Hungarian Empire. Clearly it was not only the Roman popes who legitimised power through a narrative of descent from Caesar, but Europe's new monarchs and emperors as well. From the time of the Holy Roman Empire, northern kings looked to the Italian peninsula not only for artistic education, but also territorial conquest and symbols of power. 'The representation of the Roman historical past, its explicit reproduction, constitutes it as a founding and legitimizing model.'[27]

Foucault's genealogical project is parodic: it is against history as reality; dissociative: it is against history as identity derived from continuity and the representation of tradition; and sacrificial: it is against truth and opposes history as knowledge. While traditional history may offer the possibility of alternative identities, they are simply disguises. Foucault includes Roman prototypes for the Revolution as one of history's ephemeral props. 'The genealogist will know what to make of this masquerade … he will push it to the limit and prepare the great carnival of time where masks are constantly reappearing … no longer the identification of our faint individuality with the solid identities of the past, but our "unrealization" through the excessive choice of identities … Genealogy is history in the form of a concerted carnival.'[28] The Master Plan is a key technology in constructing this carnival out of the display of power.

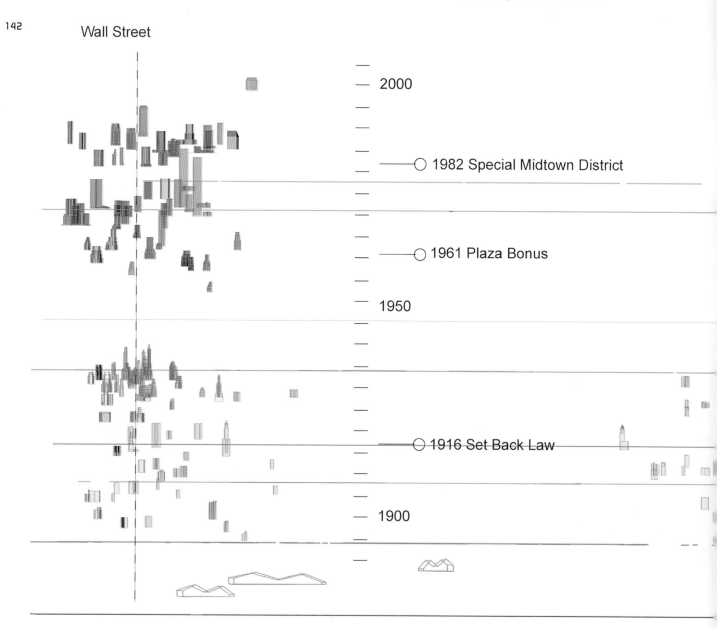

Manhattan Timeformations timeline looking west, showing Lower Manhattan on the left and Midtown on the right. The timeline divides into three building booms: pre- and post-Second World War periods, and one following the introduction of electronic trading in the 1980s. We will look at three zoning laws that shaped the skyline during those building booms: the 1916 Set Back Law, the 1961 Plaza Bonus and the 1982 Special Midtown District.

Wall Street

2000

○ 1982 Special Midtown District

○ 1961 Plaza Bonus

1950

○ 1916 Set Back Law

1900

42nd Street

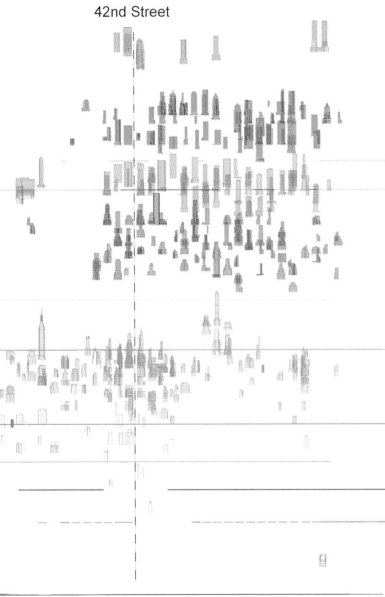

In spite of periodic calls for Master Planning, New York City directs urban design decisions through zoning rather than through a Master Plan. The instrument of zoning was instituted with the **Zoning Resolution of 1916** in reaction to both the growth of manufacturing uses in residential areas and the arrival of the skyscraper. Land-use restrictions were instituted separating manufacturing from commercial and residential use, and set-back laws required high rises to step back according to a prescribed sky plane angle to allow light to hit the streets of the city. The zoning resolution has been constantly amended, but it was only in 1961, with the radical changes that suburbanisation and the automobile brought to the city, that a complete revision was enacted. The **Zoning Resolution of 1961** 'coordinated use and bulk regulations, incorporated parking requirements and emphasized the creation of open space'.[29] The other invention of this period is incentive zoning giving added floor space to encourage the construction of public plazas. Politically contested, the zoning resolution was passed only when an agreement was made to down-zone much of the outer boroughs of the city and concentrate density in Manhattan.

144   A timeline of the descent and emergence of Manhattan's two high-rise business districts – Lower and Midtown Manhattan – reveals the boom-and-bust cycles of the real estate market, but also the way architecture, technology, planning and urban design respond to the rhythms of capitalism. After steel-frame construction and the elevator were introduced in the late 19th century, the new form of high-rise office buildings emerged along Broadway – the main commercial thoroughfare of the city.[30] The boom of construction and the shock of the effect of these new structures which rose to unlimited height up from the canyon-like narrow streets of the city, resulted in the creation of the first New York City Zoning Resolution of 1916, which dictated an inclined sky-plane, behind which all building must be set back.

This new bureaucratic regulation was an exertion of governmental authority towards an assumed public good: the availability of sunlight and fresh air on the streets of the city. The zoning resolution was well timed, because a building boom ensued with the rise of the stock market of the 'roaring '20s'. The towering new stone ziggurats grouped along Wall Street and contained within the old Dutch walled city of the 1630s, marked the first clustering of these new buildings in a distinct enclave and imprinted a new image of the modern city on the public's consciousness. The image of the skyline of Lower Manhattan, featured in countless photographs and movies, as we have seen, was the one representational trope that all the schemes for the redesign of Ground Zero repeated. The effects of the stock market crash of 1929 and the Great Depression ended this construction boom.

The Great Depression was followed by the Second World War, and high-rise office building construction in New York did not resume until the 1950s. Although the pre-war building codes and zoning resolution persisted, new technologies – such as light steel framing, glass curtain walls and air conditioning – produced strange hybrid architecture of new construction technologies and old zoning laws distinctive to Manhattan: the glass wedding cake. Some exceptional architects and corporate clients broke the mould of this awkward cross-breeding of pre-war urban planning regulations and the goals of modern architecture. Gordon Bunshaft's Lever House (1952) and Mies van der Rohe's Seagram building (1958) both created privately owned, yet publicly accessible plazas and simple cubic building forms to build a purer expression of modern architecture within the zoning regulations.[31]

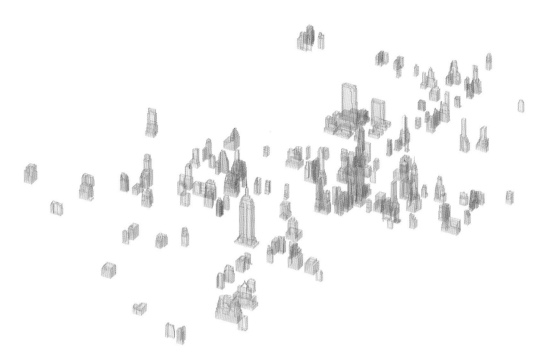

After 1916 Set Back Law

Before 1916 Set Back Law

1961 Plaza Bonus
introduced incentive zoning:
by including a public plaza in
designs, developers were
rewarded with added
allowable building bulk. The
pre-ordinance 'glass
wedding cakes' were
followed by boxy towers with
large open floor-plates.

146   These two buildings, almost facing each other on Park Avenue, connected post-war corporate civic values to the long history of public squares in Europe, as evident in our genealogy of papal Rome. Park Avenue, a street suspended over the train tracks north of Grand Central Terminal, indicates the second important clustering of high-rise office buildings – now shifted to Midtown Manhattan, as corporate America's Main Street, it became the first choice for brand-oriented companies, such as Lever Brothers or Seagram's, to locate their headquarters. Locus, as defined by Rossi as an essential aspect of urban design traced back to antiquity, is modernised by the real estate mantra of *location*, *location*, *location*. The clustering of office buildings on New York City's skyline is a physical expression of the desire of the majority of developers to build in the same location at the same time, and is therefore an indicator of the importance in understanding space/time composition in the genealogical approach.

If the headquarters of major corporations preferred a Park Avenue address, advertising firms chose Madison Avenue, and the three major national television networks were within a few blocks of each other along Sixth Avenue. The tastes of the *Air-Conditioned Nightmare* of post-war consumer America were broadcast via the boardrooms of the *Man in the Gray Flannel Suit* in Midtown. *The Organization Man* was the new figure of authority. While America's cities were dispersing into vast suburban conurbations, corporate America had its headquarters in a few-block enclave in Midtown Manhattan. The Zoning Resolution of 1961 and its amendments since continue to shape and expand this enclave through bulk controls and incentive zoning.

Building construction in Lower Manhattan remained dormant following the Second World War, and it took the combined effort of the Rockefeller Brothers to revive the financial centre. John D Rockefeller, Jr (1874–1960) built the Rockefeller Center between 1930 and 1939 on land leased from Columbia University with money inherited from his father, the founder of Standard Oil. His two sons were David (1915–), who was chairman of Chase Manhattan Bank which squeezed a huge Modernist tower also designed by Gordon Bunshaft into the canyons just north of Wall Street's ziggurats, and Nelson (1908–79), who as Governor of New York was behind the siting of the World Trade Center and Battery Park City.

The Port Authority of New York and New Jersey, which built the World Trade Center, is a public agency directed by the governors of New York and New Jersey, and Battery Park City was built by the New York State Urban Development Corporation. Both organisations are exempt from local city zoning laws and codes, and remain specially zoned sites outside city control. Government assistance supplemented the marketplace for office building construction in Lower Manhattan, and the construction of the World Trade Center's 10 million square feet between 1966 and 1973 deflated the market for decades, but also marked the end of another era of office building construction in Manhattan.

After 1961 Plaza Bonus

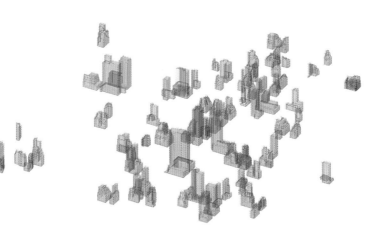

Before 1961 Plaza Bonus

In 1982, legislation allowed higher bulk in the West Midtown Special District, while downsizing the allowable bulk in the crowded East Side. The different scales of buildings on the east and west side of Manhattan are evident in the top view.

148 **The Urban Designer as Organisation Man**

Through the new mechanisms of the 1961 Zoning Resolution, the professional bureaucratic discipline of urban design was created in New York. Jonathan Barnett describes the creation of the Urban Design Group in 1967 at New York City's Department of City Planning as a new model of urban design which is clearly quite different from that of the Master Planner Edmund Bacon. Barnett even explains the difficulty in legalising urban design as a new civil servant position in the city bureaucracy. The Urban Design Group's creation of a special zoning district in the Broadway theatre district was the first attempt by New York City to enact zoning regulation within a specific district with urban design objectives. Although the oil shock of the mid-1970s witnessed a virtual halt to office building construction in New York for over a decade, when construction resumed, most of the old Broadway theatres were preserved, and new high-rise developments incorporated new theatres into their projects as a result of incentives which increased the allowable bulk of a building.[32]

Zoning incentives with professional bureaucratic urban design goals continue to evolve. In addition to the now ubiquitous corporate plaza rewarded with added bulk, amendments reward interior atria, mid-block passages and better subway connections. Developers were also encouraged to build further west, as the crowded east side had only one subway line, while Midtown West is served by three. Civic life in this new dispersed privately owned public realm was meticulously analysed by sociologist William H Whyte. The author of *The Organization Man* observed that some of the plazas of Midtown were enormously successful in promoting civic life, while others remained empty.[33] Public life was no longer organised around the triumphal or religious processions of Rome, but emerged within the cycles of the business day with the commuting rush hours, meetings, lunch and the night shift. The alternate rhythms of weekdays, holidays and weekends punctuate the work week with the different patterns of leisure and shopping. Weekend activity has increased exponentially in the last few years in New York. The public life of leisure and shopping will be discussed in more detail in Chapter 6 of this book.

After 1982 Midtown West Special District Law

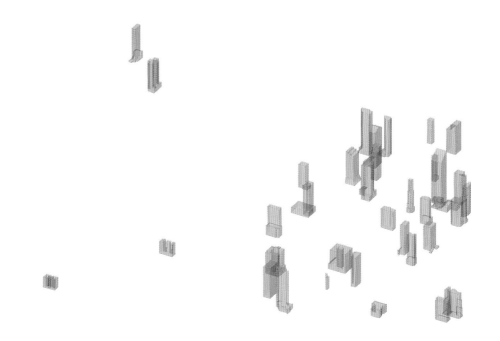

Before 1982 Midtown West Special District Law

The financial deregulations of the Reagan/Thatcher era and the computerisation of the workplace led to a new era of globalisation in the 1980s. New York has been radically altered – both spatially and socially – in the systemic reorganisation that followed the first oil shock in the 1970s. By the mid-1980s a flurry of new construction began in both Lower and Midtown Manhattan when international financial companies were allowed to compete locally, the expansion of Wall Street firms to the new World Financial Center in Battery Park City and the old water lots along the East River, NASDAQ a new electronic stock trading company and the multitude of new media corporations which have clustered along Times Square and Eighth Avenue in Midtown. Deregulations and computerisation contributed to a frenzy of both stock and real estate speculation that popular novelist Tom Wolfe chronicled in *The Bonfire of the Vanities*.

Combining archaeological and genealogical approaches, digital modelling of temporal planes shows how the lower part of Manhattan Island was developed incrementally from the walled enclave of the Dutch West Indies Company, to the Georgian British colonial town, to the post-Revolution boom of speculative land subdivision of the old farms up the island, until 1812, when a Commission of the State of New York laid out a grid of 155 streets and 12 avenues. The Commissioner's grid quickly filled with Wharton's endless chocolate-brown row houses. The two train stations, Pennsylvania and Grand Central, modelled on the late Baths of Diocletian and Caracalla of Rome, were carved from the individual properties in the grid, and anchored the skyscraper city which emerged within the train and subway network, bounded by the Third and Sixth Avenue elevated trains.

After the Second World War, the elevated trains were torn down and both Midtown and Downtown expanded towards the rivers. The image and logics of the Central Business District have become a major urban design model worldwide following the successes of the Urban Design Group at New York's Department of City Planning. Hong Kong, Shanghai, Dubai, Mumbai: all look to New York for both the image of the high-rise skyline and the mechanism and tools to shape large-scale development. Special districts and zoning are now modelled globally, yet often without the countering forces of social and environmental resistance which have marked development in New York since the 1960s.

Bangkok: A Genealogy of Lifestyle Centres

A valet opens the door of your taxi and a beautifully tailored doorman salutes as you enter Gourmet Paradise, a winding row of restaurants along an interior 'canal'. Like the royal family, who used to relax in the luxurious gardens of Sraprathum Palace, Bangkok's elite can dine on teak waterside decks – but now in air-conditioned comfort rather than relying on the lotus ponds to cool off. From there you meet your gift advisor, to help you 'plan the most memorable occasions of your life' at the many jewellery stores along Fashion Venue just one level up.[34] Exhausted by such important decisions, you retreat to the spa. Siam Paragon, 'The Pride of Bangkok', is not a mall, but a *lifestyle centre*.

Lifestyle centres first began to be noticed in 2005, as journalists reported on the new trend in retailing away from huge malls and big box discount stores towards more pampering environments.[35] In sociology, lifestyle refers to the behaviours that define the way a person lives. Advertisers and marketers 'target' lifestyles in order to match consumer desires with new products. Doctors worry about lifestyle when advising overweight or diabetic patients and environmentalists hope to change lifestyle through calls to recycle, use less fossil fuel and limit pollution. Next, we will look at the evolution of Bangkok's central shopping district as an indication of a new role for urban design in the intersecting worlds of consumption, health and environmentalism as a genealogy of lifestyle.

Social ecologist Morgan Grove uses lifestyle data called PRIZM clusters from a company called Claritas to understand people's preferences in order to develop better urban ecosystem design and management. Lifestyle, for the social ecologists in the Baltimore Ecosystem Study, is a key concept to work with people, neighbourhood groups and policy makers to move towards more resilient urban ecosystem designs. An understanding of human behaviour is necessary in an urban context dominated by private land ownership, where people are actively involved in designing their own environment. Whether in suburbs or informal settlements, lifestyle is much more than a marketing tool for developers.

Bangkok's CSD

When I first arrived in Bangkok in 1995, deep into my research on the formation of the Central Business Districts (CBD) of Manhattan, I witnessed an entire city under construction. During the decade between 1985 and 1995, Thailand was the fastest-growing economy in the world, and Bangkok was booming. However, I was never able to find a CBD in spite of all this construction activity. Western experts and American real estate executives all bemoaned the lack of a Master Plan for the city, and the fact that there was no decisive CBD. Two unexecuted American-led Master Plans sit in the offices of the Bangkok Metropolitan Administration: the Greater Bangkok Plan of 1960 prepared by Litchfield Whiting Bowe & Associates, and the Bangkok Plan of 1996, prepared with the MIT Consulting Team. In spite of the successful abandonment of Master Planning by the Department of City Planning in America's largest city, a Master Plan was deemed necessary for Bangkok. Parallel to this process, Bangkok has achieved a complexly ordered and vital urban design culture of its own. Based more on the overlay of various images and identities, Bangkok offers many new lessons for urban design in an age of globalisation.

152 Pathumwan Intersection

Ratchaprasong Intersection

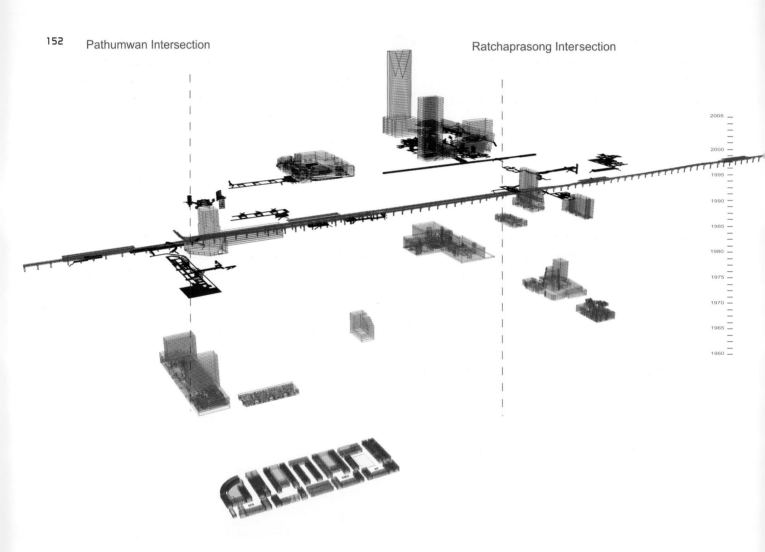

2005
2000
1995
1990
1985
1980
1975
1970
1965
1960

The equestrian statue of Chulalongkorn, King Rama V of Siam, was inaugurated in November 1908 as the culmination of a week-long series of spectacular civic pageants in honour of the 40th anniversary of his reign.[36] Pirasri Povatong has uncovered newspaper descriptions of a great carnival procession of 20,000 people and 77 floats – including papier-mâché models of major building projects constructed by Chulalongkorn.[37] The great parade proceeded down Ratchadamnoen Avenue, and Pirasri points to the design and rituals of the tree-lined boulevard, called 'the royal walk', as one of the most important new urban spaces created by King Chulalongkorn, and an example of 'hybrid urbanism in the semi colonial context of Bangkok'.[38] While the skyscrapers of Manhattan are a global city of modernity and development, Las Vegas and Disneyland have become the more preferred stops for global developers and planners in search of urban design models. This last genealogy of urban design practice will introduce symbolic image making and branding urban lifestyle as an important development in urban design practice studied in the context of the spectacular Bangkok.

In addition to his visits to the colonial cities in Singapore, Malaya, Java and India, King Chulalongkorn (1868–1910) went on two visits to the European capitals of England, Germany, Russia, Austria, Italy, Belgium, Denmark and Sweden. 'The same kind of selective acquisition of Western know-how and skills comes to expression in his recruitment of foreign experts as government advisers. During his reign their number totalled more than three hundred. Meanwhile he made sure that no single nationality would fain a monopoly over any part of the administration.'[39] If our genealogy of the Master Plan in Rome demonstrated the dispersal of the legitimacy of power through the association of European and colonial capitals with the Imperial city, in Bangkok, we see a careful selection of international knowledge, forming a modern capital city beyond the reach of colonial conquest.

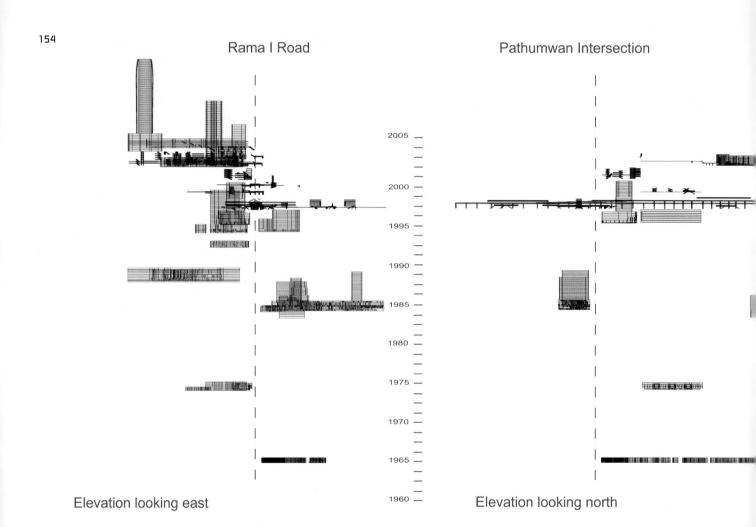

154

Rama I Road

Pathumwan Intersection

2005

2000

1995

1990

1985

1980

1975

1970

1965

1960

Elevation looking east

Elevation looking north

Ratchaprasong Intersection

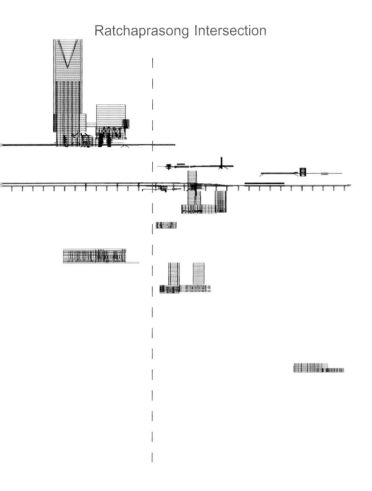

While Ratchadamnoen connected the Grand Palace and the royal moated city to the new Dusit district to the north, King Rama I Road was a long armature that connected to another royal enclave to the east of the old city. Rama I Road runs parallel to the San Saeb Canal, built as a military artery in the war against Amman over Cambodia in the 1830s. King Rama III had built a suburban palace retreat and meditation temple in this district called Pathumwan in the middle of the 19th century, but Chulalongkorn connected this district by road to the heart of the city as an eastern garden suburb. The royal family were the key actors in introducing European lifestyles into Thai society. The palaces in the garden city area east of the historical city were places where European architecture, clothing, manners and behaviour were initially introduced.

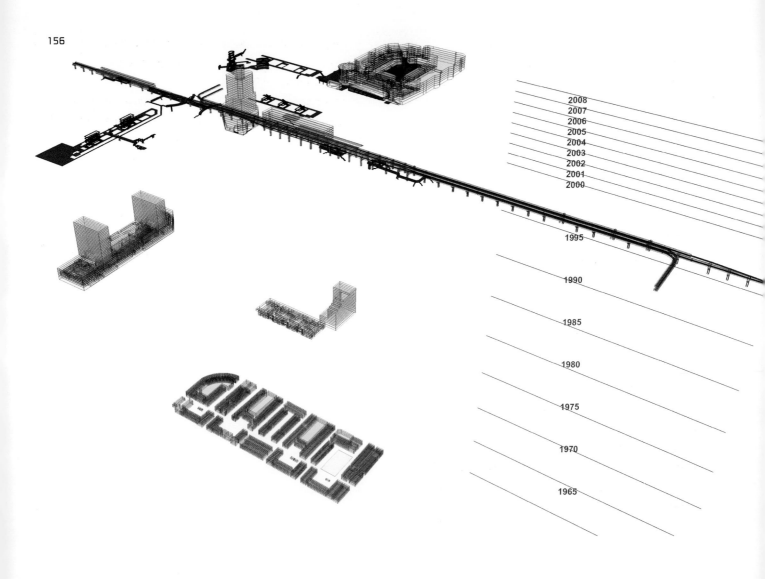

156

2008
2007
2006
2005
2004
2003
2002
2001
2000

1995

1990

1985

1980

1975

1970

1965

Following the end of absolute monarchy in 1932, Rama I Road turned from a royal garden enclave to the site of the emergence of Bangkok's central shopping district. Siam Square is a grid of commercial shop-house blocks, constructed with ample street-side parking in 1964, built on leased land from the royally founded Chulalongkorn University. It was constructed at the time American influence in Thailand was peaking, as a strategic Cold-War relation turned into a more tactical alliance to use the kingdom as the logistical base for the American war in Vietnam, Laos and Cambodia. Influenced by the concept of 'park and shop', the complex offered the convenience of diagonal parking directly in front of retail outlets. Although in congested contemporary Bangkok this parking solution is no longer adequate, the complex also introduced prefabricated concrete frame technology which still adapts flexibly to different commercial tenants' needs to expand vertically or horizontally and to continually remake their facades. Siam Square was also designed as a leisure and entertainment centre and originally included three cinemas and a bowling alley. Rama 1 Road became a locus for the introduction of American lifestyle to Bangkok – the car, music, movies and dress all began to be very influential in this period.

The university landlord encouraged its faculty to be entrepreneurs in this new commercial space, and it soon became the location for cram schools – private after-school education facilities. This concentration of the city's rapidly growing population of aspiring middle-class youth also made Siam Square the ideal location for youth-oriented clothing, food and entertainment businesses. This activity spilled over to Siam Center, first built on Crown Property by the Tourist Authority of Thailand to provide boutique shopping for the Intercontinental Hotel next door in 1974.

America withdrew from the Vietnam War and turned over its airbases and shipping ports to the Thai government in 1976, but its cultural influence continued with the introduction of a multi-level, full-scale shopping mall with structured parking, hotel and office complex. Mah Boon Krong Center (MBK) was constructed in 1984, again on University land leased, developed and operated by a rice merchant conglomerate. Now, however, Japan has replaced America as the largest foreign investor in Thailand, and a Japanese department store, restaurants and karaoke intermingle with bowling alleys, McDonald's and Starbucks. Japanese lifestyle, like foreign investment, easily filled the void created by American withdrawal.

The World Trade Center was opened in 1990 with ambitious plans to even surpass MBK as a single-destination shopping and leisure complex. Between 1985 and 1995, Thailand, in addition to being the fastest-growing economy on earth, also led the world in per capita conspicuous consumption of Rolex watches, Mercedes-Benz automobiles and Johnnie Walker Black Label whisky. The Darwinian struggle to dominate the consumer's attention in such an era referred to as the 'bubble economy' was shattered with the devaluation of the baht and the bail-out of the country by the International Monetary Fund in 1998. The World Trade Center was left partially completed, and its planned office building remained an empty concrete ruin of speculative capitalism for over a decade.

The catastrophic Asian economic crisis of 1997 began with a real estate bubble, bank failures and currency speculation in Thailand. While Thailand's economy was surging, huge glittering commercial buildings symbolised the promise of national prosperity. After '97, they turned into the counter-symbol of economic depression, as hundreds of commercial developments in central Bangkok lay empty as a result of bankruptcy, shoppers disappeared, and the city became known for its haunting hollow concrete shells. Fears of isolation and abandonment became manifest in the symbolic heart of the modern city. In this context, Thais turned introspective and began to examine the values of their own traditional lifestyles, Buddhism and a 'sufficiency' philosophy outlined by King Rama IX.

The millennium celebrations were a happy distraction for Bangkok, with a grand countdown and fireworks display in front of the bankrupt World Trade Center development diverting attention from the view of its unfinished office tower. But in the fallout from economic collapse, there were tangible transformations in the city's psyche. It was a time of national soul-searching, with the King giving a message of Buddhist self-sufficiency, and a new political party named 'Thai love Thai' – led by telecommunications billionaire Thaksin Shinawatra – achieving government control. The millennium also brought the first phase of the city's long-delayed mass transit system: two lines of the elevated Skytrain, whose concrete viaducts forcefully torque and slide by each other and meet at Siam Central Station on the long block of Rama I Road between Pathumwan and Ratchaprasong Intersections. The Skytrain initiated a renovation and building boom for a glamorous shopping district lined with constantly reconstructed shopping and lifestyle centres. Rama I Road is now covered by two massive train lines converging at Siam Central Station.

MBK Center was the first of the malls to realise the potential of both the millennial optimism and the new accessibility the Skytrain provided at their doorstep. Metallic silver defined the 21st century, and the mall was reclad in aluminium panels and a giant elliptical illuminated sign. Additionally, the interior of the shopping centre was connected directly by second- and third-level bridges to the Skytrain's National Stadium Station mezzanine, which extends a large, elevated public platform eastward across Pathumwan Intersection. However, the greatest new potential was in the social change the political philosophy of Thaksin ushered in: unrestrained, credit-based optimistic consumerism. Thaksin made shopping a national duty at all levels of society.

The immediate success of MBK's renovation started a chain reaction of architectural makeovers, as Gaysorn Plaza and Erawan were refurbished in concert with new sky-bridge connections to Chitlom Station's concourse. Now, a massive construction site stretched the entire length of Rama I Road between Pathumwan and Ratchaprasong as the two largest shopping centre and mall developers in the country both completed flagship developments east and west of Wat Pathum Wanaram.

The Mall Group recently opened the super-luxury Siam Paragon and renovated Siam Center and Siam Discovery Center as one integrated complex directly connected to both National Stadium Station and the Skytrain's main junction at Siam Central Station. The Central Group has assumed control over the former World Trade Center and the renaming of the complex World Central Plaza marked the completion of the long-abandoned office tower, a glass lantern with flat reflecting pools facing the Skytrain. Central created a lengthy extension of the Skytrain's elevated walkway system now connecting Siam Central Station through Chitlom Station at Gaysorn and Erawan, with Central's flagship department store at the opposite exit of Chitlom. The two-kilometre multi-level urban armature introduces a lifestyle and urbanism also common in Hong Kong, a city much admired by Thai visitors.

159

Ratchaprasong timeline.

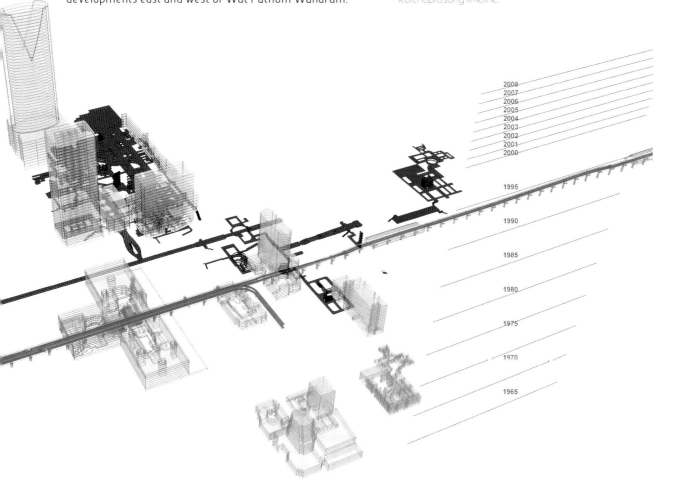

The Dispersal of Power

As an example of moving from archaeology to genealogy and from the archive to the diagram, Foucault analyses the development of the prison in order to demonstrate the transfer of the technologies of power from the centralised and absolute violent rule of a sovereign to the dispersals of power through the panoptical rule of law in the modern state. Deleuze describes Foucault's book *Discipline and Punish* as a 'new cartography' developed through a microphysical analysis of the change from 17th- to 19th-century practices of discipline and punishment which reveal this new conception of power. This conception of power is rooted in the analysis of panopticism, named after Jeremy Bentham's idea of the Panopticon, which was the design of a penitentiary house where people are kept under constant surveillance and inspection.[40]

Panoptical power is exercised rather than possessed through 'dispositions, manoeuvres, tactics, techniques, and functionings'.[41] This new conception of power, which Foucault identifies with the classical age in Europe, must be legitimised in legal institutions in the support of modern social practices such as capitalism. Our genealogical comparison of Rome, New York and Bangkok reveals this dispersion of power from emperors, popes, kings and colonial administrators to government officials, bureaucrats, capitalists, citizens, ad men and consumers.

Instead of urban design serving as a theatre for the spectacular expression of absolute power as demonstrated in the triumphal and religious processions in Rome, we now must look for power relations in 'innumerable points of confrontation, focuses of instability, each of which has its own risks of conflict, of struggles, or at least temporary inversion of the power-relations ... In brief, power is not homogenous, but can be defined only by the particular points through which it passes'.[42] This microphysics of power is exactly what circulates around any urban design process in any modern city, where advanced capitalism meets evolving forms of participatory democracy. The power to shape the city is more and more dispersed to various actors and agents, making the task of understanding the role of urban design more and more complex.

Foucault's notion of dispersed power through different forms of discipline 'cannot be identified with any one institution or apparatus precisely because it is a type of power, a technology that traverses every kind of apparatus or institution, linking them, prolonging them, and making them converge and function in a new way'. Instead it creates 'a new topology which no longer locates the origin of power in a privileged place, and can no longer accept a limited localization ... [P]ower is local because it is never global, but it is not local or localized because it is diffuse'.[43]

Urban design experienced a crisis in its origins – at the moment the design of cities was seen as a professional discipline, the power to shape the cities so admired by urban historians and planning officials was no longer centralised. This dichotomy can be seen in such urban American power brokers as Edmund Bacon, who used cities like Rome and Beijing as legitimising models for an urban design practice shaped by the Master Plan. The legitimacy of centralised decision making in a diverse, mobile and individualistic society is breaking down, and single-use Central Business Districts or even shopping centres are now being replaced by lifestyle centres. Clearly the arousal of passion around the design of Ground Zero is a sign of the emergence of another significant rupture in urban design practice, which will be the focus of the next section of this book on Schizoanalysis.

Endnotes

1 www.skyscraper.org/timeformations

2 Gilles Deleuze, *Foucault*, translated by Paul Bové, Minneapolis: University of Minnesota Press, 1988, p 74. Following the trajectory of Foucault's writing, 'the study of stratified relations of knowledge culminates in *The Archaeology of Knowledge*; the study of strategic power relations begins with *Discipline and Punish* and culminates paradoxically in *The History of Sexuality*'.

3 Michel Foucault, 'Nietzsche, Genealogy, History', *Foucault Reader*, edited by Paul Rabinow, New York: Pantheon Books, 1984, pp 76–100.

4 Deleuze, pp 70–1.

5 Ibid, p 43.

6 Ibid, p 44.

7 Brian McGrath et al, *Designing Patch Dynamics*, New York: Columbia University Books on Architecture, 2008.

8 Foucault, p 80.

9 David Grahame Shane, *Recombinant Urbanism*, London: John Wiley & Sons, 2005, p 176.

10 Foucault, p 82.

11 Shane, p 198.

12 Foucault, p 81.

13 Ibid, p 82.

14 Shane, p 231.

15 Foucault, p 85.

16 Marshall Berman, *All That is Solid Melts into Air*, New York: Viking Press, 1982.

17 Eugene Holland, *Deleuze and Guattari's Anti-Oedipus: Introduction to Schizoanalysis*, London: Routledge, 1999, p 58.

18 Iris Marion Young, 'City Life and Difference', *Metropolis: Center and Symbol of our Times*, edited by Philip Kasinitz, New York: New York University Press, 1995, pp 250–70.

19 Sigfried Giedion, *Space, Time and Architecture*, Cambridge: Harvard University Press, Sixth Edition, 1976, p 96.

20 Edmund N Bacon, *Design of Cities*, New York: Penguin Books, 1976.

21 Barbara Kruger, *Assemblage 10*, edited by K Michael Hays and Alicia Kennedy, Cambridge: MIT Press, December 1989, cover image.

22 Charles L Singer, *The Renaissance in Rome*, Bloomington: Indiana University Press, 1985, p 53.

23 Bacon, p 131.

24 Louis Marin, 'History Made Visible and Readable: On Drawings of Trajan's Column', *On Representation*, translated by Catherine Porter, Stanford: Stanford University Press, 2001, p 220.

25 Ibid, p 219.

26 James Packer, 'Politics, Urbanism, and Archaeology in "Roma Capitale": A Troubled Past and A Controversial Future', *American Journal of Archaeology*, Vol 93, No 1 (Jan 1989), pp 137–41.

27 Marin, pp 224–5.

28 Foucault, pp 93–4.

29 http://home2.nyc.gov/html/dcp/html/zone/zonehis.shtml

30 Carol Willis, *Form Follows Finance: Skyscrapers and Skylines in New York and Chicago*, New York: Princeton Architectural Press, 1995.

31 In fact, the American headquarters of Canadian (Seagram's) and British (Lever House) companies.

32 Jonathan Barnett, *An Introduction to Urban Design*, New York: Harper & Row, 1982.

33 William H Whyte, *City: Rediscovering the Center*, New York: Anchor Books, 1988.

34 http://www.siamparagon.co.th/

35 Parija Bhatnagar, 'Not a mall, it's a lifestyle centre', CNN, 12 January 2005. Andrew Blum, 'The Mall Goes Undercover', *Slate*, 5 April 2005.

36 Pirasri Povatong, 'Ratchadamnoen Avenue: Design and Rituals of Hybrid Urbanism in Bangkok, 1900–1910', *Chulalongkorn University Building & Environment: Design and Research Series*, edited by Bundit Chulasai, Bangkok: Faculty of Architecture, Chulalongkorn University, Vol 1, September 2006, p 24.

37 *The Bangkok Times*, 14 November 1908.

38 Povatong, p 23.

39 Han ten Brummelhuis, *King of the Waters: Homan van der Heide and the origin of modern irrigation in Siam*, Chiang Mai: Silkworm Books, 2005, pp 66–7.

40 Robin Evans, *The Fabrication of Virtue: English prison architecture, 1750–1840*, Cambridge: Cambridge University Press, 1982.

41 Deleuze, p 24.

42 Ibid, p 25.

43 Ibid, p 26.

Chapter 4

Trade

Between the years 1997 and 2003, when 25 million square feet of office space in New York's financial district was vacant, the Skyscraper Museum was founded and began exhibitions and public programmes in temporary spaces in vacated banking halls. During the last summer of the millennium, 3-D modeller and web designer Mark Watkins, assistants Akiko Hattori and Lucy Lai Wong, and I spent 18 days in the ground-floor retail space at 110 Maiden Lane, working on a 3-D computer model mapping the formation and deformation of Manhattan's skyscraper business districts through time. The public was invited in to witness our intensive modelling activity, in order to make this publicly funded project as accessible and informative as possible. The contributors to this open-source process included tourists, bankers, city planners, architects, students and passers-by, whom we engaged in a discussion on history, city planning, real estate markets, skyscrapers, mapping, visual communication, animation and digital technologies. The result of this exercise in participatory design, the website *Manhattan Timeformations*, will be presented in this section as a prototype and model for developing new urban design practices through creating multi-dimensional interfaces – both physical and virtual.[1]

Since going online, a variety of audiences, individuals and institutions representing different disciplines and interests have 'mistaken' *Manhattan Timeformations* for a number of things – including an online game. Art organisations have christened it digital art; a film festival gave it an award as a movie; planners, architects and urban designers have recognised it as a design tool; a journalism foundation saw it as a multi-dimensional database; graphic designers champion it as information architecture; software companies marketed their products with it; individual home pages and educational institutions link to it; and recently scientists and institutes of technology have cited it.[2] Each institutional and individual browser highlights different aspects of the digital model in the website, redefining the project through their particular disciplinary lens or individual subjectivity in terms that its designers barely imagined. The effect of this cross-disciplinary acceptance and reinterpretation is to render the project more illusive to its creators, yet increasingly more productive for imagining new forms of urban design practice.

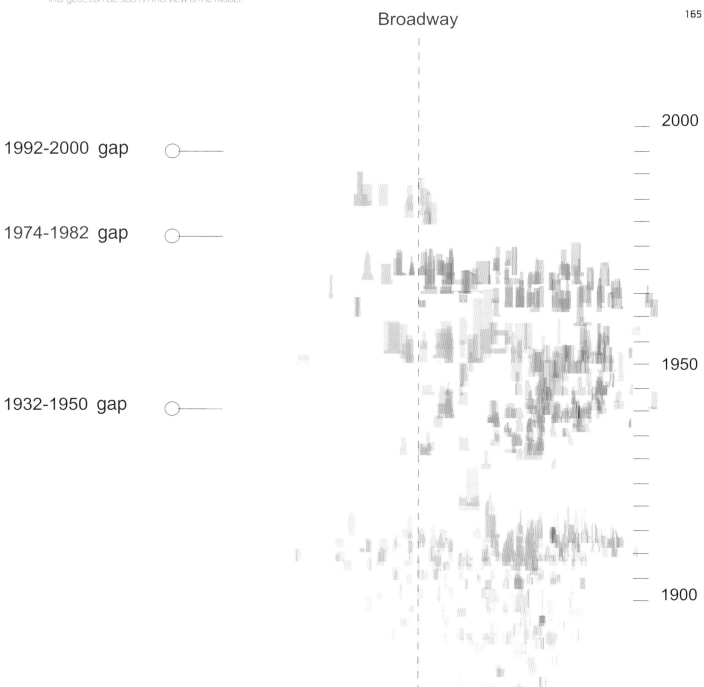

View of the *Manhattan Timeformations* model looking north. Three lulls in office building construction can be seen here: between 1932 and 1950 during the Great Depression and the Second World War; between 1974 and 1982 following the oil shock; and between 1992 and 2000 following the stock market crash of 1989. The concentration of high-rise office buildings on the east side of Manhattan before 1982, and the drift of Midtown development westward following that year, can be seen in this view of the model.

Broadway

1992-2000 gap

1974-1982 gap

1932-1950 gap

2000

1950

1900

166 Timing

Eviatar Zerubavel in his book *Time Maps* examines how narratives of time are socially constructed. Linear models of time narrate either ascending towards greatness or descending from a glorious past. Our genealogies of Rome, New York and Bangkok all exhibit a more zig-zag pattern of rise and decline, boom and bust, descent and emergence. However there are also wheels of time of different duration: days, weeks, months, years, and all repeat cycles which rhythmically repeat familiar patterns. These time cycles are layered as well. For example Pagan feasts were replaced by Christian holy days and national holidays in Rome, while New York pulses with the multiple rhythms of the diverse cultures that inhabit the city. Zerubavel also mentions how the cycle of holidays commemorating the birth, first sermon and death of Buddha are overlain with the days which celebrate the Chakri dynasty, which in turn share the calendar with the national holidays of Thailand.[3] While Rome enjoys a temperate, dry, Mediterranean climate, New York adjusts to extremes in temperature and Bangkok's rhythms are in concert with wet and rainy seasons. Historical time is also socially constructed in an uneven way as some important dates or events are given more weight than others. Non-continuous points in history are bridged in order to construct narratives of continuity.[4]

While archaeological modelling for urban design advocated a multi-layered approach to urban modelling, genealogy suggests a multi-dimensional one. Analytical layering in urban design can be traced to Ian McHarg's *Design with Nature*, which was extended through his successors at the University of Pennsylvania Anuradha Mathur and Dilip da Cunha.[5] Architects such as Bernard Tschumi in Parc de la Villette have generated rich and diverse social spaces by creating urban designs that are the result of the superimposition of layers.[6] Multi-dimensional practices are just beginning to emerge, and this chapter will intersperse new forms of teaching and practice that emerged around the issues of multi-dimensionality in time and space introduced in *Manhattan Timeformations*.

Navigating in time and space through *Manhattan Timeformations (MT)*, 2000. The following sequence of drawings will descend in time from 1990 to 1940 and move forward from Lower to Midtown Manhattan. View of the *MT* model from the 1990 time plane looking up Broadway. By the end of the 20th century only building built in the decade following the 'Bonfire of the Vanities' economic bust is the Mercantile Exchange building in Battery Park City seen to the upper right.

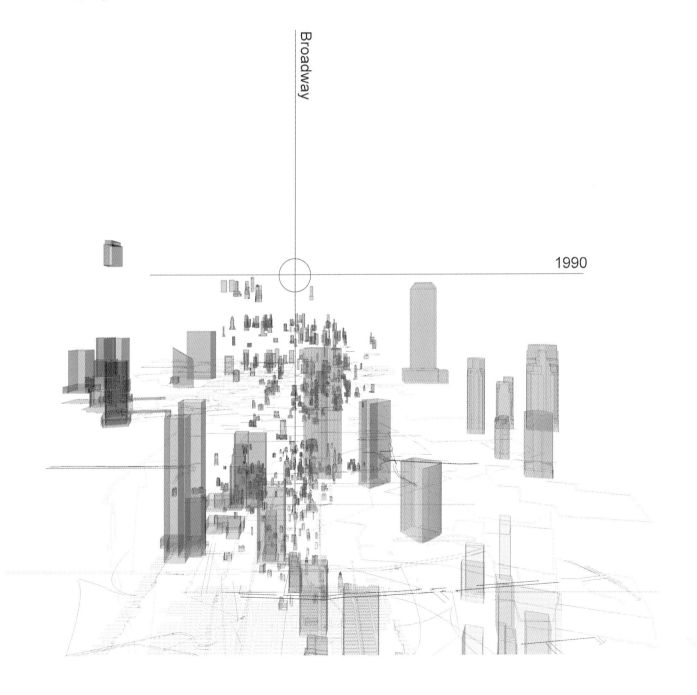

Broadway

1990

When uploaded, *Manhattan Timeformations* (*MT*) was disguised with the simple graphics of early computer games. But in fact, this digital model is a multi-dimensional urban design puzzle embedded with informational nuggets about power at work in New York City over time. Hidden texts are revealed only when the user selects specific combinations of layers, and historical narratives are created and undone by turning buildings and infrastructures on and off in various sequences. Elsewhere on the site you can rotate the x/y spatial plane of the map to the vertical z temporal dimension and construct and deconstruct the skyline of Midtown and Lower Manhattan along a timeline. Roll your mouse over office building skylines of different eras and conjure a rich cast of urban actors: 19th-century robber barons, post-war corporate men in grey flannel suits, masters of the universe igniting the 1980s 'bonfire of the vanities' or speculators in irrational exuberance at the turn of the 21st century. Finally you can horizontally fly through a perspectival representation of the city, along a particular temporal plane, or vertically ascend and descend through temporal layers.

A game-like language is employed as *MT*'s interface strategy in order to motivate interaction with the different urban models. Beginning with SimCity (1989), a city-building simulation game, computer gaming technologies have entered into urban design discourse. More recently, online virtual worlds like Second Life (2003) are attracting huge internet-based social networks, economies and new forms of virtual urban design practices. Games for Change, a movement started in New York in 2004, is dedicated to using computer and video games for social change. Conferences at the City University of New York in 2005 and Parsons the New School for Design in 2006 have highlighted projects where the massive interest in internet-based games is directed towards issues such as poverty, conflict and environmental degradation.[7] While Sigfried Giedion's book *Space, Time and Architecture* heralded in the urban designer as Master Planner, Friedrich von Borries and his colleagues have introduced the urban designer as multi-dimensional gamer in *Space Time Play*.[8]

View of the *MT* model from the 1980 time plane looking up Broadway. 1980 marks the midpoint of a 10-year pause in office building construction following the oil shock of 1974. In the interim, electronic trading was introduced on Wall Street, and a real estate boom ensued which included the construction of the World Financial Center (building cluster on the left).

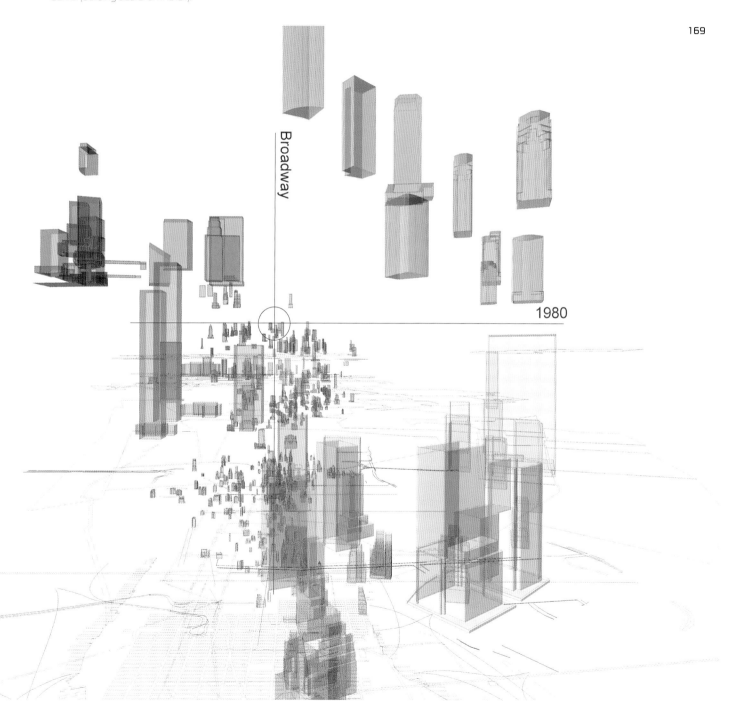

Broadway

1980

Texting

You could use *Manhattan Timeformations* as a text, since it illustrates facts about the physical history of the island of Manhattan and the construction history of the New York skyscraper – and from a check of sites linked to our site it is clear many educators use it as such. It begins with introductory 'pages' with images and text columns that are linked by buttons. However, after leaving the first interface, text is reduced to a secondary role and is limited to captions and time and space orientation guidelines. But the project is not linear like a textbook and it lacks a direct narrative point of view. It challenges readers to uncover much of the information themselves, since knowledge is gained by choosing views and combinations of layers rather than reading a sequence of words and images. Turn all the layers on and you are confronted with a chaotic overload of information, while each single map is hopelessly inadequate and incomplete. Only the acts of composing, multiplying and switching vantage point present stories and produce bits of knowledge – and no two readings can ever be the same.

View of the *MT* model from the 1940 time plane looking up Broadway. There was a long pause in office building construction between the Great Depression and the end of the Second World War. The shift in building technology can be seen by comparing the slender stone Art Deco towers of Wall Street in grey below the 1940 timeline with the blue glass curtain-wall air-conditioned buildings above.

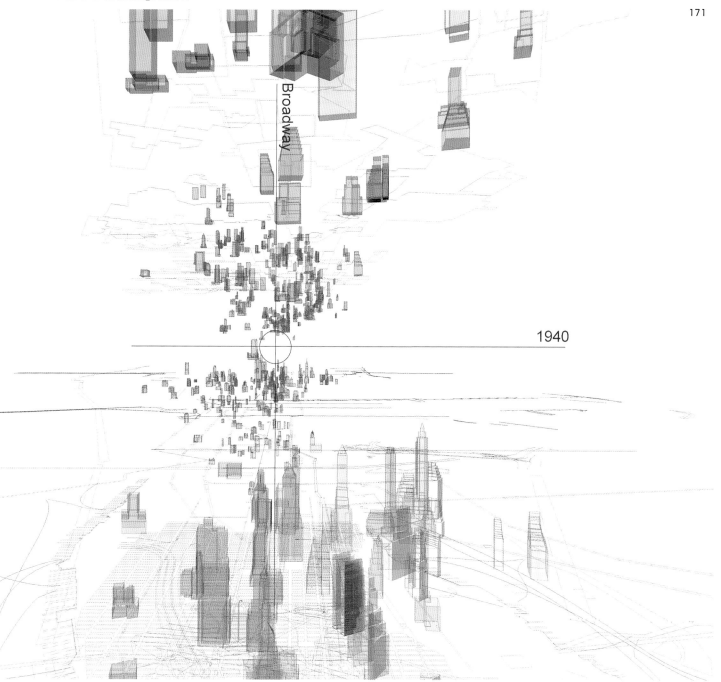

Broadway

1940

Mario Gandelsonas's book *The Urban Text* (1991) begins with the profound idea that the city itself can be regarded as a text to be both read and written.[9] Digital technology, with its ability to create hypertextual relations, provides multiple ways to read and write the city and the possibility of multiple authorships. Gandelsonas's various mapping projects with architecture students during the 1980s culminated in an opportunity to create some of the first digital urban analysis models of Chicago, beginning in 1988. The drawings generated are seen as undermining the authority of a single unifying story.

> The different configurations, layers or sequences are constantly re-arranged by these different overlapping fictions. The plan can therefore be seen as a mechanism generating drawings and stories.[10]

Agrest & Gandelsonas have realised the potential for reading the city as a multi-dimensional text most comprehensively in their Vision Plan for Des Moines, Iowa, which mixes 'readings' of the city with sites for economic development opportunity.

Digital modelling for urban design, however, opens up the possibility of spatial production through urban text messaging – texting – as well as textual readings of the city. Short Messaging Service (SMS) uses 160 characters or fewer to send text messages over mobile phones. The technology developed from 1989 via simple Motorola beepers, to the Vodafone network in the UK in 1992, and finally to the first SMS messages at Nokia in 1993. It wasn't until DoCoMo – short for Do Communications Over the Mobile Network – introduced the service in Tokyo in the late 1990s that the new technology found a broad social base, as Japan's youth and Tokyo's commuting culture embraced the convenience of arranging meetings for groups of people while moving around the city. The public broadcast of texting has reinvigorated public spaces in projects such as Antonio Scarponi's *Dreaming Wall*, a phosphorescent panel that displays telephone text messages as an 'info forum'.[11] Texting has also radically altered public space in the form of flash mobs, culture jams, and other forms of social action which are often used to mobilise protests around controversial urban developments.

View of the *MT* model from the
1990 time plane looking up 5th
Avenue in Midtown. At the time of
the construction of the model, the
state-led redevelopment of Times
Square had begun, pushing the
Midtown business district west to
8th Avenue (cluster of buildings in
the upper left of view).

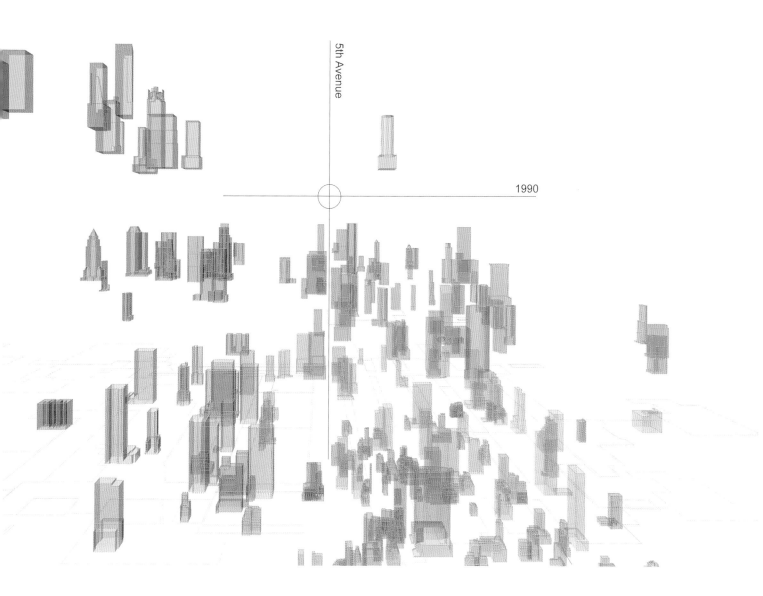

5th Avenue

1990

Mapping, Monitoring and Modelling

Digital technology may soon make conventional two-dimensional mapping obsolete. As mentioned in Chapter 1, cartography was a modern scientific discipline which replaced an indigenous spatial perception of named localities in Thailand. Global Positioning Systems in cars or handheld personal navigation devices do a better job of telling you where you are and how to get where you want to go than a conventional road map. The map archive in *Timeformations* is just one dimension of a multi-dimensional interactive tool where the final act of mapping is cognitive.[12] The act of making imaginative connections between the various layers of maps and other projections is left to the web navigator. This multi-dimensionality opens up much more space for consensus. While a two-dimensional map in a community planning charrette may limit the number of possibilities of overlaying various ideas, activities or constituencies in a space, looking multi-dimensionally in space and time allows for the coexistence of what might have ordinarily been understood as conflicting uses.

Although the interface of *Timeformations* includes a tool to overlay maps of business districts of Midtown and Lower Manhattan – streets, subway lines and zoning information are all there – its 'maps' are just flat, top-down, orthographic views of a three-dimensional model. Thinking about multi-dimensional mapping started with the simple act of plotting on a time graph the number of office buildings built in Manhattan in a given year. The result was a pattern of peaks and valleys much like the fluctuations of the stock market. This led to the idea of making the z-dimension of the computer model reflect this data. The side view of the model reveals that the vertical z-axis is a timeline. In the *Timeformations* model, high-rise office buildings were lifted to a time plane according to the year of construction. The web interface, therefore, navigates through time as well as space by toggling through different orthographic views – top and two side views – of the dense informational database of Manhattan's business districts modelled in 3-D.

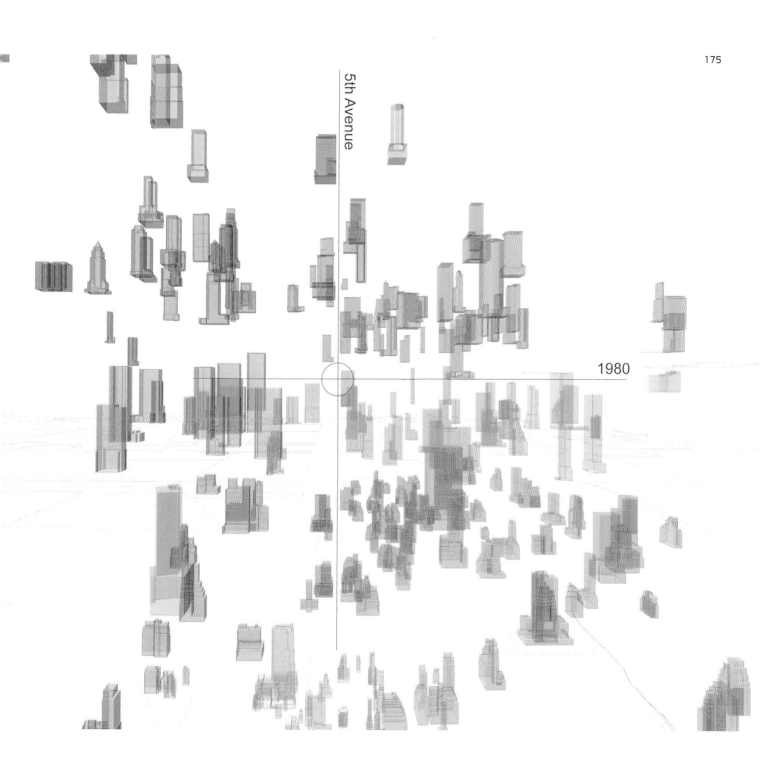

View of the *MT* model from the 1980 time plane looking up 5th Avenue in Midtown. New York City Planning instituted zoning incentives to redirect growth to the west side by decreasing allowable bulk from the overcrowded east side.

5th Avenue

1980

176 The movement image that emerged is iconic and associational, conjuring both the skyline and market fluctuations. What can be cognitively mapped onto the web interface is urban, technological, ideological and social change. Navigating through the model brings our attention to living within the historical space of modernity and change. But this knowledge is not located in any single map or view of the city. Modelling can become a way of thinking and seeing, of expanding individual cognition and attention, rather than a blinding and encrypting representation of power. The computer has fundamentally changed the art of cartography, the authority of the text and our imaginations and perceptions. It is the storytelling or *textual* dimension of cartography that the web brings forth.

Timeformations is neither map nor text, but a hybrid machine for producing personal urban cognitive models and stories in historical space.

Ecosystem scientists were one of the interested audiences for this new method of modelling, and in 2002 I met Morgan Grove, Steward Pickett and Mary Cadenasso, researchers with the Baltimore Ecosystem Study (BES). This was the beginning of a long-term collaboration between ecosystem science and design which continues today. Here the spatial and temporal measures in the *Timeformations* model are applied to the ecological theory of patch dynamics, where urban ecosystems are seen as distinct neighbourhood patches producing shifting mosaics of spatial heterogeneity while filtering the flows of water, materials, people and information. The landscape of Greater Baltimore is equipped with a network of monitoring stations that give real-time information on the ecological performance of particular patches. It is only through the visualisation of these systems through multi-dimensional models that design interventions can be proposed strategically at various spatial and temporal scales. The work of the urban design students at Columbia University between 2002 and 2005 experimented with these new methods of design in collaboration with the BES scientists. This work has been collected in a monograph called *Designing Patch Dynamics*.[13]

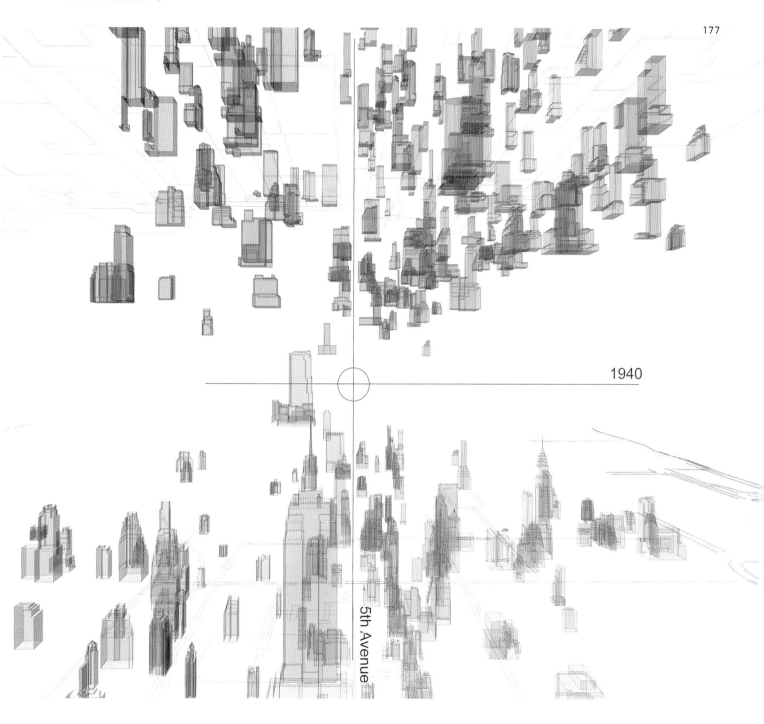

View of the *MT* model from the
1940 time plane looking up
5th Avenue in Midtown.
Rockefeller Center is the lone
office building complex built
between 1930 and 1939
during the Great Depression.
(The GE building, formerly the
RCA building, can be seen to
the left of the crosshair.)

1940

5th Avenue

Collaborating

From counting page 'hits', the most popular animated drawing in *Manhattan Timeformations* is the perspectival 'fly-through' that is presented as almost an afterthought on the site. The model and project was conceived in axonometry, in the spirit of Auguste Choisy's inverted drawings of Roman vaults and El Lissitzky's Constructivist Prouns. Flipping, disorienting, multi-dimensional drawings employ axonometric projection to explore space outside of what El Lissitsky considered 'old fashioned' perspectival projections. Western art had been stuck gazing into vanishing points for 400 years.

The following sequence of drawings will again
descend in time from 1990 to 1940, this time
looking east and moving south from Midtown to
Lower Manhattan. View of the *MT* model from the
1990 time plane looking east along 42nd Street.
The Time Warner Center (2003), Bloomberg
Tower (2005) and the cluster of towers at Times
Square represent a new era in office building
constructed for media companies, followed since
this model was constructed by the Times (2007)
and Hearst Towers (2006).

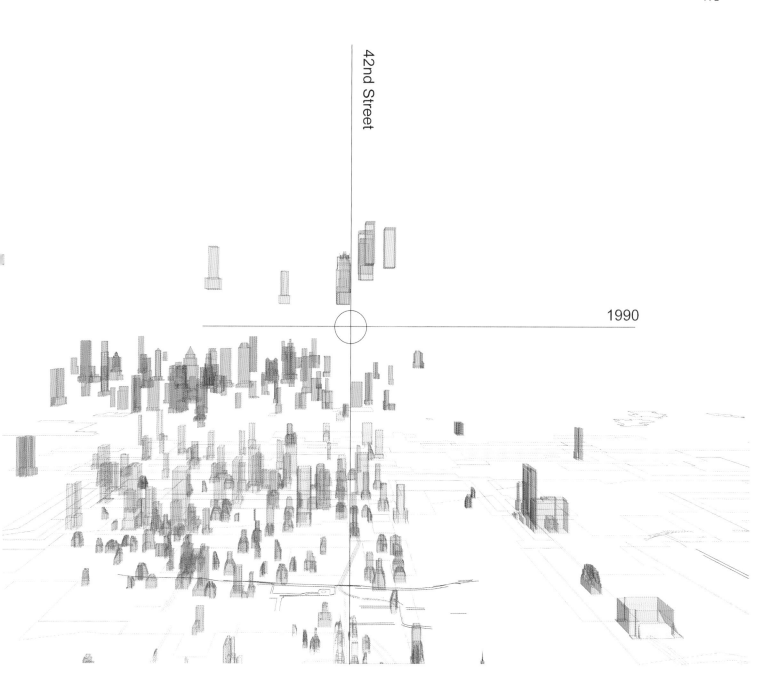

42nd Street

1990

One would never guess that this Modernist reversal of convention existed, judging from the majority of images produced from computer modelling and animation software. Highly rendered 'realistic' depictions of architectural and urban space again dominate. What the simulators seem to have ignored is a whole tradition of modern art's interest in the flatness of the picture plane as well as the new kinds of images that scientists are producing with new mapping tools. Digital technology allows for the exploration of other dimensions in mapping: the illusion of a third dimension in computer modelling, and the visualisation of temporal dimensions we see in PET scans and MRI maps of the brain or in common TV weather maps. However, modelling on the computer is never completely three dimensional, because it is always represented on a flat screen. It is only through sequence and animations that the multi-dimensionality and temporalities of computer cartography can be developed, yet most spatial depictions have gravitated towards perspectival simulations. In MT we have rejected the illusionary approach of hyper reality. The model views remain unrendered, left in 'wire' frame and are quite primitive compared with the virtual fly-throughs that dominate most urban representations generated from computer models.

While the computer has fundamentally changed the art of cartography and the authority of the text, maps and books continue to proliferate. There is now a parallel telematic reality intersecting and overlapping with the physical world. Our website demonstrates some of the possibilities in using architectural and cartographic representational languages on the internet as a new art form and practice. It is really a hope for the possibilities of new interfaces between human attention and perception within increasingly complex and insecure environmental experiences. In fact, our long vision is in developing tools to utilise information gathering and mapping technologies to enable us to inhabit the planet more intelligently. In order to accomplish this, new forms of collaborative urban design practice must be undertaken. A new generation of urban designers are experimenting with new forms of collaboration. Interboro Partners' project for the new suburbanism which is emerging in Detroit, as well as Chelina Odbert and Jennifer Toy's Kibera productive landscape project in Nairobi, both point towards new forms of collaborative urban design practice.

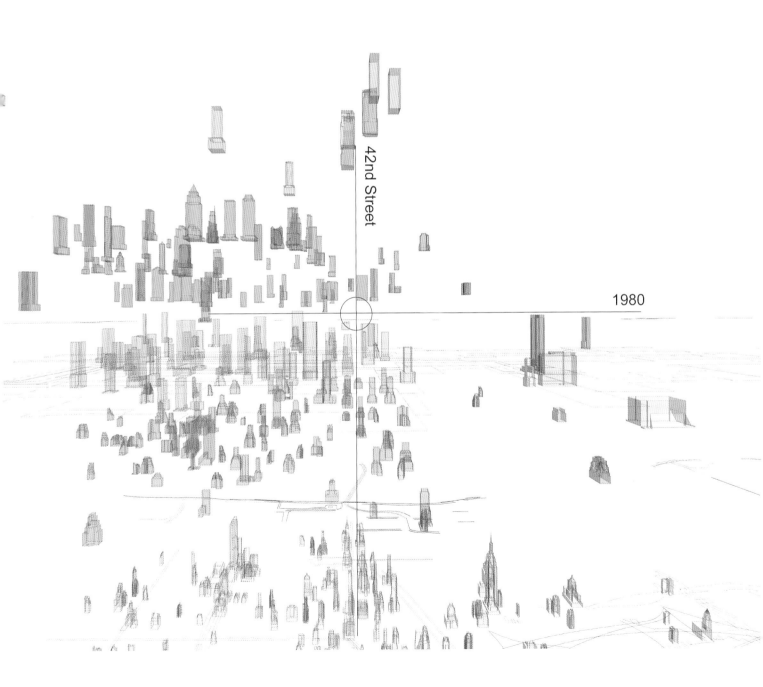

View of the *MT* model from the 1980 time plane looking east along 42nd Street. Post Second World War office building construction in Midtown has concentrated in the 20 blocks between 40th and 60th Streets.

181

42nd Street

1980

Interfacing

Manhattan Timeformations is not a game, map, text nor simulation, but an electronic hybridisation of these familiar genres and arts. Historical events, however, have thrust this website into a new role. For some this website became a memorial. The Spanish magazine *Cyber Pais* was the first to recognise it as such in an article called 'Memoria de New York', but it is the numbers of visitor 'hits' since September 11, 2001, to both the Skyscraper Museum and *Timeformations*, that has astounded me more than all the previous reinterpretations of our website. The mass general audience it received has surprised and encouraged me. Truly there is a strong and widespread desire to understand and interact with representations of complex urban systems.

Yet, all of these potential labels or descriptions remain incomplete. I want to avoid pigeonholing, but I prefer a term steeped in product and communication design. For me *Timeformations* is a prototype for an 'urban interface'. By *urban interface* I am literally referring to a mediating realm between the human sensorium and physical things in the city. For a forester the urban interface is where the urban fringe meets the wilderness. Whether built-in to familiar built environments or cheap, networked, wireless, portable, wearable device, an urban interface can be plugged into or displayed in front of your vision, enhancing your experience of your surroundings with whatever information is appropriate to your needs. How do these modelling devices create new identities, a sense of security and familiarity or mystery and wonder, how do they produce nomadic communities and localities?

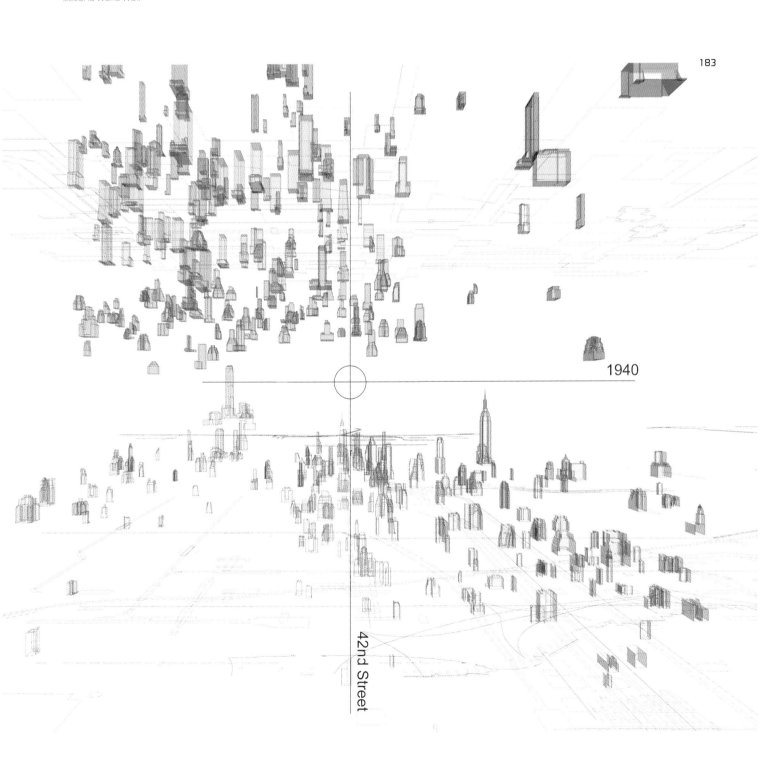

View of the *MT* model from the
1940 time plane looking east
along 42nd Street. 42nd
Street, the location of Grand
Central Terminal, was the
focus of much office building
construction before the
Second World War.

183

1940

42nd Street

Timeformations is a primitive tool for doing just that, an attempt to illustrate how such a device might work. The project is, of course, more than a mere aid to orientation. It is an analytical device for revealing hidden relationships within built space; a tool for discovering both personal and authoritative stories about the metropolis, tracing where the nodes of money and power have shifted during the 20th century and, as a result, how the city was shaped; an application that allows the user, while isolating built spaces and objects, to discover relationships which we don't normally think about but which surround us every day. Making MT has rewired my brain and refired my urban imagination.

This urban interface would extend our resources past our organic, experiential limits, to act as a means of empowerment, tracking, charting and interpreting what we can't physically see about the politics of our spatial existence. I am not the only one secretly working on such a device. Web designer Mark Watkins described to me how Atari trained a whole generation to accept simplified representations of known spaces and to interact with plans and sections. Some PlayStation titles require intense toggling between perspectival and orthographic space to achieve a high score. Cartographic information is integrated with more experientially understood representations of our surroundings. The combination, accessibility and ease of use of all modes of representation simultaneously are the information architecture being worked out now. The smart tools of the future will be built on the simple experiments of the past. Maybe these tools will help us to inhabit this planet more intelligently and allow us all to make our own cognitive models of the city.

Architect Will Alsop's project for the Bradford (UK) Centre Regeneration (2004) effectively demonstrates the ability of digital modelling to be integrated with photography and simple graphic communication techniques. The project emphasises the fine topography and heritage buildings that have been compromised by many derelict structures with less architectural value. Their animation zooms in from a satellite image to a panoramic view of the city before settling in on an inventory of the city at street level. The project identifies concrete and cars as the problems of the city, and provokes the city to consider removing all the concrete that it doesn't want. The animation proceeds to virtually subtract all the unsightly vacant buildings from the city skyline and fills the new open space with a new park focused on a lake in the centre of the city. The new park in turn inspires new architecture, housing, cinemas, markets, as well as cultural and educational institutions.[14]

View of the *MT* model from the
1990 time plane looking east
along Fulton Street.

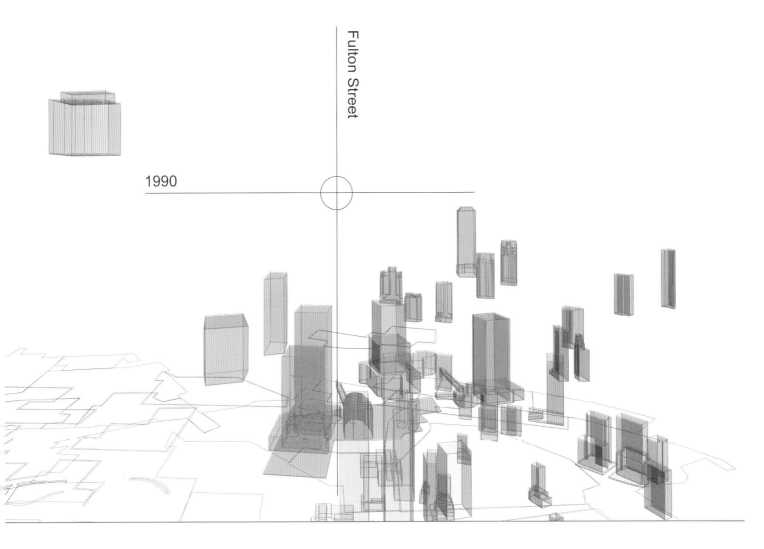

Fulton Street

1990

186 Diagramming

Manhattan Timeformations is a diagram of power in that it shows us active and reactive effects in the social, political and economic space of the city. Real estate developers endeavour to build the greatest amount of square footage at the maximum efficiency in the highest-rent location. Urban design as a governmental bureaucratic discipline is a reactive force: to situate and shape the forces of real estate for the maximum public gain – economically as well as embracing other valued attributes such as open space, light, air and amenities. While archaeological modelling for urban design revealed the historical relations between forms which constituted urban design knowledge, in genealogical modelling for urban design we see the descent and emergence of forces constituting the dispersed power of the capitalist city.

Deleuze describes the difference in nature between knowledge/form and power/force: knowledge/form is 'substance, divided segment by segment by seeing and speaking, light and language'. Archaeological modelling for urban design is therefore 'stratified, archivized, and endowed with relatively rigid segmentarity'. Power/force, on the other hand, is diagrammatic, 'it mobilizes non-stratified matter and functions, and unfolds with a very flexible segmentarity. It passes not through forms but through *points* which on each occasion mark the application of a force, the action and reaction of a force in relation to others, that is to say an affect like "a state of power that is always local and unstable".[15] The urban design diagram, therefore, marks the transmission or distribution of particular features in the balance of power between urban actors.

View of the *MT* model from the
1980 time plane looking east
along Fulton Street. The World
Financial Center, seen at the
top of the image, was built
between 1985 and 1988 on
landfill created from the
construction of the World Trade
Center (the blue twin towers at
the centre of the image).

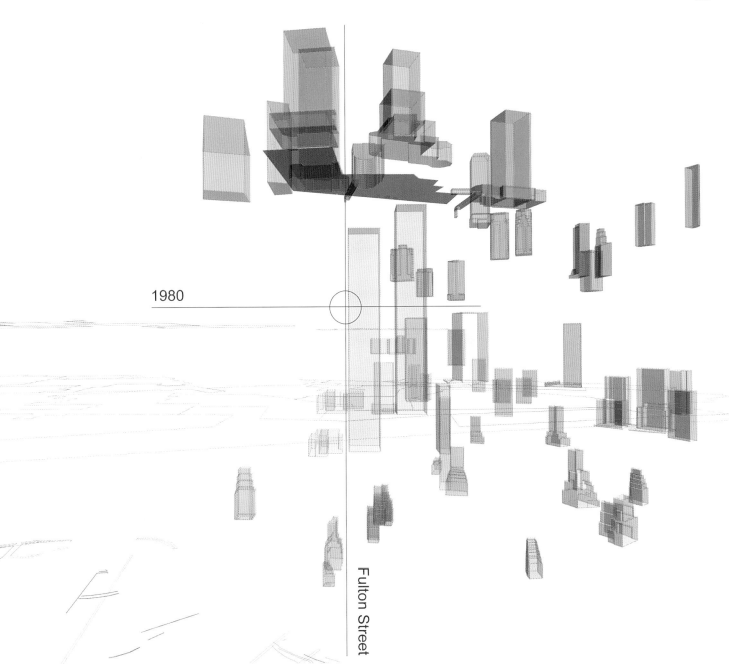

1980

Fulton Street

If power relations in the contemporary city are local, unstable and diffuse, the city cannot be formed through expert knowledge alone. The city is no longer created from a central point of authority which marks 'a unique locus of sovereignty'. Instead, it 'at each moment moves from one point to another in a field of forces, marking inflections, resistances, twists and turns, when one changes direction, or retraces one's steps'. Urban design is not 'localised' at any given moment, but constitutes a non-stratified, anonymous and disruptive strategy. 'Strategies are almost mute and blind, since they evade all stable forms of the visible and the articulable. Strategies differ from stratifications, as diagrams differ from archives. It is the instability of power-relations which defines a strategic or non-stratified environment. Power relations are therefore not *known*.'[16]

In the capitalist city, instead of urban design as an instrument of control of every physical element of the city through a Master Plan, it becomes a strategic practice of 'micro means mobile and non-localizable connections'. Urban design therefore becomes 'inseparable from the power relations which make them possible'.[17] Urban designers are trained in the techniques of architectural knowledge, but also need to learn strategies of the dispersal of power. Digital modelling for urban design ties together the complex of knowledge and power, the archive and the diagram, through the integration of archaeology and genealogy. Urban design practice, then, takes on the task of micro linkages, alignments and convergences. 'Yet there is no immediate global integration. There is, rather, a multiplicity of local and partial integrations, each one entertaining an affinity with certain relations or particular points.'[18]

Manhattan Timeformations demonstrates how these power/knowledge relations emerge over time. For each historical formation of a business district, we must examine who are the actors and what institutions are interacting in forming the city. A genealogical modelling for urban design examines how these actors, institutions and interactions transform over time. While government has presently captured many power relations in urban design, we have seen in the introduction that there is emerging a new desire from various urban actors to reclaim a greater role in shaping the city. It is in this intersection of the economic pressures to develop the city and the power apparatus of governments in shaping urban form, that digital modelling needs to emerge as an instrument to incite and provoke responses from a wider constituency.

> What a 'genealogy' shows is that moral values are subject to change, appropriation, and manipulation. The writing of history, according to Nietzsche, ought to be practiced in a way which shows that everything in human life is the product of contingent circumstances and, as such, is subject to perpetual change and contestation.[19]

Urban design is a field of knowledge that constitutes power relations in urban space. 'There is no power relation without the correlative constitution of a field of knowledge that does not presuppose and constitute at the same time power relations.'[20]

View of the *MT* model from the
1940 time plane looking east
along Fulton Street. The cluster
of Art Deco towers along Wall
Street can be seen below the
timeline in grey and the post-
war glass boxes in blue built
along Pearl and Water Street
can be seen above.

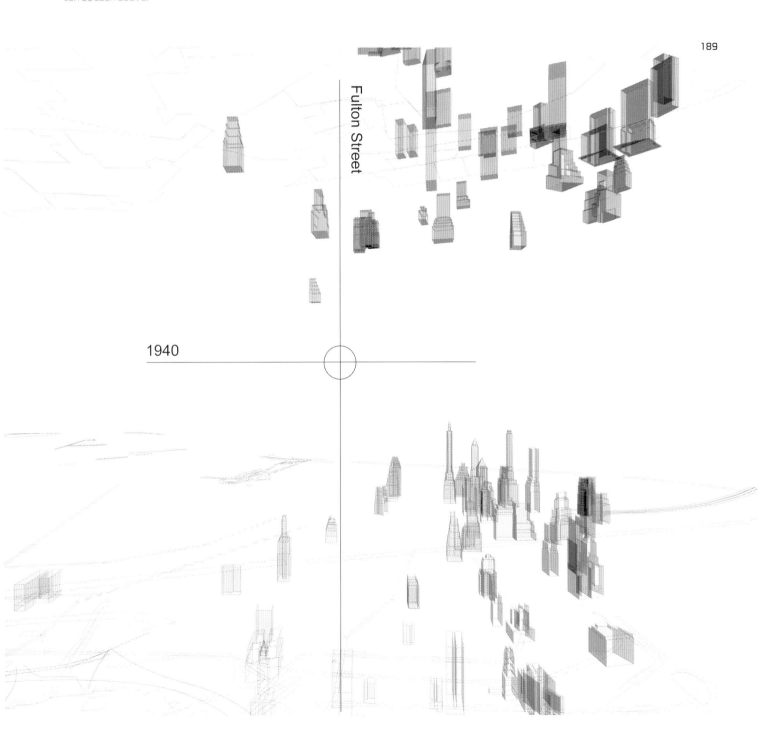

Fulton Street

1940

Back to Ground Zero

The design of Ground Zero represents a paradigmatic shift away from bureaucratic urban design practice with its dispassionate coding of special districts. There was a dramatic cry for an authoritative Master Plan, which Daniel Libeskind Studio momentarily provided. The ensuing political context of a 'War on Terror' has initiated a restructuring of American cities from heterogeneous places based on trade and the '… boundless mobility and assimilation and a national "melting pot" identity'[21] back to war and an 'anti-cosmopolitan construction of "homeland".'[22] Stephen Graham points out the contradiction between the homeland rhetoric to define, classify, border, homogenise, and the nature of financial global trade which is characterised by flows, openness and heterogeneity. At the same time, he points out that 'foreign terror cities' are dehumanised by remote imagery in the news media.[23] The tremendous allocation of resources to promote and conduct these two arenas of warfare has left cities vulnerable to natural catastrophes and ill equipped to engage in the enormous restructuring of urban space in order to address the environmental challenges of rapid urbanisation in a context of global climate change.

42nd Street

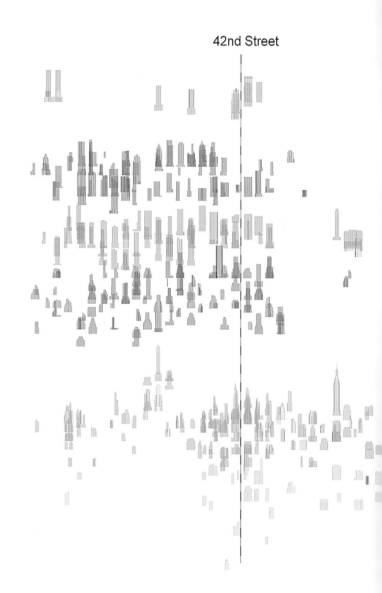

View of *MT* model looking east. This flat side view shows the consolidation of the largest Central Business District in the 20 blocks in Midtown Manhattan, between 40th and 60th Streets, following the Second World War. The clustering of the pre-war skyscrapers around Wall Street during the first stock market boom in the 'roaring '20s' can be seen in the lower right in grey.

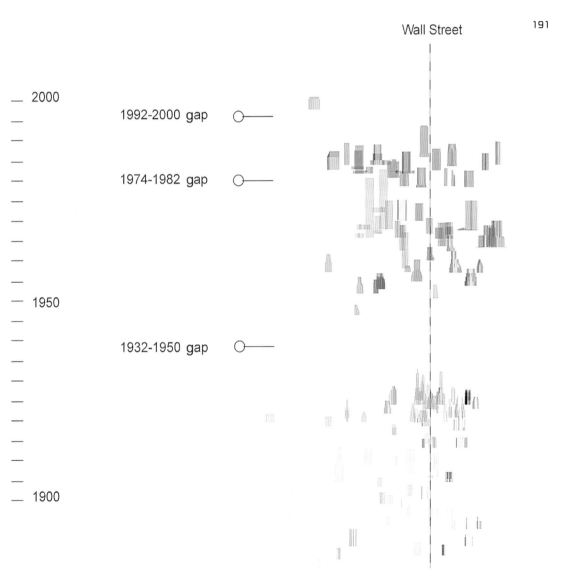

Wall Street

2000

1992-2000 gap ○────

1974-1982 gap ○────

1950

1932-1950 gap ○────

1900

New urban design models must directly address the rhetoric and ideology behind this interlinked web of social, political and ecological problems which are beyond the control of Master Planning. Urban design can play a crucial role in promoting and creating the socio-political design tools to reverse the trend in the current imagination of the urban and the environment away from a permanent *threatscape* and towards collective opportunities for change. It is crucial in constructing the current sociopolitical context to understand and unpack the mediated rhetoric in order to generate counter-logics of restructuring our cities and environments towards facing rather than fortifying real and perceived challenges and threats. Reversing the homogenising project of 'Homeland' requires tools for understanding spatial heterogeneity rather than unity and order; flows and processes rather than form in only an abstract sense; logics of flexibility and adaptation in temporal contexts of unpredictable flux; and, finally, the full engagement of a broad spectrum of social actors and agents in the making of resilient urban ecosystems.

The wartime perception of foreign cities as nests of terror, framed as target sites from above and devoid of human life, can only be confronted with an emphasis on ethnography, participant observation and 'ground truthing' through close-up informants networked globally.[24] While urban design practice is located in design studios, government offices and conference rooms, it should be balanced with substantial fieldwork based on its rich history in the social and ecological sciences. Urban design must therefore be structured around core values of urban life as the production of difference – both at 'home' and 'abroad'. This production of difference can only be understood in the nexus between psycho-socio-natural processes. Digital modelling for urban design can be the basis for the creation of new forms of networked knowledge of the relations between human, built and natural systems at micro and macro scales.

Digital modelling can begin to unpack the complex space of urban forces that express this multiple vitality by combining the urban archive with the diagram, going beyond standard practice by combining the ability of GIS data systems to store layered information and of 3-D computer modelling to diagram mutable forces and reactions. 'Diagrams communicate, above, below and between the respective strata. The diagram differs from the strata: only the stratified formation gives it a stability that it does not itself possess, for in itself it is unstable, agitated and shuffled around. Forces are in a perpetual state of evolution ... The diagram is the non-place of mutation ... transformation occurs not to the historical, stratified, and archaeological composition but to the composing forces, when the latter enter into a relation with other forces which have come from outside (strategies). Emergence, change and mutation affect composing forces, not composed forms.'[25]

Urban Design as the Production of Difference

What was understood and what served as an objective was life ... It was life far more than the law which became the issue of political struggles, even if the latter were formulated through affirmations concerning rights. The 'right' to life, to one's body, to health, to happiness, to the satisfaction of needs ... this 'right' which the classical juridical system was utterly incapable of comprehending.[26]

We have seen the diagram of power in urban design abandon the model of the authoritative Master Plan in favour of a disciplinary model, based on classification, regulation, codes and control of special districts. Foucault's late writing describes how disciplinary power has become 'bio-power' or 'bio-politics', controlling and administering all aspects of life. In this new context it is life itself that emerges as the new object of power and as a political objective.[27] Foucault provides 'a new vitalism' by saying there is no telling what we might achieve 'as living beings'.[28]

Looking south from the Hudson River piers at the World Trade Center and World Financial Center at the tip of Manhattan Island. The emerging skyline of Jersey City, New Jersey can be seen on the right (1995).

The final two chapters of this book will take this new vitalism as the site for a shift in urban design practice in order to identify new sites and types of struggle, which are 'transversal and immediate rather than centralized and mediatized ... which are specific or "particular" rather than universal'. The questions posed by Deleuze include: 'What is our light and what is our language – our truth today? What powers must we confront, and what is our capacity for resistance, today when we can no longer be content to say that the old struggles are no longer worth anything? And do we not perhaps above all bear witness to and even participate in the "production of a new subjectivity"? Do not the changes in capitalism find an unexpected "encounter" in the slow emergence of a new Self as a centre of resistance?'[29]

How do we navigate in an urban world where 'everything is subject to variables and variation: the variables of knowledge and the variation in the relation between forms; the variable particularities of power and the variations in the relations between forces; the variable subjectivities, and the variation of the fold or of subjectivation?'[30] Digital modelling for urban design must turn to one final methodology for not only the construction of the modern urban ecosystem, but the construction of identity within it. The final chapters will turn to *Schizoanalytical Modelling for Urban Design* in order to think from outside the Master Plan and the bureaucratic coding of special districts. The last section of this book will argue for immersive models which focus on understanding how the contemporary environment is designed around issues of lifestyle, marketing and branding – in other words the space of *desire* rather than war or trade.

End Notes   195

1 www.skyscraper.org/timeformations
2 Marcus Friedl, *On-line Game Interactive Theory*, Hingham, MA: Charles River Media, 2002, p 105. Rhizome Art Network, January 2001, Prix Ars Electonica, 2001, Flash Film Festival, 2001, *Wired*, November 2001, Digital Salon, 2001, Pew Center for Civic Journalism, 2001, *Architectural Record*, June 2002, National Science Foundation Digital Library Selection, June 2002.
3 Eviatar Zerubavel, *Time Maps: Collective Memory and the Social Shape of the Past*, Chicago: University of Chicago Press, 2003, p 32.
4 Ibid, p 82.
5 Ian McHarg, *Design with Nature*, New York: John Wiley & Sons, 1992.
6 Bernard Tschumi, *Event Cities*, Cambridge: MIT Press, 1994.
7 http://www.gamesforchange.org/
8 Friedrich von Borries et al, *Space Time Play*: *Computer games, architecture and urbanism*, Berlin: Birkhäuser/Springer, 2007.
9 Mario Gandelsonas, *The Urban Text*, Cambridge: MIT Press, 1991.
10 Ibid, p 26.
11 Antonio Scarponi, 'Info-Forum – The Dreaming Wall: Milan', *Sensing the 21st Century City*, B McGrath and DG Shane, eds, London: *AD Architectural Design*, Vol 75, No 6, Nov/Dec 2006.
12 Fredric Jameson, *Postmodernism: or the logic of late capitalism*, Durham: Duke University Press, 1991.
13 Brian McGrath et al, *Designing Patch Dynamics*, New York: Columbia University, 2008.
14 http://www.alsoparchitects.com/<movies >Bradford Master Plan
15 Gilles Deleuze, *Foucault*, translated by Paul Bové, Minneapolis: University of Minnesota Press, 1986b, p 73.
16 Ibid, pp 73–4.
17 Ibid, p 74.
18 Ibid, p 75.
19 Friedrich Wilhelm Nietzsche, *The Genealogy of Morals*, translated by Francis Golffing, New York: Anchor Books, 1990, p xxi.
20 Michel Foucault, *Discipline and Punish: the birth of the prison*, translated by Alan Sheridan, New York: Vintage Books, 1995, p 271.
21 A Kaplan, 'Homeland Insecurities: Reflections on language and space', *Radical History Review*, Vol 85, 2003, p 85.
22 Stephen Graham, 'Cities and the "War on Terror"', *International Journal of Urban and Regional Research*, Vol 30.2, June 2006, p 259.
23 Ibid, p 263.
24 Brian McGrath and Grahame Shane, *Sensing the 21st Century City: close-up and remote*, London: John Wiley & Sons, special issue of *Architectural Design*, Vol 7, No 6, Nov/Dec 2005.
25 Deleuze, pp 84–7.
26 Michel Foucault, *History of Sexuality*, Vol 1, New York: Vintage Books, 1990, p 145.
27 Deleuze, p 92.
28 Ibid, p 93.
29 Ibid, p 115.
30 Ibid, p 117.

Chapter 5

Schizoanalysis

The twin escalators glide silently up from opposite sides of King Rama I Road, rising three storeys to the passenger mezzanine of the Siam Central Interchange Station where the two lines of the Bangkok Transit Systems (BTS) Skytrain meet. The escalators bring passengers up from the hot and crowded street, under the massive concrete viaduct where the lines torque, to converge two levels above. Arriving at the crowded mezzanine before the electronic entry, there is a profusion of small shops and advertisements. A call on your cell phone tells you that your friends are waiting by the fountain in the square in front of Siam Paragon. Descending half a flight of stairs leads you through the giant glass wall of Siam Center, where your bags are checked by security guards. Another stair to the right leads down again to the second-level plaza of Paragon. The crowd has swelled in anticipation of the grand opening of Siam Paragon. A rock band is performing in front of the giant glimmering blue aluminium Christmas tree sponsored by Visa cards. Cell phones are recording digital photographs of the event broadcast live on TV.

Grand openings of new or renovated malls in Bangkok are usually timed for the beginning of December when the King's birthday can be honoured and the stores readied for Christmas and New Year holidays. February brings sale banners emblazoned in red to celebrate both the lunar Chinese New Year and Valentine's Day. April brings Songkran, the Thai New Year timed with the beginning of the rainy season. The rains stop in October, when the Queen's birthday can be celebrated, and in November small votive boats made from banana leaves and containing offerings and a candle are floated downstream at Loy Krathong.

While Bangkok ignored decades of calls for a Master Plan, and has yet to create a Central Business District, in the decade following the 1997 economic crisis a Central Shopping District emerged along the two-kilometre stretch of Rama I Road under the BTS interchange. Bangkok residents were amazed at the cosmopolitan space created around the privately owned public spaces on Crown Bureau and Chulalongkorn University property. While we have traced the genealogy of the Master Plan to Pope Sixtus V's Rome, and the zoning of the Central Business Districts in Manhattan, as well as the emergence of the central shopping district of Bangkok, in this final section on *Schizoanalytical Modelling for Urban Design* we will look at the immersive space of each city's time geography.

Schizoanalysis, while initially a difficult term in relation to its reference to the psychological ailment of schizophrenia, is in fact a call for a more creative, subversive and playful response to capitalism by its inventors – philosopher Gilles Deleuze and psychologist Félix Guattari. The provocation in subtitling their two books *Anti Oedipus* and *A Thousand Plateaus 'Capitalism and Schizophrenia'*, is that capitalism is by its nature a schizophrenic system that substitutes psychological repression for creative desire. Guattari developed schizoanalysis as a tool to uncover the repressive aspects of capitalism in order to create social experiments to recreate human relations with Nature by unleashing the creative capacity of desire. In urban design, a schizoanalytical approach splits our analytical framework into a comprehensive multi-layered and multi-dimensional analysis of cities, as well as an immersive and embedded understanding of the psychological dimensions of the multi-layered and multi-dimensional urban space of late capitalism.[1]

Rather than focusing on the descent and emergence
of urban design practices as outlined in the second
section with the exploration of genealogical modelling,
we now analyse the spatial and temporal capacities and
restraints on individual social behaviour in the global city.
Our schizoanalytical models will take us back to the
Forum in Rome, Ground Zero in Manhattan and Rama I
Road in Bangkok, utilising the time geography of Torsten
Hägerstrand as a guide. Hägerstrand examines human
migration and flows based on three limitations or
constraints. **Capability** includes the limits of human
movement based on physical or biological factors, but
also includes the technological means which increase
human mobility such as cars and skytrains. **Coupling**
refers to the need to interact with other people. Finally,
authority considers the constraints on movement
controlled by other people or institutions.[2]

Street section in front of Siam Paragon. A broad terrace of fountains and coconut palm trees descends from Paragon's main plaza to the taxi drop-off from Rama I Road. The Skytrain mezzanine can be seen on the right leading to a pedestrian bridge connecting to the mall in the background.

Movement will not be considered only in relation to the physical, social and authority constraints, but also in relation to the city as an archive of stratified knowledge.

The world is made up of superimposed surfaces, archives or strata. The world is thus knowledge. But strata crossed by a central fissure that separates on the one hand the visual scenes, and on the other the sound curves: the articulable and the visible on each stratum, the two irreducible forms of knowledge, Light and Language, two vast environments of exteriority where visibilities and statements are respectively deposited. So we are caught in a double movement. We immerse ourselves from stratum to stratum, from band to band; we cross the surfaces, scenes and curves; we follow the fissure, in order to reach an interior of the world. But at the same time we try to climb above the strata in order to reach an outside, an atmospheric element, a 'non-stratified substance' that would be capable of explaining how the two forms of knowledge can embrace and intertwine on each stratum, form one edge of the fissure to the other. If not, then how could the two halves of the archive communicate, how could statements explain scenes, or scenes illustrate statements?[3]

The spatial archive of archaeology and the temporal diagram of genealogy together form a basis for a third analytical technique in digital modelling for urban design: schizoanalysis. While archaeological modelling situated urban design knowledge within the collateral space of strata, and genealogical modelling diagrammed the correlative space created by exertion of forces of various urban actors and agents over time, schizoanalytical modelling will analyse the complementary space of the disjunctive flows which comprise our rapidly urbanising and globalising world. Schizoanalytical modelling cuts multiple sections through the layered archaeological and genealogical time frames to evaluate the disjunctive space of global flows of information, people, material and media. While we referred to Aldo Rossi's theories of the city through archaeological modelling, and Grahame Shane's theories of recombinant urbanism with genealogical models, Robert Venturi, Denise Scott Brown and Steven Izenour's *Learning from Las Vegas* will assist us in developing a schizoanalytical model for urban design based on the role urban design plays in situating symbolic language in space.[4] Since its publication, the new Las Vegas has become a destination not just for gamblers, but on the new Grand Tour for public officials as well as architects, urban designers and their developer clients from Dubai to Shanghai.

For psychoanalyst and activist Félix Guattari, the schizoanalytical project is both modest, because it just requires observation of the here and now, and also broad, in that it has the potential for becoming a discipline for reading other systems of modelling. Guattari sees schizoanalysis not as a general model, but as a tool for deciphering the way various fields or disciplines construct models.[5] Schizoanalysis is therefore presented, not just as a way to revolutionise his field of psychoanalysis, but as a *meta-model* for examining the everyday world around us. Meta-modelling – a kind of model that exists to look above and beyond specific disciplinary models – brings us back to a re-examination of Kevin Lynch's different definitions of modelling outlined in the Prelude of this book. Can urban design look beyond the limits of any particular discipline and construct a way of understanding how urban space is generated through multiple forces and flows acting at different speeds and intensities?

Schizoanalysis primarily examines human desire released by capitalist consumerism. Today's dense and complex urban contexts continually present divergent choices rather than unitary directions. Schizoanalysis in urban design leads to the production of difference and diversity rather than singularities and uniformity based on the *polyvocal* nature of contemporary society. Desire is seen as a positive force rather than a lack or a need. Desire sets the psyche in motion to make new connections and trajectories – in other words to actively create new urban design models. However, according to Eugene Holland, desire gets tricked by representations and the critical task of schizoanalysis is to destroy and critique the power of representation in all its forms.[6]

Guattari defines the analytical aim of schizoanalysis as a shift away from prescribed ways of thinking within disciplinary structures of representation, by instead 'fashioning new coordinates for reading and for "bringing to life" hitherto unknown representations and propositions'.[7] Urban design, as we have seen in our archaeological and genealogical analyses, is a system of representation – it makes knowledge, power and the exertion of social forces concrete over time. What happens when the world explodes with multiple and conflicting signs, languages and images? Robert Venturi, Denise Scott Brown and Steven Izenour, with their students from Yale, developed a revolutionary method of analysing such a world by exploring the Las Vegas strip in 1972 as an assemblage of enunciation. In the decades since they published their work, Las Vegas has become an urban design model for much of the urbanising world. Through an analysis of the space, scale and speed of the strip *in section* through serial photography and analytical diagrams, Venturi, Scott Brown, Izenour and their students developed a basis for a schizoanalytical approach for urban design.

For Guattari, 'the task of Schizoanalysis is that of learning what a subject's desiring-machines are, how they work, with what syntheses, what bursts of energy, what constituent misfires, with what flows, what chains, and what becomings in each case. This positive task cannot be separated from indispensable destructions, the destruction of ... the structures and representations that prevent the machine from functioning.'[8] Ultimately, the revolutionary transformation and redirection of this vast reservoir of human psychic energy for Guattari is a new environmentalism, creating a 'new earth'. 'A revolution may occur only after capitalist super-exploitation of resources has so severely impaired or even reversed its ability to continue developing productive forces and energies that some other mode of social relation to the earth shows visible signs of doing better.'[9]

There is no consistent schizoanalytical protocol for urban design, but only constant re-evaluation of urban mutations and assemblages at various scales, created through effects of environmental, social and psychological feedback. This feedback can take positive and negative forms. For Guattari, negative feedback leads to a simple re-equilibrium, while positive feedback engages splitting processes, such as disturbance or catastrophes.[10] Guattari's distinguishing between equilibrium and disturbance ecologies mirrors contemporary urban ecosystem science. As ecologists Steward Pickett and Mary Cadenasso have demonstrated, disequilibrium is the 'natural' state of ecosystems.[11] Pickett and Cadenasso are disturbance ecologists, and their theories provide a radically different view of nature, one in which equilibrium is just one state in an ecosystem of constant dynamism and flux. For them, the city is a network of patches in which human movement is just one of many types of flows.

1745–1778: A Schizoanalysis of War

Approaching from the Coliseum, the pile of marble forming a triumphal gate leans on a brick buttress at the eastern entry to the Forum. A prominent billboard-like inscription can be seen on top of the arch announcing the gate as built by the Senate and People of Rome in honour of the divine Emperor Titus, son of divine Emperor Vespasian. The arch, in a half-ruined state, does not encourage a triumphal march under it, but a dramatic sky looms over the deep space of the monumental ruins of the Forum to the left, and behind the arch, a heavy masonry retaining wall recedes into the distance. Through an elaborate Renaissance gateway, a series of symmetrical ramps climb to a hilltop botanical garden and orchard. Such is the way into the Roman Forum as depicted in an etching by Giovanni Battista Piranesi.

Piranesi's second etching of the Arch of Titus shifts our point of view to the opposite side of the triumphal arch from inside the Forum. The vault of the arch dominates the left edge of the etching, its top and left side disappearing outside the edge of the frame. This composition is more dramatic and complex, and an index of building names and explanatory text runs across the bottom of the etching and guides us through not only the view, but the space of the Forum and the layers of Roman history. Marguerite Yourcenar, however, is critical of Piranesi's use of indexed keys:

To the last, he docilely follows custom, which consists in numbering on the plates each part of the structure, each fragment of ornament still in place, and making certain explanatory notes in the lower margin correspond to them, without its ever occurring to him, as it certainly would to an artist nowadays, that these schoolbook specification or engineering diagrams might diminish the aesthetic or picturesque value of his work.[12]

However, this prosaic system of numerical indexing invites a closer inspection of the *View* and invites our eyes to wander over the Forum like an 18th-century visitor to Rome and read multiple messages through its complex juxtapositions of landscape, social activity and buildings. Flickr is a website that allows individuals to form a social network and a discussion group to tab or mark photographs in the same way that Piranesi tagged his. His pictures are not just eye candy, but framed sets of information.

Giovanni Battista Piranesi's
View of the Arch of Titus at the
entry to the Roman Forum.
Copper plate etching, 1760.
The print is keyed to the letters
A to G embedded in the view.

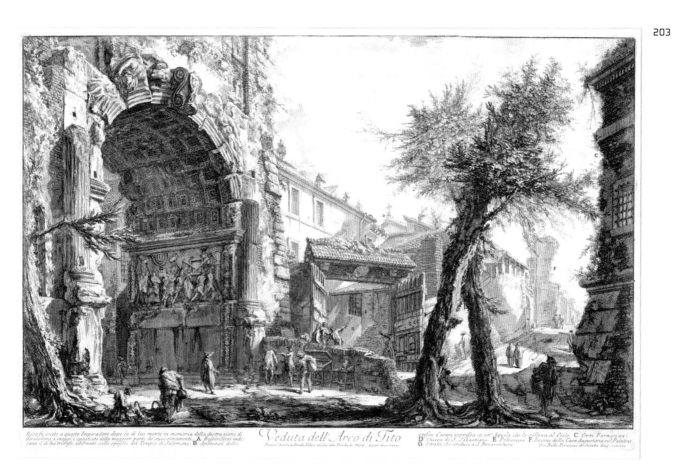

204

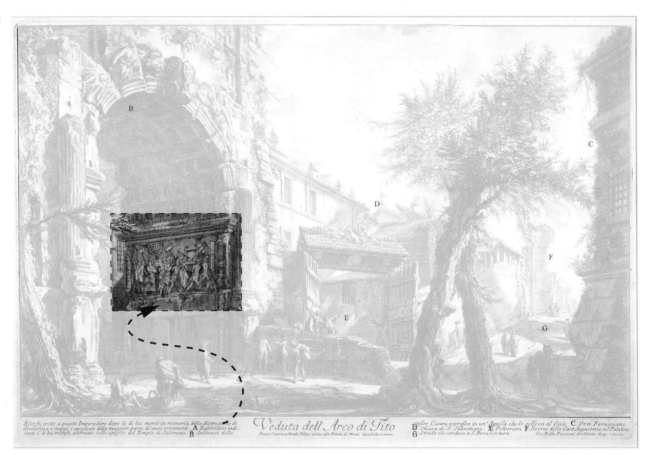

Veduta dell' Arco di Tito

The title, *View of the Arch of Titus*, runs along the bottom margin of the etching and is followed by a brief description of the scene. Piranesi writes that the arch was erected after the death of the Emperor in memory of the destruction of Jerusalem, and today the spoils form a major part of the ornament. With that simple introduction to the dramatic events which are monumentalised in the arch, we go on to read the print guided by the lettered index.

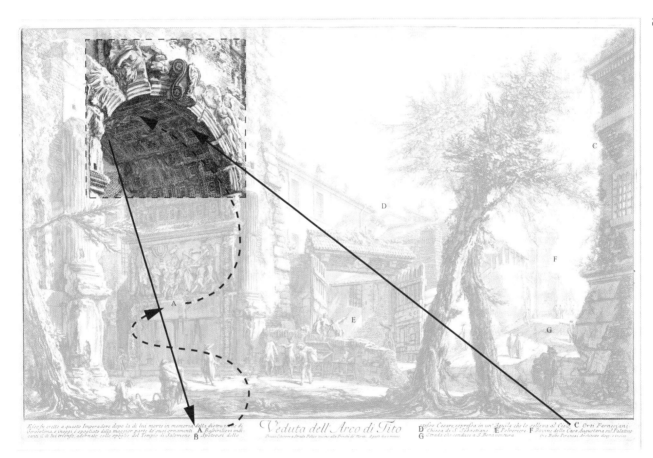

Veduta dell' Arco di Tito

The letter **A** points to the bas-relief inside the arch not seen in the previous view. Piranesi identifies this as a bas-relief indicating Titus's triumph, adorned with the spoils from the Temple of Solomon. A frame within the frame of the etching, Piranesi juxtaposes a representation in stone of the events one thousand five hundred years before the time he prepared his etching with the comings and goings of his contemporaries in the foreground. The bas-relief shows the people of Rome celebrating the conquest and sack of Judea and Piranesi invites us to participate in the triumphal march. The soldiers, walking left to right, are carrying the spoils of war, which include the seven armed candelabrum and the silver trumpets from the temple of Jerusalem. The signs carried by some soldiers display the names of the conquered cities and people. The letter **B** redirects our view to the underside of the arch's vault where we see the 'Apotheosis of the same Caesar on an eagle that ascends into heaven' – an event which mythically occurred after his death, some 10 years after Titus's triumph.

206

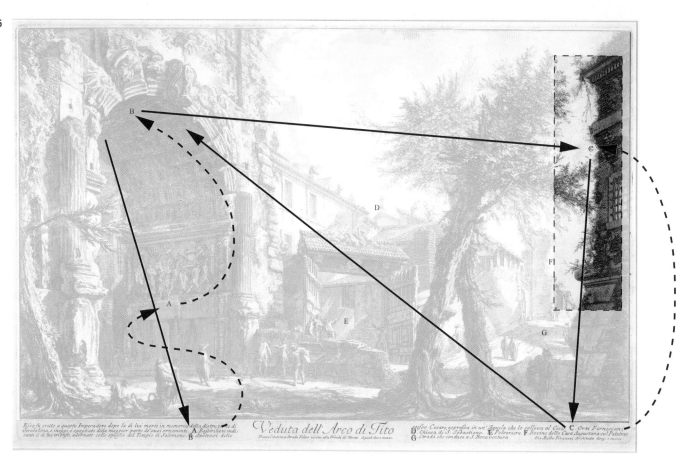

Veduta dell' Arco di Tito

After some searching we see the letter **C** indexing the Farnese Orchards – in fact just a corner of the retaining wall of Vignola's villa that was so prominent in the previous view, this time disappearing outside the right edge of Piranesi's frame. We are next directed to the centre of the plate, near a cross in the background, which is labelled **D**. The text below indicates it is the Church of St Sebastian. This church, referred to by Richard Krautheimer as San Sebastiano alla Polveriera, was built in AD 970 as Santa Maria in Pallara,[13] but renamed in honour of the Roman soldier whose stripped body was famously depicted during his martyrdom pierced by multiple arrows.

207

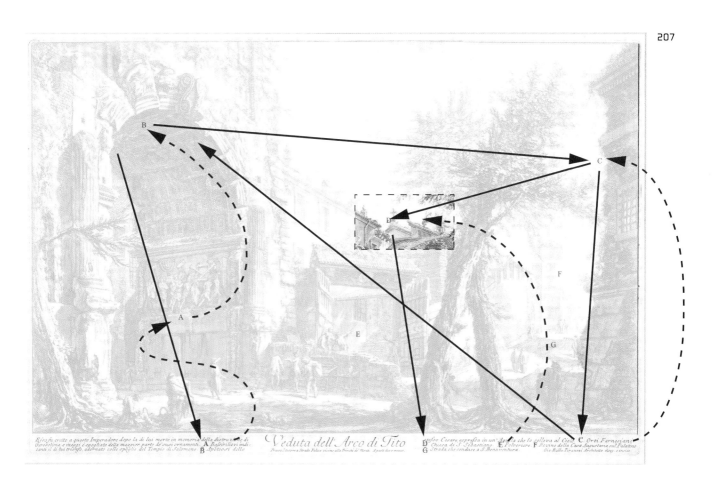

The letter **E** directs our eye to the compositional centre of the etching; two simple wooden doors are opened to reveal piles of material – an old warehouse with two men outside pointing in. This is merely labelled 'Polveriere' without further explanation. **F** guides us further up in the right background where we see the ruins of Emperor Augustus's house on the Palatine. Finally **G** indicates the road connecting to St Bonaventure, and we see ecclesiastically robed cardinals walking up the inclined path. Again the view is populated by various animated figures from Piranesi's era, frozen in time like the stone soldiers in the bas-relief. Piranesi's etching is a guide through the complex histories of the Roman Forum, but not one that takes a linear path through space or time. Drawing from his experience as a stage designer, architect and painter, Piranesi depicts the recombinant theatre of 18th-century life in Rome in the context of the multiple histories of the site.

Letter **E** is located in the centre
of the view inside a
warehouse behind an open
pair of wooden doors.

208

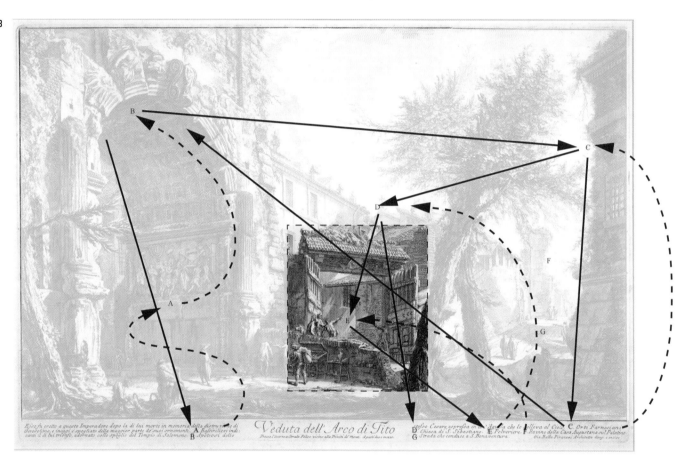

Piranesi was born on 4 October 1720 in Mestre outside
Venice and died 9 November 1778 in Rome. He was an
architect, archaeologist, master designer and engraver.
His *Views of Rome* provide a critical rendering of urban
design as the representation of power legitimised
through historical narrative. Piranesi's work provides a
rupture away from the Renaissance and Baroque
representational models of the city and introduces a new
and more complex modern sensibility in reading urban
space. For Yourcenar, Piranesi 'the observer on the prowl
for the ineffable' is in fact, the 'interpreter and virtually
the inventor of Rome's tragic beauty'.[14]

Piranesi's successful engraving enterprise captured
the 18th-century market of the educated classes of
Europe taking their Grand Tour of Italy.

To see Rome, after having learned so much about
its important role in history for the culture of the
Western World, was the high point of any
traveller's dream. And as they saw the ancient
city's treasures, they discovered Piranesi's
renderings of them in print ... The voluminous
series of *Views and Antiquities* represented, for
the eighteenth-century dealer and connoisseur,

209

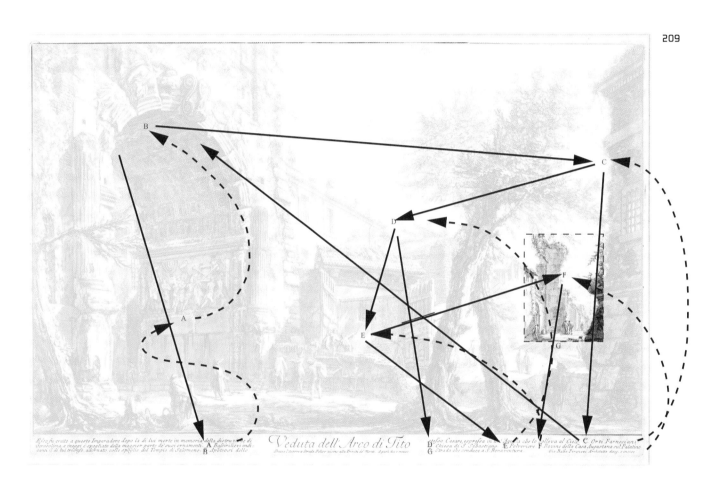

the equivalent of the coffee-table albums of artistic photographs offered nowadays to the tourist eager to confirm or complement his memories, or to the sedentary reader who dreams of faraway places.[15]

But do Piranesi's images faithfully represent the historical narrative sought by the princely travellers? An engraver takes many liberties in reconstructing reality on the etching plate, and Piranesi's images need to be *read* as critical subjective texts instead of being *seen* as literal representations of reality. The prints are much larger

than can be reproduced here. Our face enters into the space of the page and our eyes dart from one corner of the image to another like a spectator at the theatre – Piranesi was trained as a stage designer – scanning the surface of the page like the large screen of the cinema darting from edge to centre and back. The engraver of these images uses a technique that the filmmaker Sergei Eisenstein likened to montage. The revolutionary Russian film maker's analysis of Piranesi's prison engravings recognises the 'cuts' and 'explosions' in the engraver's frame.[16]

210

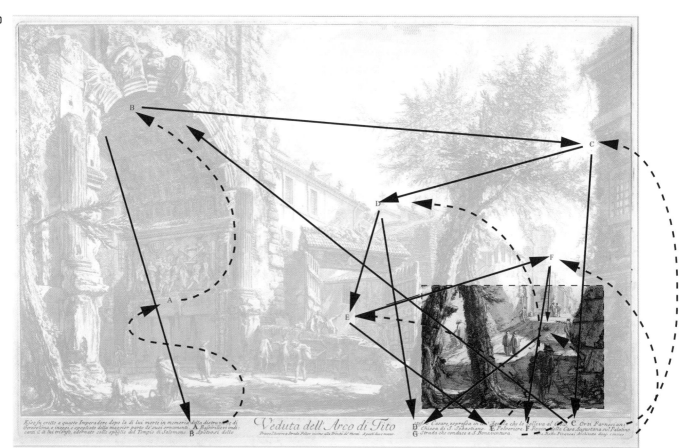

Consider the method in creating these views, a complex mechanical process with many steps. First, Piranesi drew from life. His biography is filled with anecdotes about his immersion into the streets and sites of the city, especially those abandoned or buried, and often at night.[17] He was not just a studio artist of ideal and abstract compositions, but a collector of material artefacts – the classical fragments he found or unearthed and sold often supported his family. But he was also a collector of subjects of everyday life, the grave robbers, beggars, aristocrats, cardinals, the spectrum of personages from 18th-century Rome were as vivid as the 20th-century characters of Fellini's *Roma*. Society of 18th-century Rome is not frozen in some official ceremony, but caught spontaneously, almost like a documentary photographer of urban life.[18]

From his collection of sketches of palaces, churches and ruins and the actors in Roman society, Piranesi assembled populated stage sets that can be read as constructed urban scenes telling not just historical narratives, but stories of everyday life.

> Nowhere has the artist attempted ... to harmonize human nobility and gravity with architectural dignity. It is a rare thing if, here and there, a small figure of a handsome youth standing or prone, solitary wanderer, dreamer, or simply local guide, suggests among these human will-o-the-wisps the equivalent of an ancient statue.[19]

His assembled compositions are not balanced Renaissance compositions, but marked by the dynamic composition and disequilibrium of the Baroque. For Yourcenar, 'the grotesque contrast between papal pomp and antique grandeur on the one hand, and on the other the miseries and absurdities of contemporary Roman life', are felt and express the majesty of Rome's ruins in relation to the Baroque will to power. In fact a close observation of a pair of Piranesi's etchings situated in the Forum establishes the basis for an understanding of schizoanalysis as a critical rather than triumphal modelling for urban design as described in Chapter 2. The art of etching involves drawing images in reverse on a copper plate, placing the plate in an acid bath so the drawn lines are inscribed in its surface, and then running it through an etching press to create multiple copies for mass distribution. This modern technology involves an assemblage and distribution process of images and it would be useful to consider both in order to understand Piranesi's etching as schizoanalytical digital modelling for urban design.

212   Although Piranesi's *Views of Rome* provided him with
steady income from the aristocratic travellers from
northern Europe who were eager to learn the symbols of
power from the ancient city, this market for the *Views*
does not explain the elaborate montage of images that
Piranesi collapses in this particular etching. Certainly the
composition is a guide to what a visitor to the Forum
would sequentially confront after passing through the
arch, a close-up view of the bas-relief, including the
sacred objects from the Temple of Solomon in Jerusalem,
then looking across they would see the physical evidence
of a much more recent power, the Farnese's sumptuous
botanical gardens located on the ruins of the Imperial
palaces. The visitor might then turn to see the Church of
St Sebastian in the distance, the informal trading
activities, and then proceed up the street to St
Bonaventure with the cardinals.

However, as a two-dimensional montage-like
composition, the etching is strikingly modern and less
prosaic: the dramatic asymmetry of the sharp angle of
the arch and the group of buildings receding across the
plate, and the way the viewer's eye crosses transversally
from corner to corner. Piranesi's *View* is not a snapshot of
a moment in 18th-century Rome, but his construction of a
new reality by creating various sketches from multiple
site visits and assembling them on a single copper plate.
Hence we see the schizoanalytical juxtaposition of the
spoils of the sack of Jerusalem with the warehouse
workers and the cardinals on a stroll.

The distribution of the images was well known to
Piranesi – he knew his clients, the princes and aristocrats
from London, Paris, Berlin and Vienna would soon be
building palaces, monuments and institutions of these
new capital cities. One can imagine these future
architects and builders carrying their bound portfolio of
favourite views to pore over back in their home countries
for inspiration. But why did Piranesi complicate his views
so much and why would a view titled *View of the Arch of
Titus* actually centre on a humble warehouse? It is useful
to remember Lanciani's statement that 'every ruin was
accompanied by a lime kiln' and his reference to the
periodic appearance of laws to prevent the plundering of
ruins and the use of kilns to burn pulverised marbles
down to lime.[20]

Perhaps we are intended to wonder what activity is
actually taking place in the *polveriera* indicated by the
letter **E**. In fact, Lanciani's archaeological evidence and
archival research tells us what is actually happening in
Piranesi's constructed view. We are witnessing the
dismantling of the Arch of Titus by the Roman people
themselves in order to produce construction material.
Piranesi critically juxtaposes in his etching an image of
the carved bas relief of the historical looting of the
temple of Solomon with the looting of the Forum in his
time. He also frames this composition with the Farnese's
Villa, one of the aristocratic families who formed the
ruling class in Piranesi's Rome. Finally, the reproductions
of his etching circulated across European capitals to the
new centres of political power. A *polveriera* is, in fact, a
gunpowder magazine, and the centre of his view of the
triumphal Arch of Titus is literally about to explode.

There is a more recent call to 'speak truth to power'. Piranesi, a struggling architect making a living out of selling etchings, certainly spoke both to his contemporaries and to us about the transience of power, order and might. Unfortunately, that spirit is not in evidence in the many images of Ground Zero and its redevelopment assembled and distributed today. For Yourcenar, it is '... the City itself, the City in all its aspects and in all its implications, from the most banal to the most unwonted, that Piranesi has fixed at a certain moment of the eighteenth century, in a thousand plates at once anecdotal and visionary'.[21] For her, what Piranesi gives is the sense of a great natural metamorphosis, but by reading the index which Yourcenar casually dismisses, one can see also a powerful political critique as an anti-triumphal message embedded in these popular images.

Chapter 5 in Deleuze and Guattari's *A Thousand Plateaus* is titled '587 BC – AD 70: On Several Regimes of Signs'. The historical dates that bracket the chapter refer to the two stages in the destruction of the Temple of Solomon in Jerusalem: by Nebuchadnezzar in 587 BC and by Titus in AD 70. For them, the wandering, tribal Jews, the history of the temple and the mobility and fragility of the ark and the House of Solomon represent deterritorialisation as a regime of signs – proceeding through lines of flight rather than marking territory through circular expansion. They oppose this nomadic realm of signs to the territorial empires of both Persia and Rome. After the Jews, Deleuze and Guattari trace two more realms of signs: Christian or modern philosophy epitomised by Descartes in opposition to ancient philosophy – the idea of the infinite – 'I think therefore I am'; second, 19th-century psychiatry with its realm of signs emerging from passional delusion.[22]

This collapsed history of the world also outlines the trajectory of this book. Following this discussion about Rome, we will explore modernity in New York and 'passional delusion' in Bangkok in order to understand digital modelling for urban design as a realm of signs. This includes the analysis of how the layered and multi-dimensional landscape of cities is already embedded with potent symbolic material, but also how digital simulation enriches our understanding of inhabiting a forest of signs. Empires contain the machinery of their own destruction. Resistance and lines of flight are always present. Remarkably the messages, signs and symbols around Ground Zero repeat those which recur around the Forum. The descent below ground, then from the cenotaph of Trajan and spiralling up to an apotheosis at the top of the column is mirrored in the Foster journey from the depths of underground September 11 Memorial to the top of what is now the Freedom Tower. The levelling of the ground and the planting of lines of trees by Pope Alexander VI in Rome is repeated by the Lower Manhattan Development Corporation in New York with the design of the grove of trees which was added to the memorial design. While Libeskind's initial proposal for Ground Zero was closer to the archaeologically excavated Forum we see today, the current plan is more aligned with the spirit of 17th century Rome.

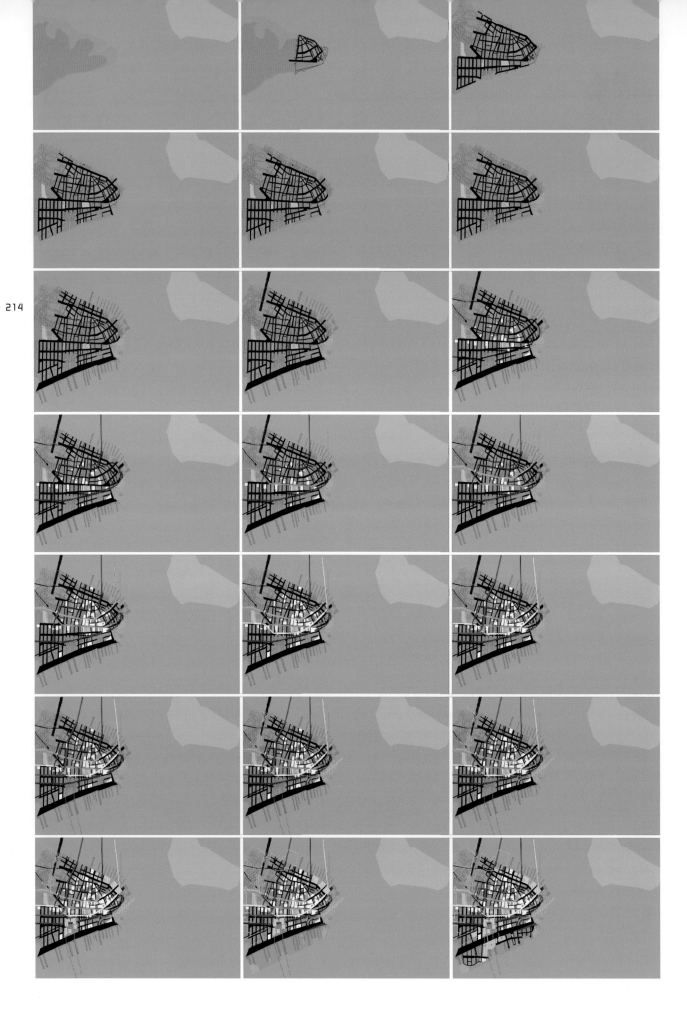

1978–2008: A Schizoanalysis of Trade

Seven months prior to the opening of the mass spectacle of the Innovative Design Study, nine artists were invited by the Lower Manhattan Cultural Council and the World Financial Center Arts & Events Program to participate in an Artist Residency at the World Financial Center. This residency was part of the process of restoration and reoccupation of Lower Manhattan which culminated in the reopening of the Winter Garden with an exhibition of the art works, developed during the residency, in September 2002 at the one-year anniversary of the terrorist attacks on the World Trade Center. My own digital installation *New York: Here and Now* in the upper level of the Winter Garden looking over both the void of Ground Zero and down across the new giant palm trees towards the Hudson River, provides the basis for an argument about the rich potential of digital technologies in supporting a polyvocal urban design practice.

Battery Park City (BPC) was constructed on landfill at the mouth of the Hudson River estuary on earth excavated for the basement parking levels of the World Trade Center. Ground Zero straddles three rail transit lines and sits within a concrete bathtub holding back the Hudson River estuary and the landfill under BPC. As soon as emergency efforts were completed, and the red-zone that police established around Lower Manhattan was slowly reduced to the immediate perimeter of Ground Zero, visitors began arriving to visit the site as if participating in a sacred pilgrimage. The images of the towers' collapse were broadcast and mediated repeatedly into a global collective consciousness. Millions of tourists, visitors and mourners still circle the site's perimeter, attentive to every minor change in this large hole despite efforts to screen most direct views of the site.

The installation was shown on a horizontally displayed plasma screen within an elliptical Plexiglas frame encouraging viewers to orbit the animation. In sequence 2, the layered plan view rotates to reveal a timeline of the Lower Manhattan skyline.

BPC's Winter Garden is a huge glass-roofed room dominated by a grove of giant palm trees. Windows overlook the Hudson River to the west, and, from a second-level mezzanine, Ground Zero to the east. The digital animation *New York: Here and Now* was displayed horizontally on a flat plasma screen surrounded by an elliptical transparent frame. The colour of the frame and the background of the animation were Caribbean blue – a nod to the giant palms and climate change predictions. The installation was visible during the exhibition of the Innovative Design Studies, and offered a hypnotic space of reflection and relief from the grand designs and virtual simulations offered below. The intention of the installation was not just to provide thoughtful art for the thousands of visitors who now included the Winter Garden and World Financial Center as part of their promenade around Ground Zero, but also to create a contemplative moment in the working day of the thousands of employees who witnessed the events of September 11 and had only recently returned to their offices at the site of horrific trauma.

From a distance the plasma screen table looks like a blue reflecting pool with small colourful tropical fish swimming across the screen with the giant palm trees in the background. An approaching viewer discovers that the screen in fact is displaying a map of Lower Manhattan animated with layers to illustrate the development of the Financial District over time. When finished loading, the layered map rotates to reveal 3-D models of Lower Manhattan's high-rise office buildings arrayed along vertical time planes. The tropical fish are in fact miniature skyscrapers moving across the screen. The rotation completes a 360-degree loop revealing the history and geology of the area from above and below. The view from below is washed by the Hudson River Estuary in which all these monumental yet fragile buildings submerge, float and then fly.

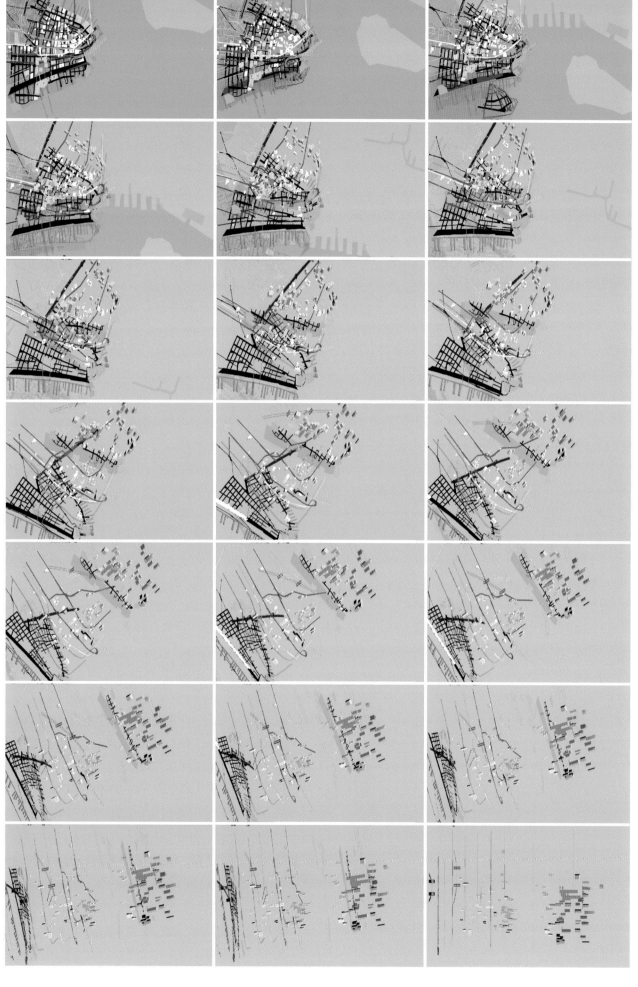

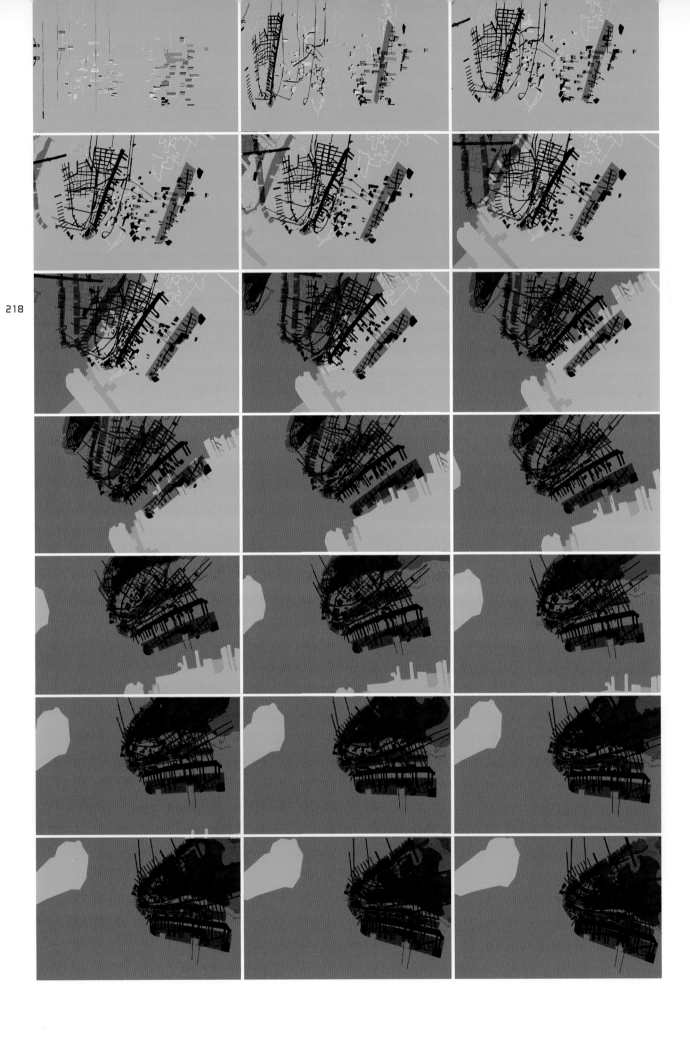

In sequence 3, the timeline flips to a view from below the model, as if one were going underwater. While the first sequence showed the successive landfills in Lower Manhattan, this sequence suggests a water-submerged future for the island.

The installation refers to navigational maps of the world's oceans which are incised into the marble floor of the Burgerzaal in Amsterdam. This hall was the meeting place of the first modern-world capitalists, where they could discuss financial deals and shipping routes while walking on the giant map of the globe and pinpoint locations of the East and West Indies Corporations' outposts. Similarly, in the Winter Garden of the World Financial Center, the employees of Merrill Lynch and American Express would have the orbit of their usual trajectories through the commercial complex of the World Financial Center diverted by the gravitational pull of the elliptical disc. For a moment in their working day, financiers can engage in this illusive and hypnotic work as a moment of reflection of their place among other participants in recreating Lower Manhattan as a world financial centre, and over time grow to understand its reference to the concrete-lined void in the city just outside the installation. For the ellipse also directs views to the giant windows overlooking Ground Zero, and creates a larger context for the discussions of rebuilding on the site. In addition to all the actors who have already played a part in the discussion – the families of the victims, the Port Authority, Silverstein Properties, the architects and the neighbourhood – the installation also shows the Hudson estuary and New York Bay as a major actor on the site, given sea-level rise and the predictions of flooding from storm surge in the near future.

From the opening in September 2002 to the end of January 2003, all the art works engaged issues of public space, viewing, nature, ruin, renewal, memory and life. *New York: Here and Now* served as a modest orientation device overlooking the open wound of Ground Zero, as witness not only to the reopening of this vital node of New York's financial industry, but also to the dawn of a new era for urban design. As introduced in the Prelude, the Critical Art Ensemble (CAE) promotes a digital cultural resistance to authoritarian cultural production. Combining Crick and Watson's discovery of DNA and Claude Shannon's invention enabling the transmission of digitally coded information over wires at Bell Labs, recombinant theatre and digital resistance utilise advances in molecular biology and communication technology not as specialised knowledge, but as the 'foundation of a new cosmology – a new way of understanding, ordering, valuing and performing in the world'.[23] Was Piranesi's recombination of experiences and drawings from the Forum, in etchings distributed around the world, not a form of recombinant theatre and mechanically reproduced resistance through the technology of print? Capitalism is primarily a digital political-economy, much as the medieval economy was primarily analogic. Digital aesthetics, for CAE, 'is a process of copying – a process that offers dominant culture minimal material for recuperation by recycling the same images, actions and sounds into radical discourse'.[24]

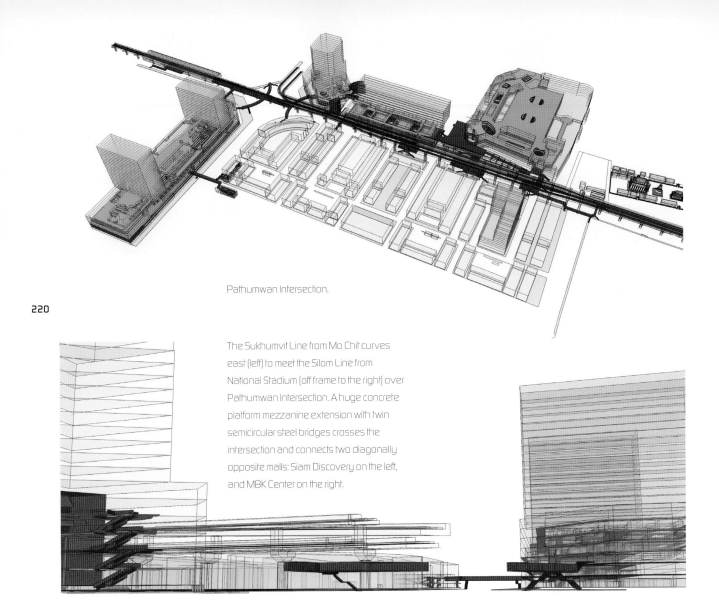

Pathumwan Intersection.

The Sukhumvit Line from Mo Chit curves east (left) to meet the Silom Line from National Stadium (off frame to the right) over Pathumwan Intersection. A huge concrete platform mezzanine extension with twin semicircular steel bridges crosses the intersection and connects two diagonally opposite malls: Siam Discovery on the left, and MBK Center on the right.

2000–2005: A Schizoanalysis of Desire

Following the shock of the Thai economic crisis of 1997, thousands of people were out of work, many fortunes lost, bankruptcies were rampant and hundreds of halted construction sites across Bangkok were stark reminders of the end of the 'Asian Miracle Economy'. With the crisis came a period of widespread self-evaluation, especially when the economic remedies instituted with assistance from the International Monetary Fund (IMF) and the World Bank only worsened the crisis. King Bhumibol Adulyadej introduced the concept of the 'Sufficiency Economy' in the year following the collapse, based on the Buddhist principle of the 'middle path', a guiding principle for all people pursuing their livelihood. 'Sufficiency means moderation, reasonableness, and the need for self-immunity for sufficient protection from impact arising from internal and external changes.'[25]

Sufficiency economy is both a philosophy and a basis for policy making that operates in three arenas of application. For individuals and households, application of the philosophy asks for reasonable behaviour in investment and consumption. For the corporate sector it recommends risk awareness as well as good corporate governance and responsibility. Finally, for government economic policy makers it outlines the need for fiscal discipline, sustainable growth, fair competition and distribution, immunisation against global risk and the strengthening of impoverished rural communities. 'The effective application of the sufficiency economy requires a holistic perspective, encompassing the environmental, cultural, and social dimensions.'[26]

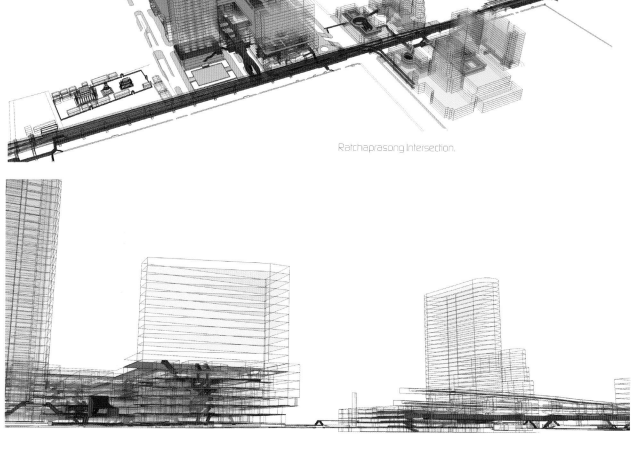

Ratchaprasong Intersection.

Thaksin Shinawatra was elected Prime Minister in 2001 – on a platform that rejected Thailand's dependence on IMF loans and requirements – heading a political party called 'Thai love Thai'. 'Thaksinomics' represents a distinct break from the past and the demise of the neoliberal economy of 'The Washington Consensus'.[27] Pasuk Phongpaichit and Chris Baker argue that the transformation of Thai institutional structures to conform to the mandates of the Washington Consensus with limited state economic intervention was the primary cause of the Thai crisis of 1997.[28] Thaksin was elected by rejecting the Washington Consensus and outlining ways the government could intervene to promote domestic competition, regulate financial transactions, promote education and stimulate the inward transfer of technology. Thaksinomics included farm assistance and a one-million-baht-per-village loan fund, urban relief, new sources for micro credit, the one village one product' project, and affordable public medical care for all Thai citizens.

At Ratchaprasong Intersection, the Silom Line turns south (to the right) while the Sukhumvit Line continues east. Zen department store at Central World Plaza to the left is connected by a sky walk to Gaysorn Plaza and Erawan to the right.

Thaksinomics led to a growth rate for the Thai economy that increased from 1.9 per cent in 2001 to 6.5 per cent in 2003.[29] The wider availability of credit and government stimulus produced for the first time in Thailand a mass-consumer society completely at odds with the dictates of the Sufficiency Economy. Thaksin was the first Thai Prime Minister to complete a full term, and was re-elected by an overwhelming mandate of the rural poor in 2005. It was during those years that the emergence of Bangkok's central shopping district became both a symbol of Thaksinomics and its basis in consumer spending, and the site of Thaksin's ultimate political demise. Almost immediately after Thaksin's re-election, his consolidation of power and signs of corruption brought the Bangkok middle class to the front door of Parliament House, the great square at the end of Ratchadamnoen Road.

After months of growing unrest, the protesters gathered in Rama I Road, in the shadow of the Skytrain, and brought Bangkok's CSD to a halt, forcing Thaksin to resign. Thaksin regained power as caretaker Prime Minister, but on 19 September 2006, a coup d'état placed Surayud Chulanont as Premier with a mandate to institute the Sufficiency philosophy. Elections in December 2007 replaced the interim government with the People's Power Party led by Samak Sundaravej based on a platform which allied itself with Thaksin and the banned 'Thai love Thai' political party.

Spectacular Feedback

Bangkok's CSD is not just a shopping district, but a symbol of all the conflicts inherent in the global city of disjunctive flows. In the following chapter, we will present a schizoanalytical model of Bangkok's central shopping district as a final example of digital modelling for urban design. While urban design has traditionally prioritised the physical context of an urban site, schizoanalysis looks at contextualisation in a deeper sense by considering the micro-politics of subjective meaning. There is never any correct interpretation of an urban context, and schizoanalysis uncovers the multiple assemblages of codes and meanings which constitute an urban site.

Schizoanalysis is located within the various disjunctive flows which pass through any urban context. These include the ecosystem fluxes of water, materials, nutrients and organisms, but also the mechanical flows which convey these materials as well as people, information and ideas through cities. The informational and media flows which constitute the semiotic flux of contemporary life are accompanied by a continual sound and visual track which complements the material and human flows. It is the intersections and interstices between these flows which constitute the object of schizoanalytical modelling. Human perception and social organisation occurs also at the intersection of these flows, and schizoanalytical modelling can begin to capture the relationship between human subjectivity and the mechanics of flows. Urban design captures the transformational capacity of redirecting these flows in relation to human agency and social life.

View looking east along Rama
1 Road from the municipal
pedestrian bridge across Henri
Dunant Road. Central World
Plaza office tower is the lit
beacon seen through the
Skytrain concrete viaduct.

Endnotes

1 Félix Guattari, 'Schizoanalysis', translated by Mohamed Zayani, *The Yale Journal of Criticism*, 11.2, 1998.
2 John Corbett, *Torsten Hägerstrand: Time Geography, Center for Spatially Integrated Social Science*, http://www.csiss.org/classics/content/29
3 Gilles Deleuze, *Foucault*, Minneapolis: University of Minnesota Press, 1986, pp 120–1.
4 Robert Venturi, Denise Scott Brown and Steven Izenour, *Learning from Las Vegas*, Cambridge: MIT Press, 1972.
5 Guattari, p 433.
6 Eugene Holland, *Deleuze and Guattari's Anti-Oedipus: Introduction to Schizoanalysis*, London: Routledge, 1999, pp 54–7.
7 Guattari, p 433.
8 Ibid, pp 338/404.
9 Ibid, pp 277/329.
10 Ibid, p 435.
11 Steward Pickett and Mary Cadenasso, 'Meaning, Models and Metaphor of Patch Dynamics', *Designing Patch Dynamics*, edited by Brian McGrath et al, New York Columbia University Books on Architecture, 2008, pp 18–31.
12 Marguerite Yourcenar, *The Dark Brain of Piranesi and Other Essays*, New York: Farrar, Straus and Giroux, 1980, p 98.
13 Richard Krautheimer, *Rome: Profile of a City, 312–1308*, Princeton: Princeton University Press, 1980, pp 317–19.
14 Yourcenar, pp 88 and 93.
15 Ibid, p 95.
16 Sergei Eisenstein, 'Montage and Architecture', *Assemblage 10*, Cambridge: MIT Press, Dec 1989, pp 110–31.
17 Yourcenar, p 92.
18 Ibid, p 101.
19 Ibid, p 102.
20 Rodolfo Lanciani, *The Destruction of Ancient Rome*, New York: Macmillan, 1901, p 206.
21 Yourcenar, p 98.
22 Gilles Deleuze and Félix Guattari, *A Thousand Plateaus: Capitalism & Schizophrenia Vol 2*, translated by Brian Massumi, Minneapolis: University of Minnesota Press, 1987, pp 111–48.
23 Critical Art Ensemble, *Digital Resistance: Explorations in Tactical Media*, Brooklyn: Autonomedia, 2001, p 83.
24 Ibid, p 85.
25 Thai Embassy, News Division, Department of Information, 23 April 2007, http://www.thaiembassy.be/pdf/sufficiency_economy.pdf
26 Ibid, http://www.thaiembassy.be/images/stories/sufficiency_economy/sufficiency_economy.pdf, p 6.
27 http://www.thaksinomics.com/
28 Pasuk Phongpaichit and Chris Baker, *Thailand's Boom and Bust*, Chiang Mai: Silkworm Books, 1998.
29 http://www.thaksinomics.com/

Chapter 6

Desire

Commuters head to the centre of Bangkok on the San Saeb Canal ferry.

The early call to prayer drifts with the morning fog on the Saen Saeb Canal. A taxi boat's engine idles for a few moments while picking up commuting passengers. As the boat takes off, its wake splashes into the tiny lanes which wind to the mosque. Across the canal, the monks from Wat Pathum Wanaram make their morning rounds through the Buddhist monastery community that lines the small *soi* – or alley – that connects the canal to the broad Rama I Road. People sit quietly meditating on the cool floor of the temple. The first Skytrain of the morning crosses the canal, a slowly moving arch of light turns over Pathumwan Intersection before pulling into Siam Central Station. The sound of train wheels on a steel track barely filters through the thick temple walls. Traffic is stopped at Pathumwan Intersection for a moment to allow Princess Maha Chakri Sirindhorn to leave Sra Pathum Palace to perform her Royal duties.

The icemakers on the narrow Soi Kasemsan 1 have ground and bagged the blocks of ice which have been stored in the ground floor of the shop house all night, cooling the workers in their dormitory above. As they have for four decades, they load their bicycle *samlors* to deliver crushed ice for cool refreshment to the vendors diagonally across in the shopping centre Siam Square. The snack vendors have gathered in front of Siam Paragon Mall, where they are allowed to sell freshly prepared food, in small plastic bags wound tightly with rubber bands, to the workers who will serve the customers arriving after 10am, among them university students coming for a coffee and doughnut before heading off to class. This is morning in *Bangkok Simultopia*, as the great arenas of globalisation, the huge malls of Bangkok's central shopping district, prepare to open again for the hundreds of thousands of daily visitors, alongside diverse local activities from earlier times which still persist.

Simultopia

Simultopia is a purposely ambiguous term coined to give meaning to the complex experience of place in late capitalist global cities. While -*topia* means place, *simul*- implies both the Modernist dream of *simultaneity* – the ability to understand multiple actions in one place – and Post-Modern theories of *simulation* and the *simulacra*, which refer to copies without an original. *Simultopia*, therefore, describes the mediated experience of globalisation which includes both that of speed, movement, transparency and simultaneity which captivated historical Modernist aesthetics, and revisionist notions of the phenomenology of place which grew in reaction to 'placelessness' of Modernist technological space.[1] The term resonates critically in two directions, towards regressive utopian Modernisms which still imagine heroic possibilities of human physical overachievement, and theories of place which are inadequate in describing the mediated experiential possibilities of contemporary environments, societies and psyches. In Bangkok it is used to describe the coexistence of extremely localised environments along canals and alleyways (*sois*), juxtaposed with the huge commercial spaces of globalisation.

In this sense, *simultopia* resonates between Baudrillard's concept of the simulacra[2] and the vast knowledge embedded in Bangkok's Theravada Buddhist scriptures and practices. The *Traibumikatha*, Thailand's Theravada Buddhist canon, describes three worlds – one formless, one comprising form but no sensation, and finally the world of form and sensation – divided into 34 levels of existence.[3] For eight centuries, Siam has constructed symbolic urban realms embodying modes of behaviour which interpret this cosmological model in architectural details, ritual space as well as city planning and design. *Simultopia* also dreams of inventing new paradigms for city production, ones which neither transcend nor simulate place, but inhabit space as different layers of reality. Furthermore, *simultopia* embraces a philosophy of the new and the now, to understand a world of changing perceptions and experience, rather than symbolically fixed representations and signs of place.

Through careful self-examination, the philosopher Henri Bergson found himself split into two individuals, one an actor in his role, the automaton, and the other an independent spectator, free and real, who observes the other like on a stage.[4] For Bergson, time and memory are not inside us, but it is the interiority that we are in, in which we move, live and change. The actual and the virtual, physical and mental, present and past are inseparable ongoing coexistences. Theravada Buddhist meditation practice, likewise, enables the attainment of such perception by the development of a separate consciousness which surveys sensory-motor stimulations from a floating, detached, non-reacting vantage point. This practice is most ideally developed in isolation – the most learned priests in the ancient capitals in Siam were located in the forest monasteries. In modern Thailand, wandering ascetic monks still seek enlightenment in the forests; equipped only with a tent-like umbrella they live off the land and offerings from villagers. Wat Pathum Wanaram, now surrounded by the forest of signs of Bangkok's Central Shopping District, was originally a forest meditation retreat, outside the royal city of Bangkok and accessible only by canal. Even today temple monks with offering bowls make their rounds in the small streets leading to Rama I Road, and cross Pathumwan Intersection before the malls open.

Radical contemporary Buddhism now interprets the *Traibumikatha*'s super-mundane realms as psychological states in the here and now.[5] The repeating cycles of human existence based on suffering, death, karma, merit-making and rebirth can be understood best through meditation practices which still the body and mind in order to bring attention to reality as constant flux and change. Contemporary ecological thinking has also been radicalised through new open, non-equilibrium, disturbance models. Rather than seeing ecologies as closed systems in balance, ecosystem science today conceives of the world as comprised of an open impermanent system of patches in constant flux.[6] The global context in which both contemporary Buddhism and disturbance ecology are imagined has radically shifted as well. For the first time in human history, the majority of people are urban dwellers. Nature can no longer be conceived as the wild 'other' of the city, isolated from human disturbance, and cities can no longer be conceived as closed human systems outside Nature.

Bangkok Simultopia revisits the mediated human ecosystem which comprises the large commercial blocks surrounding Wat Pathum Wanaram. This conjunction of historical space and time is an architectural expression of Bangkok's current collective psyche at a time of social, political and economic uncertainty. Félix Guattari has said that schizoanalysis is setting all objects in relation to connectivity, disjunctive and conjunctive value.[7] While Grahame Shane[8] has examined the **connective** architecture of urban armatures, here in addition to the connective value of urban design, its **disjunctive** and **conjunctive** value will be analysed in Bangkok central shopping district as a schizoanalytical model of globalisation. We will employ digital modelling to cut through the spatial and temporal compression within this corner of contemporary Bangkok – a collapse of histories, geographies and cultures. As Foucault reminds us:

> History becomes 'effective' to the degree that it introduces discontinuity into our very being – as it divides our emotions, dramatizes our instincts, multiplies our body and sets it against itself. 'Effective' history deprives the self of the reassuring stability of life and nature, and it will not permit itself to be transported by a voiceless obstinacy toward a millennial ending. It will uproot its traditional foundations and relentlessly disrupt its pretended continuity. This is because knowledge is not made for understanding; it is made for cutting.[9]

Blocks of ice are delivered every night under the red neon light of a short-stay motel. The ice workers sleep in cool comfort above the refrigerated shop house

230 Pathumwan Intersection

We begin our digital cutting at the National Stadium Station, the terminal station of the Bangkok Transit System's (BTS) Skytrain Silom Line. The broad concrete platform completely covers congested Rama I Road – the most direct connection to the heart of Bangkok – and after crossing the three city moats to the west, ends at the gates of the Grand Palace. But the concrete viaduct of the BTS Skytrain terminates abruptly here, and you have to contend with a multitude of road-based vehicular options to travel to the historical centre of the city, unless you know about the hidden municipal canal boat service tucked at the end of the narrow *sois* that line Rama I Road. Travelling eastward, however, has become quite easy with Bangkok's first mass transit system. The Silom Line travels east for two kilometres before turning south past Lumphini Park, and snaking along the business districts of Silom and Sathorn Roads, before terminating at the Thaksin Bridge pier, where the Chao Phraya express boat provides another way to the palace and temple enclaves of Rattanakosin Island.

The station platform looks over the old National Stadium and the green oasis of Chulalongkorn University to the south, and the short, crowded *sois* of shop houses, guest houses, bungalows and street vendors which end at the Saen Saeb Canal. More than just a transit stop, National Stadium Station is the beginning of a schizoanalytical journey through the heart of *Bangkok Simultopia*. This chapter will travel by cutting through the layered space of the multi-level armature, as the Silom Line transfers to the Sukhumvit Line at Siam Central Station, before coming to a rest at Chitlom Station and Central Department Store.

Just south of National Stadium Station, across the street from Soi Kasemsan, is MBK Center, one of the largest shopping malls in Asia. Two thousand micro stores and services, a hundred eating places and a large entertainment complex consisting of a cinema city, karaoke complex and bowling alleys extend south from Pathumwan Intersection. Locals and tourists come here because it is a multi-level souk – prices are negotiable and brand products are reproduced at a fraction of their original prices. The east end of National Stadium Station's mezzanine extends to a bridge leading to MBK through the Tokyu Department Store. MBK Center's website boasts that 150,000 customers, including 30,000 tourists, circulate through eight floors of the 330-foot-long mall every day. The complex also contains an office building and the Pathumwan Princess Hotel above, as well as a 4000-space car parking deck. The mall's exterior was renovated in 2000, in celebration of both the new millennium and the opening of the Skytrain. It is the success of MBK's direct connection and resurfacing that led other businesses to follow suit along the entire length of the BTS, creating one continuous interconnected multi-level shopping armature.

Hawkers spread out their goods on the BTS mezzanine outside National Stadium Station platform after the malls close. Central World Plaza is the lit tower in the background, and two steel bridges to MBK Center can be seen in the foreground and middle ground.

Section through National
Stadium Station with bridge to
MBK Center on the right.

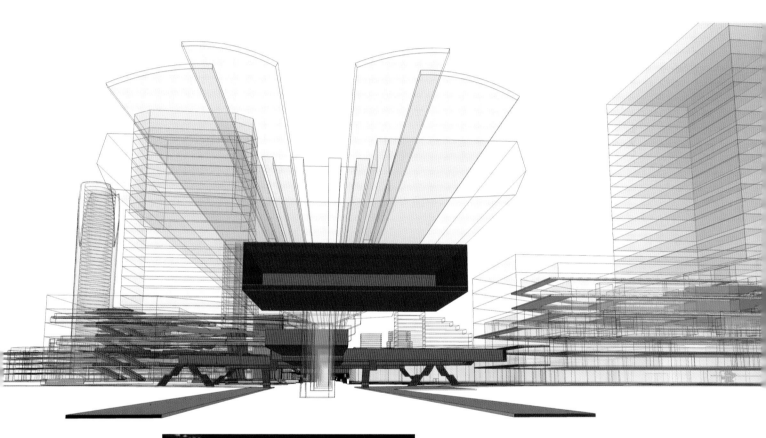

The giant concrete National Stadium Station mezzanine extends across Pathumwan Intersection, and two semicircular steel bridges lead to curving stairways descending to the four corners of the intersection. The bridge at the south-west corner has a second stair which climbs up to provide direct access to the third floor of MBK. After MBK closes, the raised mezzanine platform is filled with hawkers, entertainers and people just enjoying the cool evening breeze. Food vendors, taxi, motorcycle and tuk-tuk drivers strategically congregate in shifts at the points where the transit system stairs touch the ground. A journey along the Skytrain not only demonstrates how developers have reorganised their large commercial spaces around the new infrastructure of the city, but how the micro economic and informal sectors adapt to these new urban flows as well.

Diagonally opposite Pathumwan Intersection from MBK Center, the north-east corner of the semicircular bridge from the National Stadium Station mezzanine extension provides direct access through the shiny aluminium facade of Siam Discovery Center. The bridge leads to a glittering six-storey atrium, consisting of overlapping circular walkways. Siam Discovery Center opened in 1997, just as the Thai economy collapsed, initiating a financial crisis across East Asia. However, it was positioned to serve a more sophisticated and mature clientele than the bargain hunters at MBK. Riding the exterior glass elevator you ascend from the plaza entry level, past the pedestrian bridge level, above the Skytrain mezzanine, lower track, and finally above the upper tracks to the 'gold class' cinemas on top. Above the cinemas sits a 36-storey office tower.

Section through Pathumwan
Intersection with Siam
Discovery Center on the left.

Events plaza located
between Siam Discovery and
Siam Center.

Siam Discovery Center was built to complement Siam Center, constructed in 1973, and the two malls are interconnected to Siam Car Park, which was built in 1994. They share an events plaza and are interconnected by a bridge on the fourth level. Four-storey Siam Center extends for 900 metres eastward along Rama I Road. It introduced novelties such as air conditioning, interior atria and escalators. While originally designed as an austere glazed tile box for international tourists who stayed in the adjacent Intercontinental Hotel, it instead became a fashion centre for teenagers and college students. It has recently been renovated to present to the Skytrain a 'magical glass box' with giant advertisement billboards, graduated lighting and projections on the criss-crossing escalators, which can be seen through large windows facing Rama I Road and the Skytrain.

A redesigned pedestrian bridge crosses Rama I Road, connecting Siam Center to Siam Square, one of the first modern shopping and entertainment areas in Bangkok. Siam Square consists of six Manhattan-scaled blocks and streets, bisected by a connecting road. Constructed with the latest in French precast concrete technology in 1965, Siam Square introduced the American concept of 'park and shop'. The precast concrete frames allow for a variety of shop sizes on three levels, and customers could diagonally park directly in front of the stores. In addition to bowling alleys and three cinemas, Siam Center became populated with 'cram' tutor schools. A new 'education centre' called The Style by Toyota instructs the many students in the area on the intricacies of the Toyota brand by offering membership complete with entertainment, cafés and events. This captive audience of young people has made Siam Center the 'Shinjuku of Thailand', and some of the on-street parking has been replaced by open plazas, one named Centre Point where concerts take place and new products are introduced. Music provides a background soundtrack for all the activities offered at Siam Square and The Style by Toyota features a giant LED video screen which can broadcast the events and messages to the crowds outside.

Pedestrian bridge across Rama 1 Road leading to Siam Center from Siam Square.

Rama I Road pedestrian
bridge connecting Siam
Square (right) to the third floor
of Siam Center (left).

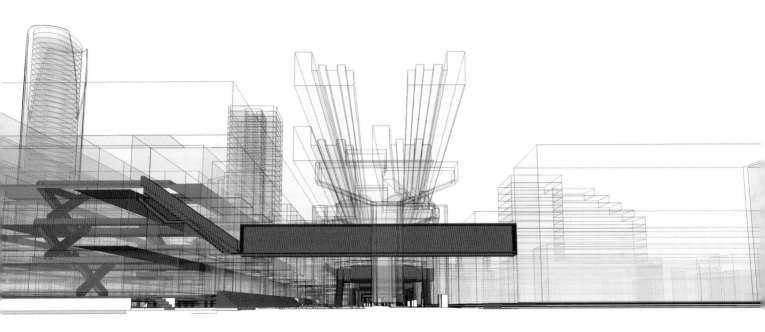

236 Siam Central Interchange Station

Straddling Rama I Road between Siam Center and Siam Square is the giant Siam Central Interchange Station connecting the two BTS Skytrain lines. While all the other stations along the Skytrain face inward towards parallel tracks, here two platform levels face outward – both north and south – towards the city. Both Siam Center and Siam Square responded to this greater public exposure with new glass walls, billboards and media screens facing the BTS. The north platforms faced the lush gardens of the old Intercontinental Hotel, which stretched to the Saen Saeb Canal to the north, the Sra Pathum Palace to the west and the Buddhist monastery and temple complex, Wat Pathum Wanaram, to the east. Twin escalators lead directly up to the station mezzanine from Rama I Road, and a broad raised covered plaza and grand staircase runs the entire length of Siam Center. With the Skytrain viaduct above, the entire effect between the two shopping centres is of an outdoor living room for the city, usually filled with traffic, although for a few days before the 2006 coup it was the site of massive political demonstrations.

The grand opening of Bangkok's glittering new upscale shopping mall, Siam Paragon, was broadcast throughout the kingdom in December 2005. The mall replaced the verdant Siam Intercontinental Hotel, torn down in 2002 on Crown Property Bureau land next to the royal gardens of Sra Pathum Palace, just west of Wat Pathum Wanaram. The grand entrance to the mall, according to its website, is a faceted glass 'jewel' meant to glitter like diamonds in the day and glow with the colours of gems – from ruby, sapphire and emerald to topaz – in the evening. Inside Siam Paragon are luxury car showrooms, a food court, fountains and the largest aquarium in South-East Asia – Siam Ocean World. The mall as jewel has nine different 'facets': Luxury, Fashion, Lifestyle, Leisure, Technology, Living, Divine Dining, as well as Education and Exploration. The 300,000-square-metre mall expects to draw, like MBK, 100,000 visitors a day.

Siam Paragon (left) second-level plaza provides a stage for the passengers awaiting trains on the two platforms at Siam Central Interchange (right).

The faceted jewel-like entry to
Siam Paragon (right) faces a
raised plaza with direct
access to Siam Central
Interchange Station (centre).

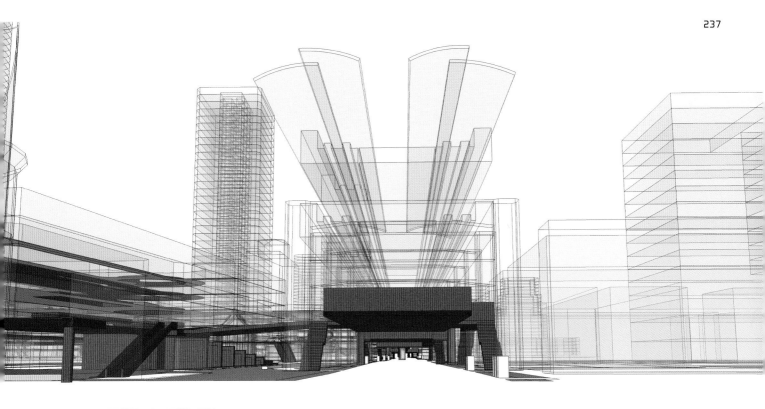

While all the other shopping centres along the Rama I Road adapted older structures to take advantage of direct connection to and visibility from the new Skytrain, Siam Paragon was the first mall to be designed and built after the opening of the BTS, and in fact the station platforms provided the best view of the construction site for a number of years. Now the two levels of north-facing platforms face a giant raised plaza that separates Siam Paragon from Siam Center and the Skytrain itself. Instead of connecting directly to the Skytrain, Paragon attracts more attention to itself by setting itself apart and inverting the standard mall typology by placing its atria and vertical circulation on the outside, and embedding the department store in the core. Further east is Siam Paragon's multi-level parking deck for 4000 cars.

The eastern exit of Siam Central Interchange Station connects to a pedestrian bridge which crosses the intersection of Rama I and Henri Dunant Roads. Instead of proceeding in a direct line, the mezzanine ramps down to the municipal walkway and takes a 90-degree turn around the intersection before joining a long elevated walkway constructed by the Central Group, owners of Central World Plaza located at the next intersection. This disjointed walkway passes under the twisting and torquing viaduct of the Skytrain as the stacked train platforms of Central Siam Interchange Station flatten to the parallel tracks of the two separate Silom and Sukhumvit Lines. The Central Skywalk passes above Wat Pathum Wanaram – the Buddhist monastery complex to the north, and the Thai Military Police enclave to the south.

Ratchaprasong Intersection

While the spiral ramps to Siam Paragon's 4000-space car park loom above Wat Pathum Wanaram's western flank, the expansive site of an even larger mall, Central World Plaza, rises to the east. Central World Plaza is the remaking of the financially troubled World Trade Center, whose hollow concrete office building shell stood empty over its shopping mall for a decade. The complex was redeveloped by Central Group, who first finished the 63-floor office tower in shiny aluminium in 2005. A large reflecting pool and orchard separates the office tower from the Skywalk, covering a large multi-level underground parking deck. This reflecting pool replaces the royal water gardens which surrounded the temple. A ship prow-shaped glass bridge connects the Skywalk to the office building and the rear of the old World Trade Center mall.

Ship-shaped bridge connecting Central Skywalk to Central World Plaza (left).

Central Skywalk wraps around Henri Dunant Intersection past Wat Pathum Wanaram (left). Central World Plaza can be seen in the background right. The concrete train viaducts converge above.

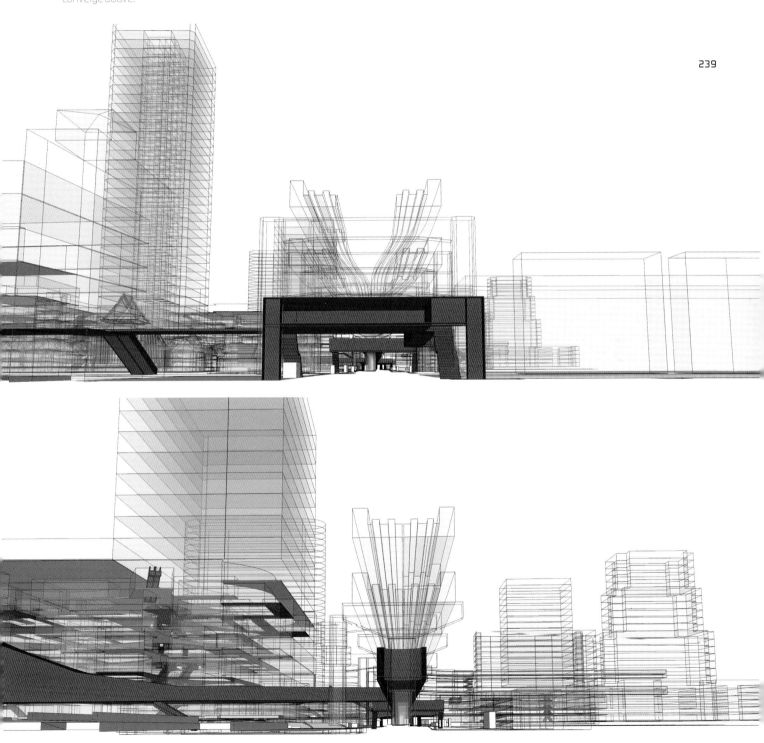

The World Trade Center mall has been completely wrapped both inside and out with a new layer in its transformation to Central World Plaza. The wrapper includes a seven-storey-high, 350-metre-long glass digital media wall, with the capability to project multiple LED images and lasers. The new High-Tech face of the greatly expanded centre looks out on a revitalised plaza – which, like Times Square in New York, serves as the gathering space for the annual New Year's countdown, and in the cool winter months serves as an enormous German beer garden. The architects claim that among the new offerings that will flash across the big screens are a variety of retail 'rooms' or precincts, an Olympic ice rink, bowling, a fitness centre, a convention centre, high-rise hotel, office space and multiple entertainment spots. The redesign turns the eight-storey mall inside out by moving the vertical circulation including stairs, escalators and elevators to the interstitial space between the wall of the building and the media screen, which hangs from the existing facade.[10]

Chitlom Station

When the World Trade Center opened in 1990 it anchored a second shopping node at Ratchaprasong Intersection – a cluster of boutique shopping malls that grew around the Erawan Hotel, one of Bangkok's first luxury hotels. Erawan Mall, Gaysorn Plaza, Amarin Plaza, Maneeya Centre, the relocated Intercontinental Hotel and Holiday Inn jointly built an extension of the Chitlom Station further east on the Sukhumvit Line to Ratchaprasong Intersection. Facing each other as sentinels across the intersection are Louis Vuitton, the shrine to luxury leather goods, and Erawan Shrine. Above the shrines, the two Skytrain lines again split as the Sukhumvit Line heads east, and the Silom Line diverts to the south.

Inside Central World Plaza's new glass wrapper which takes pedestrians directly off the Skywalk and up six flights of escalators to 'Heaven on Six'.

The viaduct splits as the Silom
Line heads south and the
Sukhumvit Line continues
east over Ratchaprasong
Intersection.

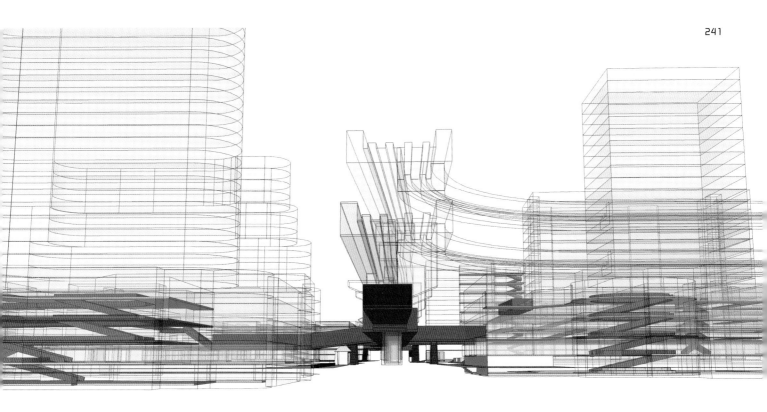

The Erawan Shrine was built in the 1950s following construction problems at the government-built luxury Erawan Hotel. The bad luck was reversed by the erection of a shrine to the four-faced Brahmin god Than Tao Mahaprom. Since then, the shrine has become a popular place to ask for favours of the god by offering carved teak elephants, flowers, fruits or sticks of incense, or even by purchasing a live Thai classical music and dance performance. The shrine has outlasted the hotel, which was rebuilt in 1992 as the Grand Hyatt Erawan.

Amarin Plaza has five floors of shops, spas and restaurants and is known for its many Thai handicrafts geared towards tourists. Its Tourist Information Centre brags that it has the widest range of visitor information available in Bangkok. The Ratchaprasong elevated walkway connects directly to Chitlom Station but, other than the small commercial building Maneeya Centre, has no direct connections along the length of the station. This is because it is bordered by the public utility headquarters of the Telephone Organization of Thailand to the north, and the private Mater Dei School for girls to the south. The school protested at the location of the station in their front yard, but were only able to gain a modesty wall to block the view of the school from passengers waiting at the train platform.

Immediately east of Chitlom Station is a direct connection to Central Chitlom, Bangkok's largest department store which opened in 1973. Its themed eight floors begin at 'Heaven of Luxury' and move up to the 'Top of the World' and the Food Loft beyond. But the Central Group has purchased the land in front of the British Embassy further east on Ploenchit Road, and the CSD is destined to continue to grow, especially in light of plans to dramatically expand and integrate the Bangkok Mass Transit System in the future.

Ratchaprasong Skywalk looking west towards Rama I Road. The bridge to the left connects to Erawan and Amarin Plazas.

The shopping centres at Ratchaprasong built the Skywalk over Ploenchit Road to Chitlom Station. The Intercontinental Hotel is on the left and Amarin Plaza is on the right.

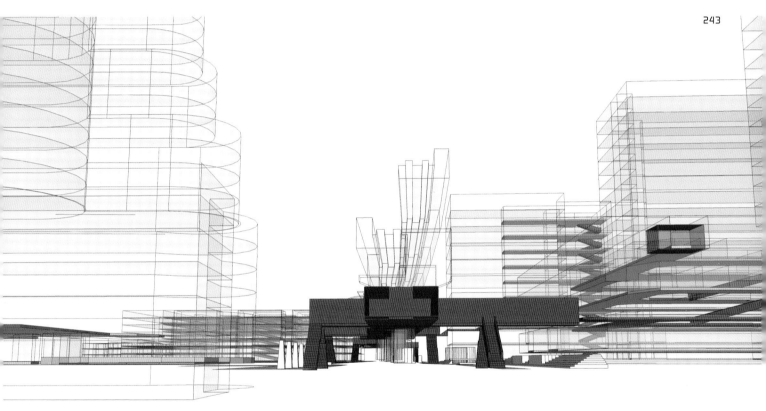

Complementary Space

This two-kilometre-long stretch of Rama I Road, under the converging lines of the Skytrain, also parallels the Saen Saeb Canal, built in 1837 as infrastructure to transfer military supplies and soldiers to Cambodia in the war with present-day Vietnam. A string of Muslim settlements line the canal and informal settlements have grown around these old Islamic villages and the Buddhist temples which line the canal and Bangkok's central shopping district. Wat Pathum Wanaram was constructed within a water lotus garden during the early 19th century by King Rama IV, the first part of a royal enclave of villas, accessible from the Saen Saeb Canal. With the expansion of the kingdom of Siam and growing commercial contacts with Europe, the Grand Palace at the centre of Bangkok grew overcrowded, and the Thai elite began to experiment with the architecture, landscapes, dress codes and decorum of colonial Europe, while simultaneously rediscovering rituals and pleasures from the historical capitals of Sukhothai and Ayutthaya. Today the site continues to experiment with new architectural and life styles. It is no surprise then that in addition to the big real estate companies and institutions such as the Crown Property Bureau and Chulalongkorn University responding to the new spatial configurations of the Skytrain, the informal economy has adapted as well.

Food vendors visit wholesale markets in the hours before dawn, and prepare food before the hot sun rises. Early in the morning, the monastery drums, howling of dogs and the call to prayer from the mosques greet the new day. Meditators and merit seekers visit the monastery, while some monks make the rounds to the canalside neighbourhoods to accept food offerings from residents. Mobile vendors are allowed to take up positions on the sidewalks near Skytrain and mall entrances, providing cheap food for the mall workers. When the malls open, most pack up, but motorcycle, tuk-tuk and taxi drivers still swarm in concert with the new mass transit flows. When the malls close, again vendors and sidewalk restaurants appear, and people enjoy food and the cool night air.

In addition to the informal rhythms of life which line the canal and complement the commercial and social activities of the mall, there is a virtual and mobile social network around that is created by both the internet and cell phones. As noted above, all the shopping centres maintain websites in English and Thai languages, and both advertise and guide new visitors to the malls, but also engage residents through club memberships, frequent events and online social networking. Before the Skytrain, it was impossible to move between these few congested blocks by car, but the complementary relationship between the mass transit system and the cell phone, like in Tokyo, allows for spontaneous shifting of social gatherings as friends meet or avoid each other through strategic cell phone calling and text messaging.

Bangkok Simultopia is the setting for new mass consumer desires marketed through a potpourri of historical and contemporary references, situated within a diverse and rich social and ecological context. The monastery complex now shares this stretch of Saen Saeb Canal with four major shopping mall/mixed-use commercial complexes comprising the central shopping district of Bangkok. Surprisingly, the recent profusion of reflective and transparent architectural skins and surfaces come to resemble, more and more, the aesthetic dematerialisation – if not spiritual dimensions – of Wat Pathum Wanaram's glimmering illusionary shutters. Digital screen printing as well as new glass and LED technologies create new luminescent images and reflections back to city inhabitants wandering through the malls or gliding above the city on the elevated Skytrain.

Virtual Itineraries

A virtual itinerary through the websites of the various malls in Bangkok's central shopping district provides another complementary space of online social networking. MBK's website in English guides residents and tourists through a clearly designed site – with pop-up map marking the Skytrain and bus stops, and an online directory which virtually moves up its eight levels – while the Thai-language website reflects the micro-diversity of the mall itself with lots of animated buttons announcing sales, promotions, activities, concerts and an e-shopping mall, a blog, as well as an invitation to join MBK Club.[11] Siam Piwat maintains a slick English-language website which collects Siam Discovery, Siam Center, Siam Tower and the computerised Siam Car Park together with a link to its membership programmes. Members are given an S-Club card for discounts, receive a newsletter and can get a Citibank Discovery Visa card if they qualify. The website offers a Thai language option, a link to activities and movie previews.[12]

Siam Square's website displays a night-time image of the Skytrain taken far from Siam Square itself. Its site – with English-, Thai- and Swedish- language versions – directs tourists to hotels, shopping, history, dining and other helpful links.[13] The Style by Toyota maintains its own stylish website where its giant LED screen is in constant animation with a hip musical background. A text skirts around the virtual building inviting web browsers to 'explore the style'. Rolling your mouse over the menu button shifts the animation and allows online visitors to navigate through the four floors of the building learning about different events. The site is polyglot, mixing English and Thai text rather than maintaining separate language sites.[14] Siam Paragon's website features a night-time view of the square in front of the mall during the dazzling media display in the first televised New Year's celebration in 2006. Geared to a more mature audience, the site offers guidance, orientation, privileges, careers, investment, as well as special services such as 'ambassadors', personal stylists and gift advisors. The general information brags that Paragon is 'beyond precious, beyond peak, beyond performance, beyond perfection, beyond paradise, beyond prestige, beyond premium, beyond phenomenon, beyond pinnacle, beyond passion, and beyond pride – the Jewel of Asia'.[15]

Central World's website appeals to the broader audience it seeks to attract to the 'The Bangkok Lifestyle Landmark'. Colourful advertisements to sales and shops split the screen with product placements. A calendar tells you 'what's happening', in both English and Thai. Buttons link to 'what's new' promotions and events, 'services' include tourist privileges and press tours, 'member zone' allows you to log in or join, 'our location' guides the visitor to the Jewellery Zone, Asian Senses and Balcony on 3rd, and finally there is a contact button for the advertising programme and partnerships. A virtual 3-D model here provides a microscope to scrutinise the urban context, complete with animated trains moving on the BTS lines.[16]

Louis Vuitton anchors Gaysorn Plaza – 'Bangkok's premier lifestyle shopping centre' – whose English and Japanese website describes the shopping centre as 'the home of choice for international high-end brands to showcase their flagship stores. One could say that it is Thailand's very own Champs Elysées'.[17] While Erawan Bangkok's website displays its recent renovation to accommodate fashion and accessories, a wellness and beauty centre and an 'urban kitchen',[18] Amarin Plaza's website announces a 'refreshing new look and our Amarin "Kolors of Style" concept, we are Bangkok's best-kept secret for shopping, dining and entertainment'.[19] Ratchaprasong shopping district maintains its own website with a virtual 3-D model of all the hotels and shopping centres around Ratchaprasong Intersection, from Amarin Plaza to Zen. Roll your mouse over it and click on each building to get a pop-up of information. The group organises the annual New Year Countdown and maintains an archive of photographs since 2005. The elaborate decorative lighting rededicates the intersection the 'Times Square of Bangkok' for a few weeks every year.[20] The Central Department Store website completes our complementary virtual tour of Bangkok's CSD with its multi-screen animations of print and television ads simultaneously running in both English and Thai.[21]

Attentive Circuits

Walter Benjamin has described architecture as experienced in a state of distraction.[22] However, according to Henri Bergson's concept of *attentive recognition*, when we consciously reflect on an object, we summon up a remembered image and superimpose it on the perceived object.[23] Bergson carefully analysed the connection between recognition and attention. To recognise an object is to revive a past memory of it and note its resemblance and presupposes a reflection, an external projection of an actively created image onto an object. Attentive and automatic recognition do not differ qualitatively, in both we summon up a memory image and project it onto the object. In attentive recognition, the object and each memory-image we summon up together form a circuit. As we pay closer attention to the object, we summon up memory-images from broader and more distant past contexts. Deeper, reflective attention represents a higher expansion of memory and deeper layers of reality.

An architectural understanding of circuits of recognition, attention, reflection and memory is evident in the great monastery architecture and planning of Siamese cities. No greater evidence of architecture built to create distraction exists in contemporary themed commercial space. Bangkok seems poised in-between these two conditions of distracted and attentive reflection. The question Bangkok now poses to architects and urban designers is how to make contemporary sensate environments in a world that is more and more mobile, fast-paced and mediated? Contemporary architecture provides a wide array of attention-grabbing forms as well as new materials and technologies. The spectacle of the mediated modern metropolis with its privileges and delights is broadcast to every village in the kingdom of Thailand and neighbouring countries as well, continuing to fuel rural/urban migration.

Street vendors prepare noodle soup for a sidewalk restaurant on Henri Dunant Road.

Wat Pathum Wanaram Temple with Siam Paragon under construction in the background. From left to right are the *vihran*, the principal Buddha hall, the *chedi* or stupa, where the main relics are buried, and the *ubosot*, the ordination hall.

246

The question ecosystem science poses for contemporary architecture and urban design is: how can newly attentive urban citizen be directed to larger systems and process to create new urban models based on new urban experience. The opportunity to connect these worlds as complementary rather than conflicting spaces is everywhere present. In the heart of Bangkok the water gardens of Wat Pathum Wanaram and Khlong Saen Saeb sit beside and behind giant shopping malls which deploy water and media as themes and signs. The malls, shopping and 'lifestyle' centres which constitute Bangkok's central shopping district are no longer following American norms, but are inventing new branded and themed environments where water, Thai culture and exoticism play key roles. The new social space emerging in-between the malls and the websites suggests the possibilities of urban designs which engage the human psyche at multiple levels and sites. The rich past of Siamese urbanism is continually mined for source material to entice the world to an environment of tranquillity, wellbeing and sensual luxury and rural migrants to the informal settlements that line Saen Saeb Canal immediately behind the malls.

Endnotes

1 Brian McGrath, 'Bangkok Simultopia', *Embodied Utopias: gender, social change and the modern metropolis*, edited by Amy Bingaman, Lise Sanders and Rebecca Zorach, London: Routledge, 2002, pp 204–17.

2 Jean Baudrillard, *Simulacra and Simulation*, translated by Sheila Faria Glaser, Ann Arbor: The University of Michigan Press, 1994.

3 Pinraj Khanjanusthiti, *Buddhist Architecture: Meaning and Conservation in the Context of Thailand*, PhD Dissertation, York: University of York Institute of Advanced Architectural Studies, 1996.

4 Roland Bogue, *Deleuze on Cinema*, London: Routledge, 2003, p 118.

5 Sulak Sivaraksa, *A Socially Engaged Buddhism*, Bangkok: The Inter-Religious Commission for Development, 1988.

6 Steward Pickett and Mary Cadenasso, 'Meaning, Model and Metaphor of Patch Dynamics', *Designing Patch Dynamics*, New York: Columbia Books on Architecture, 2008.

7 Félix Guattari, *The Anti-Oedipus Papers*, edited by Stéphane Nadaud, translated by Kelina Gotman, New York: Semiotext(e), 2006.

8 David Grahame Shane, *Recombinant Urbanism*, London: John Wiley & Sons, 2005, p 198.

9 Michel Foucault, 'Nietzsche, Genealogy, History', *Foucault Reader*, edited by Paul Rabinow, New York: Pantheon Books, 1984, p 88.

10 http://www.altoonporter.com/

11 http://www.mbk-center.co.th/en/Profile/Pro.asp

12 http://www.siamdiscoverycenter.co.th/

13 http://www.siam-square.com/

14 http://www.toyota.co.th/thestyle/main.htm

15 http://www.siamparagon.co.th/

16 http://www.centralworld.co.th/

17 http://www.gaysorn.com/

18 http://www.erawanbangkok.com/

19 http://www.amarinplaza.com/

20 http://www.ratchaprasong.or.th/

21 http://www.central.co.th/

22 Walter Benjamin, 'One Way Street', *Reflections*, translated by Edmund Jephcott, edited by Peter Demetz, New York: Harcourt Brace Jovanovich, 1978.

23 Henri Bergson, *Matter and Memory*, translated by NM Paul and WS Palmer, New York: Zone Books, 1991, p 105.

247

Crushing ice on Soi
Kasemsan 1.

Modelling Urban Design Futures in India and China

Informal garment factory in an
urban village, Hangzhou, China.

250 Near the end of the line of the Hangzhou Bus Rapid
Transit (BRT) system, we headed into one of the urban
villages outside the city. We heard a lot about the
problem of urban villages in China for government
officials and city planners. While the utopian fantasies of
Ebenezer Howard's *Garden Cities of Tomorrow* and Le
Corbusier's *Ville Contemporaine* were only partially
realised in the West, in China, all its cities were being
rebuilt to fulfil the Modernist dream of the Master
Planned city. The urban villages of China do not fulfil
ideals of rationality and order mandated from above, but
exist as vital, messy reminders of urban growth initiated
by actors below. In spite of repeated efforts, we were not
able to visit any urban villages on our official trip, so we
took advantage of the new BRT line, modelled on
Curitiba, Brazil, to see this urban problem ourselves.

The narrow road followed an irrigation canal, fouled
with waste and garbage, through some abandoned fields
to the dense cluster of four-storey houses beyond. The
houses were uniform in height, material and design, and
all had miniature copies of the Oriental Pearl TV Tower in
the Pudong district of Shanghai atop a square attic
cupola. A young man was washing his clothes from a
pump along the dirty canal, and the ground water rushing
up was surprisingly clean. The houses formed a neat grid,
and most had ground-floor shops – pool halls, grocery
stores, or small garment and printing factories. Other
ground-floor spaces were used by groups of women to
shell beans, and one storefront accommodated a
Buddhist prayer group – a dozen ancient women chanting
with prayer beads and incense around a table. As we
wandered deeper into the village, we could see that
migrants were renting rooms, not just in the upper floors
of the town homes, but in small one-storey barracks that
surrounded the village. We sat in one such dorm with
some migrants enjoying a sunny afternoon and counted
the 20 bunks with mosquito nets neatly lined up in a
single 100-square-metre room.

Factory 798 in Beijing was transformed from a forested factory complex to an art enclave.

The urban villages economically thrive because of the *hukuo* residency system, in which household registration marks one as either a rural or city inhabitant. Mary-Ann O'Donnell has written that under Mao, urban and rural areas were distinct social and administrative entities. While in urban areas, property was owned by the state, in rural areas, collectives owned property. Until 1980, the *hukuo* required you to stay where you were registered.[1] Urban villages are developed by the rural communes, now as holding companies which distribute shares. As such they are outside the Master Plan of the city, and remain in tension with official urban design protocols. However, Jane Jacobs's *The Death and Life of Great American Cities* was translated into Chinese recently, and the current National City Planning Law mandates reasonableness, participation and harmony. China has begun to realise the enormous problems its planners have created by using only one urban design model for the entire country.

The old cotton mills in the heart of Mumbai mushroomed during the American Civil War, when new sources of cloth for Europe were suddenly needed. The old factories are gated, and suspicious guards discourage unauthorised snooping around given the controversy over the planned redevelopment of the mill lands. The huge area of old factories and workers' housing is to be recycled for new development. While the Mumbai Metropolitan Region Development Authority's Regional Plan for the Mumbai Metropolitan Area for the years 1996 to 2011 includes directives on growth rates, land use, housing and water management, development is proceeding in the city without any specific plan. In spite of much evidence of a vibrant democracy and a strict adherence to the rule of law, India has not demonstrated a capacity to involve reasonableness, participation or harmony in most current urban redevelopment.

Empty cotton mills in the heart of Mumbai are the site of rampant real estate speculation.

The easy demolition of the mills ignores the potential of culturally based uses such as Factory 798 in Beijing. I talked with the manager of Factory 798, who has seen the transformation of this urban work unit from a place of manufacturing to the locus of the Chinese global art scene. The new galleries, bookstores and cafés now support the pension of the factory workers in a neat arrangement rarely seen in the gentrifying post-industrial sites in the West. The tall mature trees dominate the site, planted by the same East German builders who created the magnificent concrete vaulted factory structures. Behind Factory 798, a new industrial site will feature fashion companies and runway shows among the scrubbed coal furnaces and cranes.

This book has presented a design perspective that has been influenced by my experiences of living, working and teaching in the 1980s in both Rome and New York, and for the past decade between New York and Bangkok. Over the past two years I have had the opportunity as a Fellow at the New School's India China Institute (ICI) to participate in a trilateral discussion on globalisation and urbanisation with scholars, activists, professionals and government officials from India, China and the US. This final chapter, with its shifting lenses from Chinese to Indian to American perspectives, draws from this multi-national, cross-disciplinary and collaborative experience. The challenges and opportunities ahead for urban design in India and China are enormous, and some initial observations and questions will be posed in this final concluding chapter. Asian urbanism, as Bangkok serves as a vivid example, is both a radically new contemporary phenomenon, given the scale and speed of urbanisation across the continent, but also exists within a long historical and cultural context of urbanisation which has just begun to be understood from multilateral and indigenous perspectives. This concluding chapter will ask the question how the three methods outlined in this book – archaeological, genealogical and schizoanalytical modelling – might be assimilated in practice and applied as design tools.

Commuters wait outside Kurla Station in Mumbai.

Liberalisation

The rapid pace of urbanisation in China since Deng
Xiaoping's shift to socialist modernisation in 1978 and the
decision to centre the restructuring of the Chinese
economic system on cities in 1984. The resulting pace of
urbanisation is unprecedented in the history of the world.
Even a cursory examination of the results of China's initial
'great leap forward' reveals its new cities are a massive
realisation of the 20th-century Modernist dream of
totalitarian Master Planning. Car dependent and
uniformly based on a single urban design model – a blend
of Ebenezer Howard's *Garden Cities of Tomorrow* and Le
Corbusier's *Ville Contemporaine* – the results of China's
recent urbanisation are currently being redirected and
reevaluated. New urban design models which incorporate
historic preservation, ecological issues, public
participation and experimental architectural design are
emerging in almost every Chinese city. Additionally, in
October 2007, the Ministry of Construction issued a new
urban and rural planning law which now dictates that a
city's Master Plan should be reasonable, should include
public participation and contain a controlling detailed
plan that cannot be revised.[2]

Since Manmohan Singh's economic liberalisation of
1991, India is not just following China's lead, but is closely
examining the urban design results of China's rapid
development. While China is now focusing on the theme
of social harmony to bring more economic development
to the rural interior of the country, India is attempting to
'leapfrog' into the 21st century through high technology
and financial industries and developing the rural along
with the urban. ICI Fellow Aromar Revi sees Indian cities
as sites for serious emerging conflict due to the large
populations of poor and vulnerable people, growing
disparities, limited access to resources, declining State
legitimacy, and the rapidly rising aspirations of the
young.[3] But India, with its institutions of legislative and
judicial checks and balances, is inventing more
fragmentary urban design forms and processes to bypass
the slow process of democracy. Revi sees four necessary
urban transformations: a social transformation for caste,
gender and minority inclusion and empowerment, an
economic transformation where 'markets' work for poor
people, an ecological transformation which balances
ecosystem services between rural and urban demands,
and an institutional transformation leading to a
functioning and responsive decentralised government.

The new highway from Delhi
to Agra.

254   ICI Fellow Yang Yao summarised the many
discussions about democracy in India and China in the
final conference in Beijing on 'Urban Futures'. Indian
democracy with its focus on tolerance and stability in the
face of great diversity is greatly respected in China, but it
cannot be characterised as a liberal democracy. It is
overly politicised, lacks accountability and is marked by a
prevalence of populism. While India is procedure based,
and government gains legitimacy through voting, rule of
law, due process and the right to challenge authority,
China is performance based, where social harmony is
ensured by the perception of government efficiency. The
ability of a local government to improve economic
development while avoiding unrest is the main goal. For
Yang Yao, the question for China is how to move to a
procedure-based democracy, how to go from
ruling to governing?[4]

    What became clear in this exchange is that
democracy is a cultural practice being tested differently
in both India and China at local levels, and that in the 21st
century, it will be Asia that defines what democracy and
capitalism will be. The implications for urban design are
enormous. State-directed Master Planning in both India
and China is being replaced by many competing local
arenas that must adjust development to specific
ecological and social realities in an unpredictable world.
New School Professor Ben Lee told the audience in
Beijing that these are the 'wicked problems' of the 21st
century, and the crisis in higher education is the
specialisation which separates the Humanities and the
Sciences rather than joining them in practical problem
solving in a context of environmental degradation and
urban poverty.[5] Wicked problems are non-linear, socially
complex feedback loops, and urban designs require
collaborative frameworks and continuous reframing.
Digital modelling for urban design can provide important
tools to begin to test new processes and models of
remaking localities.

255

Gentle Arrivals: Fatehpur Sikri and West Lake

The ICI delegation arrived at Delhi Airport from China early in the morning of 24 November 2006, and we were whisked by bus to Agra and a tour of Fatehpur Sikri, the Mughal Emperor Akbar's capital city from 1571 until 1585. A UNESCO World Heritage Site, the city is a three-dimensional maze-like puzzle of red sandstone sprawling over the dry hills of Uttar Pradesh. In fact, the city is said to have been abandoned due to a lack of water. This first encounter with the spatial intricacies of Mughal architecture thrilled and surprised the Chinese Fellows, especially those from Beijing. The shifting axes and great variety of views were in sharp contrast to the relentless symmetry of the Forbidden City. However, Chinese urbanism is not only represented by the absolute order of the Mongol or modern Beijing, and the ICI Fellows received a hint of the subtlety of 13th-century Song Dynasty landscape urbanism at West Lake in Hangzhou.

West Lake offers countless walks among its artificially sculpted landscape of water gardens, causeways, artificial islands, bamboo and cypress forests. Constructing the Hangzhou water body consisted of converting a swamp at the bend of the Qiantang River into a freshwater lake, and the construction of a merchant city at the end of the Grand Canal. Many canals drained though the city, hydrologically connecting the Grand Canal to West Lake and the Qiantang, and a bronze scale model fills a plaza by the Lake, allowing one to wander and imagine the city Marco Polo visited and called the most beautiful in the world. West Lake must be continually dredged to keep it from reverting to a swamp, and each dredging in the past provided an opportunity to create a public amenity which today comprises the famous *Ten Scenes of West Lake*: Dawn on Su Causeway in Spring, Curved Yard and Lotus Pool in Summer, Moon over the Peaceful Lake in Autumn, Remnant Snow on the Bridge in Winter, Leifeng Pagoda in the Sunset, Two Peaks Piercing the Clouds, Orioles Singing in the Willows, Fish Viewing at the Flower Pond, Three Ponds Mirroring Moon and Evening Bell Ringing at the Nanping Hill. The *Ten Scenes* form a vivid example of urban design as attentive circuits outlined in the previous chapter. Sites are revisited at particular moments in time – the day, season – in order to sharpen the senses in relation to subtle environmental changes.

'Silicon Valley in Paradise' is the evocative urban branding of civic boosters in Hangzhou, China which neatly collapses the city's ancient scenic reputation as 'paradise on earth' and promotes its ambition to plug into a new economy that links Palo Alto and Bangalore.[6] While the Southern Song Dynasty (1127–1279) capital carefully crafted a lake-front garden city in the foothills of the Tiantai Mountain scenic area, its recent embrace of the information economy now fuels another Howard *Garden Cities of Tomorrow* imagination. The city of Hangzhou – which means the city across the water – has always been identified by hydrological relationships: politically, economically and aesthetically. Located near the mouth of the Qiantang River, the Grand Canal made Hangzhou accessible to both the Yangtze and Yellow Rivers, ensuring its strategic economic and political position as first a regional capital, seafaring market town, and later the Southern Song Dynasty capital city. Now, economic planners are tuning this fluid imagination to the digital age as the city leverages its physical charms towards a post-industrial future based on branding and lifestyle rooted in a rich historical past.

Prof Wang Xiangrong and Dr Zhang Hao, ecologists from Fudan University in Shanghai, are preparing a plan for the designated greenbelt of the new Hangzhou Master Plan. Their approach marks a significant redirection of urban design in China. The two ecologists recognise the mistake of borrowing Western urban design models. Instead of the uniform green space generally directed to limit sprawl at the perimeter of the city, they have analysed the sensitivities of specific ecological zones in greater Hangzhou. Instead of a Garden City green belt, the plan envisions six sub-ecological regions called eco-belts providing specific ecological services and where human activities are directed towards biological and natural systems conservation. Scientific principles and priorities include: harmonious framework, natural water bodies, eco-agricultural zone, forest, eco housing, wetlands for natural conservation and waste water treatment. They plan not one green belt like Ebenezer Howard, but six eco-zones each with its own ecosystem processes and different features.

World Financial Capitals: Mumbai and Shanghai

Our visits to the National Stock Exchange of India (NSE) and the Shanghai Stock Exchange were both memorable by the remarkable lack of any physical trading activity. Both exchanges run almost invisibly through virtual online trading networks. The difference is that the Shanghai exchange has built a giant, ghostly trading floor in its signature building in Pudong that crystallises the desire to participate in – in fact lead – the 21st-century world, while at the same time needing the symbolic architecture and urban design of the 20th century. Shanghai Pudong New Zone was founded in 1992 in order to create a modern CBD facing the old colonial banks along the Bund. As a special zone, it creates a tax-free area for foreign financial institutions to open local offices. Pudong and Bandra-Kurla Complex are both planned commercial enclaves as Mumbai dreams of being the next Shanghai. The Mumbai Metropolitan Region Development Authority (MMRDA) was appointed as the 'Special Planning Authority' for planning and developing the Bandra-Kurla Complex back in 1977 in order to relieve the development pressures on South Mumbai where the Bombay Stock Exchange, the oldest in Asia, has been located since 1875. The 'G' block in Bandra-Kurla is designated the International Finance and Business Centre and is seen as the Pudong of Mumbai.

According to the MMRDA website, 'The main objective of International Finance and Business Centre (IFBC) planning is to create new office locations of international standards, ensuring easy accessibility and high quality of amenities for employees, safe environment and a distinct character and image. The main users in IFBC are: 'The National Stock Exchange, the securities and exchange board, the Diamond Bourse, Convention and Exhibition Centre, Banking and financial institutions, housing, hotels and amenities, the American consulate and an indoor cricket academy, City Park, and parking for 15,000 cars'.[7] The IFBC includes a direct link to both the western and central railways, new highway and airport. Shanghai's Pudong and Mumbai's Bandra-Kurla Complex are not the only planned Central Business Districts in Asia. As ICI Fellow Adriana Abdenur has pointed out, hundreds of new CBDs are being built as special districts around the world today.[8] Every city with aspirations looks to the skylines of New York, Hong Kong and now Shanghai dreaming of globalisation.

Just across the Mithi River from the IFBC is Dharavi, the sprawling informal settlement that grew from a fishing village in the mangrove swamps to the north of the island city of Bombay, but now located in the centre of modern Mumbai. What is remarkable about Dharavi is how its micro economies are prospering in association with the new economy in parallel with the new financial centre just to the west. Potteries, tanneries, apparel piece work and the recycling of much of Mumbai's solid waste occur here. While the city has been incrementally replacing settlers with new housing, a new plan will replace the entire area with new development. As a result, Dharavi has been the focus of much media attention, including the May 2007 issue of *National Geographic*, a BBC report and YouTube accounts.[9]

Indian architect Prakash M Apte, in the planning blog *planetizen*, says 'Dharavi is not "outside" Mumbai. It is in the heart of it, just across the Bandra-Kurla Complex close to the Mumbai domestic and International airports. Dharavi is not a "shantytown", it is a unique vibrant, thriving cottage industry complex, the only one of its kind in the world where all the raw materials produced and processes (lining cloth, sewing needles & thread, colors & dyes, pigments, skinning, tanning, cutting & tailoring) of the final product (leather bags, fancy ladies' purses) are carried out at the same location and the value added is very high! Families have been engaged in this industry for generations. The very nature of the process of making fine leather goods requires large tracts of open land for the activity. This is in fact the kind of self sufficient, self sustaining "village" community that the Father of the Nation – Mahatma Gandhi – dreamt of and wrote about in his books on the path India should take for its development.'[10]

257

A potter and her children in Dharavi, Mumbai.

New corporate headquarters at the Bandra-Kurla International Finance and Business Centre, Mumbai.

Children in an East Delhi slum
resettlement area.

Governance: Delhi and Beijing

Chen Gang, Vice Mayor of Beijing, appeared at the final ICI conference, 'Urban Futures: People and Planning in India and China' in shirt sleeves. Chinese government officials have abandoned Western suits along with air conditioning as a way to decrease energy consumption. Chen explained that Beijing – a 3000-year-old city that had been the capital of China for 800 years – was planned as a modern city with Russian assistance in the 1950s. With Moscow as its model: ring roads and industrialisation were promoted. Beijing is currently moving its industrial sector and looking to simultaneously fulfil four identities to characterise the city of the future: a National, Global, Cultural and Livable city. The major problem is how to control the population size. The city would like to cap the population at 18 million people, and to plan it like Los Angeles as a cluster rather than concentric city.[11]

Chen argued that while controversy swirls around the symbolic aspects of Beijing – it is accused of being a lab for foreign design – the open design market promotes the technical expertise of local designers. Much more pressing is how to ensure the livelihood of 15 million people. There are estimated to be three million migrant farmers in the city, and education and housing are pressing needs. Some 70,000 new low-rent units are currently planned, but how do farmers adapt to high-rise housing in the city?

Migration and Resettlement

We were able to visit a private migrant school outside Beijing. Rural migrants in China are not able to receive social services such as medical care or education for their children under the *hukuo* residency card system. Non-governmental organisations are struggling to fill that gap. Huang He, Headmaster and founder of Xingzhi School, proudly showed us the converted one-storey brick factory building that is now a migrant school. With playgrounds, an art class, even a computer classroom, the school is fully accredited by the government, but the students when they graduate will have to go back to their home provinces for high school and national examinations for university placement.

New Delhi faces tremendous pressures of migration and millions of informal housing dwellers have been resettled in the periphery of the city. We had a chance to visit one resettlement community in East Delhi and talk to activists at Parivartan – a people's movement that is fighting for the rights of the resettled poor. Parivartan recently used the new Indian Right to Information Act of 2005 to ensure the delivery of food rations to the resettlement community. By gaining access to government records, the non-governmental organisation was able to prove that food had been delivered to local merchants who in turn had been selling it on the black market, telling the residents that the government had not delivered it. This small demonstration in activism and the power of access to information deeply impressed the ICI Fellows from China.

Short- and Long-Term Plans

While New York City has not had a Master Plan for decades, Hangzhou has had three in 25 years. None could be completed, approved or implemented quickly enough to stay ahead of the growth of the city. The Master Plan of 1983 covered an area of 405 square kilometres and cleared the way for the demolition of the old city in order to create a new CBD. It was continually modified before it was finally implemented in 1992. The inherent limitations of the Master Plans of 1983 and 1992 became obvious, and the Master Plan of 1996 covered an area of nearly 900 square kilometres and directed growth to two city subcentres. It was approved by the Ministry of Construction in 2000 and was meant to be effective up to 2010 with an estimated population of fewer than two million people. However, in March 2001, two cities were annexed as new urban districts in Hangzhou; the administration of over 3000 square kilometres required a new Master Plan. Master Plan 2001 was submitted to the State Council for approval and approved in February 2007. City growth has now been directed across the Qiantang River, making the riverfront the new city centre.[12] A new regional ecological plan promises to address the failure of Master Planning to keep up with the speed of change in China.

Goa 2030 also looks beyond traditional Master Planning for urban and rural design insights through a long-term vision based on regional ecological knowledge. Aromar Revi argues that urban and infrastructure systems in India must be designed for the long-run – 50 to 100 years. He believes a sustainability transition is technically, financially and economically viable for India in the next 30 to 50 years, but socio-cultural and institutional obstacles pose larger challenges than technical or economic concerns. Revi proposes to invert conventional planning by designing the ecosystem services first and then locating settlements within the interstices. Long-range planning requires a designed urban and rural integration of energy, water, biomass, mobility, economic and governance systems, and a framework for unbundling risk.[13]

259

Street vendor in Hangzhou.

New Urban Design Models in Asia: Happiness, Harmony and Sufficiency

Rae Kwon Chung, the Director of the Environment and Sustainable Development Division of the United Nations Economic and Social Commission for Asia and the Pacific, greeted our students in Bangkok in January 2008 with a stern critique of the Asian cities which looked to America for urban design models. Chung argued that Asia has a much larger population and much scanter resources than the US, and it is folly for Korea, Thailand and now China to continue to follow the American model. Instead of measuring national development by gross national product, he argues for a happiness equation. Recent government directives for social harmony in China and the Sufficiency Economy in Thailand point to a new direction in Asian urban thinking.

The New York residency of ICI established friendships between Fellows from India and China and the US which were prompted by the ability to talk frankly about generational traumas – the Cultural Revolution in China and the ethnic/religious riots in Mumbai. While there is much merit in the argument for Asian cities not to follow generic American urban models, there was also a great deal of excitement in the first ICI residency at using New York as an urban design model, in particular given its long history of the integration of immigrants and a rich culture of tolerance of difference. This will continue to be an important legacy of the programme. The New York residency also dissolved differences between Fellows through commonalities found after long detailed discussion, especially around the link between the need for legitimacy and accountability through the delivery of government services by the widely different political systems of India and China.

Residencies in India and China were exhaustive, thorough and comprehensive. Comparative observations of the workings of financial institutions such as the stock exchanges of both Mumbai and Shanghai were combined with insights into governmental operations at both the national level in Delhi and Beijing and locally in Hangzhou and Mumbai. Visits with high-ranking officials were accompanied by an immersion into the difficult life worlds of all these cities on the ground. Visits to the NGO Parivartan in a relocation settlement in East Delhi, the Dharavi settlement in Mumbai, a school for migrant children outside Beijing as well as farmer resettlement and migrant factory housing complexes in Hangzhou presented individual human faces to enormous challenges.

But detailed observations and discussions also led to disagreements and highlighted the differences between India and China. China Fellows accused India of being a place of all talk and no action and questioned the ability of civil society and slow democratic processes to keep up with the speed of change. Meanwhile, India Fellows found that in China development has reproduced the environmental problems of 20th-century Western development at a huge scale, through its automobile and fossil fuel dependence. A stratification of disciplines emerged too as a result of the collaborative groups: foreign investment, planning, governance, and marginality – the topics of individual group research – were difficult to integrate by any single discipline. The promise and challenge of the India China Institute is to more substantially bridge these disciplinary and nationality gaps once more, but now based on much more solid knowledge of the enormous challenges both countries face.

Master Plans, Special Districts and Lifestyle brandings are present everywhere in India and China, but it is archaeological, genealogical or schizoanalytical knowledge, analysis and self reflection that is necessary to sort through the debates and conflicts. If urban designers have a role to play, it is as transdisciplinary and transcultural mediators in the conversations around the future of cities in India and China. This is where the three approaches outlined in this book might help – a multi-layered, multi-dimensional and inter-subjective approach based on archaeology, genealogy and schizoanalysis. Instead of Master Planning – even ecologically sensitive design – based on land, or zoning based on bureaucratic controls, or lifestyle branding based on the seduction of consumerism, the layered, temporal and psychological approaches facilitated by digital modelling provide tools for a deeper analysis and engagement by a larger arena of actors. *Digital Modelling for Urban Design* advocates the creation of archives, timelines and multiple personal narratives as the raw ingredients necessary in designing the city.

Endnotes   261

1 Mary Ann O'Donnell, 'Vexed Foundations: An Ethnographic Interpretation of the Shenzhen Built Environment', paper presented at the 'Shenzhen: On and Beyond China's Fastest Growing City' symposium at The New School, New York, 13–15 February 2008.
2 Yao Yang, 'Aspiration and Agency', paper presented at the 'Urban Futures: People and Planning in India and China' conference at Central Academy of Fine Arts, Beijing, 16 June 2007.
3 Aromar Revi, 'Urban Futures: Limits to technological and formal innovation-led change', paper presented at 'Urban Futures', 16 June 2007.
4 Yao Yang, 'The Emergence of Property Rights and the Re-orientation of City Planning', paper presented at 'Urban Futures', 16 June 2007.
5 Ben Lee, opening remarks presented at 'Urban Futures', 16 June 2007.
6 Kathleen Hartford in 'West Lake Wired: Shaping Hangzhou's Information Age', *Chinese Media, Global Contexts*, London: Routledge (in press).
7 http://www.mmrdamumbai.org/planning_ifbc.htm
8 Adriana Abdenur, 'Build and They Shall Come?: Central Business Districts in Beijing and Mumbai', paper presented at 'Shenzhen: On and Beyond China's Fastest Growing City', 13–15 February 2008.
9 http://ngm.nationalgeographic.com/ngm/0705/feature3/index.html
http://news.bbc.co.uk/2/shared/spl/hi/world/06/dharavi_slum/html/dharavi_slum_intro.stm
http://www.youtube.com/watch?v=o9r1lclT9Os
10 http://www.planetizen.com/node/21539
11 Chen Gang, keynote address presented at the 'Urban Futures: People and Planning in India and China' conference, 16 June 2007.
12 Yang Zuojun, 'The Master Planning Practice in Hangzhou City', presentation to India China Institute, 9 June 2007.
13 Aromar Revi, 'Urban Futures: Limits to technological and formal innovation-led change', paper presented at 'Urban Futures', 16 June 2007.

Street vendor in Mumbai.

Glossary

The Glossary is presented in relation to the sequence in which the key concepts of the book are presented.

Introduction

Digital as used in the title and the book refers not only to the technical aspects of computer modelling software, programming and scripting, but also to the broad and accessible array of popular digital technologies: web browsers, workflow software, open-sourcing, outsourcing, offshoring, supply chaining, insourcing, in-forming, and a new generation of digital, mobile, personal and virtual technologies.[1]

Modelling is used in the title and the book in every sense of the word. Designers use the term to refer to a 3-D miniature, this year's new car, and a person who shows off new clothes. A science model is a quantitative demonstration of a theory of how something functions. For policy makers, a model is a picture of how the environment *ought* to be made, a proscription of a 'good' form or a 'fair' process which is a prototype to follow.[2]

Urban design refers to the academic and professional discipline formed between architecture, landscape architecture and urban planning. It includes both the concerns that architects and landscape architects have for the built environment, and the social, economic and policy concerns of planning.

Spectacle/spectacular/spectacularisation is introduced in the sense Guy Debord has popularised it as a reading of an entertainment- and media- centric society lulled into passivity by the dream world of high production value imagery. This book advocates a more active social role for digital modelling, engaging a wider range of people in urban design decision making.[3]

Chapters 1 and 2: Archaeology and War

Archaeology/archaeological modelling Michel Foucault's archaeology of knowledge distinguishes between the formation of statements and the 'non-discursive' formation of environments in order to uncover the relationship between words and environments unique to every era. This book analyses the formation of urban design as a disruptive discipline and a practice and advocates examining urban form as embodying ideas specific to every place and time. *Archaeological modelling* is therefore a method in analysing ruptures in physical urban strata as a way of uncovering what Foucault refers to as the stratification of knowledge.[4]

Archive Creating an archive is the main task of archaeological modelling. This archive is a layered and transparent three-dimensional modelling of all aspects of an urban site that can be uncovered: geological, natural, historical and social.

Artefact An urban artefact is the element of the archaeological archive that persists beyond a single formation of urban strata. As defined by Aldo Rossi, urban artefacts demonstrate the 'intimate and protracted relationship' between urban architecture and its specific site or locus.[5]

Locus refers to the formation of a distinct place over time through close and intimate relations between geography, topography, natural resources, climate, local materials and construction techniques and social practices.

Archaeological archives can be organised into three different kinds of analytical space: collateral, correlative and complementary.

Collateral space is 'an associate or adjacent domain formed from other statements that are part of the same group'.[6] Archives of collateral space focus on successive layering of geological, topographic and historical building information within one limited area. Examples here include the Roman Forum, Manhattan's high-rise business districts and Bangkok's central shopping district.

Correlative space is naturally and reciprocally related linkages between non-adjacent subjects, objects, and concepts.[7] Archives of correlative space are comparisons between related cities and sites. Examples here include the implicit relationship between spaces which celebrate military victory in Rome, capital accumulation in New York and symbolic representations of globalisation in Bangkok.

Complementary space is the creation of non-discursive statements.[8] Archives of complementary space are classified according to mediated ideas or concepts which are applied on top of physical spaces. Examples include the triumphal march and religious processions of Rome, the psychology of speculation in New York and the role of global media images in Bangkok.

Transparent/transparency is used according to the aesthetic description of Gregory Kepes: 'If one sees two or more figures partly overlapping one another, and each of them claims for itself the common, overlapped part, then one is confronted with a contradiction of spatial dimensions. To resolve this contradiction, one must assume the presence of a new optical quality. The figures are endowed with transparency: that is, they are able to interpenetrate without an optical destruction of each other. Transparency, however, implies more than an optical characteristic; it implies a broader spatial order. Transparency means a simultaneous perception of different spatial locations. Space not only recedes but fluctuates in a continuous activity.'[9]

Chapters 3 and 4: Genealogy and Trade

Genealogy/genealogical modelling 'Genealogy is based on the premise that historical institutions and other features of social organization evolve not smoothly and continuously, gradually developing their potential through time, but *discontinuously*, and must be understood in terms of difference rather than continuity as one social formation appropriates and abruptly reconfigures older institution or revives various features of extant social organization by selectively recombining them to suit its own purposes.'[10]

Genealogical modelling operates in two directions:

Descent uncovers the 'unstable assemblage of faults, fissures, and heterogeneous layers that threaten the fragile inheritor from within or from underneath ... The search for descent is not the erecting of foundations: on the contrary, it disturbs what was previously considered immobile; it fragments what was thought unified; it shows the heterogeneity of what was imagined consistent with itself.'[11]

Emergence is 'the moment of arising. It stands as the principle and the singular law of an apparition. As it is wrong to search for descent in an uninterrupted continuity, we should avoid thinking of emergence as the final term of a historical development' ... Emergence is always produced through the generation of forces and the analysis of emergence 'must delineate this interaction, the struggle these forces wage against each other or against adverse circumstances'.[12]

Disturbance ecology introduces a way to look at archaeological ruptures according to ecosystem thinking. In line with this thinking, urban design ruptures are by their nature disturbances to an urban ecosystem, and create pockets or patches of order by displacing, reorganising and resorting energy, matter and people.[13]

Zoning emerged as a key tool for professional urban design practice through its legislated separation of different land uses, its three-dimensional sculpting of urban skylines through set-back laws, and its promotion of public amenities through the incentive of larger allowable bulk to developers.

Schizoanalysis/schizoanalytical modelling Félix Guattari developed schizoanalysis as a tool to uncover the repressive aspects of capitalism in order to create social experiments to recreate human relations with Nature by unleashing the creative capacity of desire. Schizoanalysis primarily analyses human desire released by capitalist consumerism. For Guattari, 'the task of Schizoanalysis is that of learning what a subject's desiring-machines are, how they work, with what syntheses, what bursts of energy, what constituent misfires, with what flows, what chains, and what becomings in each case. This positive task cannot be separated from indispensable destructions, the destruction of ... the structures and representations that prevent the machine from functioning.'[14]

Simultopia is a purposely ambiguous term coined to give meaning to the complex experience of place in late capitalist global cities. While -*topia* means place, *simul-* implies both the Modernist dream of *simultaneity* – the ability to understand multiple actions in one place, and Post-Modern theories of *simulation* and the *simulacra*, which refer to copies without an original. *Simultopia*, therefore, describes the mediated experience of globalisation which includes both the experience of speed, movement, transparency and simultaneity which captivated historical Modernist aesthetics, and revisionist notions of the phenomenology of place which grew in reaction to 'placelessness' of Modernist technological space.[15]

266 **Globalisation** here refers to the disjunctive financial, technological and human flows which have marked the world since the 1980s, and the new cultural imagination thereby unleashed.[16]

Locality varies from Rossi's concept of locus in that it is socially produced rather than emerging out of the 'genius' of a particular place. The production of locality in the era of globalisation is therefore as much about media and image flows as topography or climate.

Disjunction/disjunctive flows Anthropologist Arjun Appadurai finds that the financial, informational, media, technological and human flows in the contemporary age are disjunctive and create the particular cultural dimension of globalisation.[17]

The connective value of urban design is based on its origins in Master Planning such as Sixtus V's radial streets of Rome which connected the dispersed Christian basilicas into an urban system. The impulse to connect nodes in the city continues unquestioned today.

The disjunctive value of urban design has risen in importance in relation to the disjunctive space of flows which Arjun Appadurai has identified as constituting the cultural dimension of globalisation.[18]

The conjunctive value of urban design is a connection in a linguistic or symbolic sense instead of in a physical sense. European kings gained legitimacy for their neoclassical urban design schemes by connecting to the sensibility as well as the construction of Imperial Rome as shopping mall developers create a conjunctive value by symbolic association with global branding and lifestyle.

Endnotes

1 Thomas L Friedman, *The World is Flat: A brief history of the twenty-first century*, New York: Farrar, Straus and Giroux, 2005, Critical Art Ensemble, *Digital Resistance: Explorations in Tactical Media*, Brooklyn: Autonomedia, 2001, p 85.

2 Kevin Lynch, *Good City Form*, Cambridge: MIT Press, 1984, p 277.

3 Guy Debord, *The Society of the Spectacle*, translated by Donald Nicholson-Smith, New York: Zone Books, 1995.

4 Michel Foucault, *Archaeology of Knowledge*, New York: Routledge, 2002.

5 Aldo Rossi, *Architecture of the City*, translated by Diane Ghirardo and Joan Ockman, Cambridge: MIT Press, 1982, p 119.

6 Gilles Deleuze, *Foucault*, translated by Sean Hand, Minneapolis: University of Minnesota Press, 1988, pp 4–6.

7 Ibid, pp 6–9.

8 Ibid, pp 9–12.

9 Gregory Kepes, *The Language of Vision*, Chicago: Theobald, 1944, p 77.

10 Eugene Holland, *Deleuze and Guattari's Anti-Oedipus: Introduction to Schizoanalysis*, London: Routledge, 1999, p 58.

11 Michel Foucault, 'Nietzsche, Genealogy, History', *Foucault Reader*, edited by Paul Rabinow, New York: Pantheon Books, 1984, p 81.

12 Ibid, p 82.

13 Steward Pickett and Mary Cadenasso, 'Meaning, Models and Metaphor of Patch Dynamics', *Designing Patch Dynamics*, edited by Brian McGrath et al, New York Columbia University Books on Architecture, 2008, pp 18–31.

14 Félix Guattari, 'Schizoanalysis', translated by Mohamed Zayani, *The Yale Journal of Criticism*, 11.2 (1998), pp 338/404.

15 Brian McGrath, 'Bangkok Simultopia', *Embodied Utopias: gender, social change and the modern metropolis*, edited by Amy Bingaman, Lise Sanders and Rebecca Zorach, London: Routledge, 2002, pp 204–17.

16 Arjun Appadurai, *Modernity at Large: the cultural dimensions of globalization*, Minneapolis: University of Minnesota Press, 1996.

17 Ibid, pp 178–99.

18 Ibid.

Index

Photographic Credits

272 The author and the publisher gratefully acknowledge the people who gave their permission to reproduce material in this book. While every effort has been made to contact copyright holders for their permission to reprint material, the publishers would be grateful to hear from any copyright holder who is not acknowledged here and will undertake to rectify any errors or omissions in future editions.

Cover image by Brian McGrath

pp 17-19, 23, 25, 27, 29, 55, 58-59, 61-62, 65-69, 70-77, 80-89, 91-99, 100-106, 111-118, 122-132, 135-138, 140, 142-3 145, 147, 149, 152, 154-5, 156, 159, 165, 167, 169, 171, 173, 175, 177, 179, 181, 183, 185, 187, 189, 190-1, 214-5, 217-8, 220-1, 230, 233, 235, 237, 239, 241, 243 illustrations by Brian McGrath

pp 29, 56, 87-88, 109, 193-4, 199-201, 223, 226-7, 229, 230, 233, 235, 237, 241, 243, 250, 246-7, 250-61 photographs taken by Brian McGrath

p 10 The Beijing Organizing Committee for the Games of the XXIX Olympiad (BOCOG)

p 12 Provided by the National September 11 Memorial & Museum at the World Trade Center, Rendering provided by Sauared Design Lab, LLC

p 35 © Redux Pictures Photo by Librado Romero, The New York Times

p 37, 47 Courtesy of the Port Authority of New York and New Jersey and Beyer Blinder Belle Architects & Planners: Renderings by PB

p 39 © Foster & Partners

p 40 © Peterson/ Littenberg Architecture and Urban Design

p 41 © Skidmore, Owings + Merrill

p 41 Courtesy of Richard Meier & Partners, Eisenman Architects, Gwathmey Siegal & Associates and Steven Holl Architects

p 42 Courtesy of United Architects

p 43 © Frederic Schwartz /THINK: Frederic Schwartz, Shigeru Ban, Rafael Vinoly and Ken Smith

pp 44-45 © Studio Daniel Libeskind

p 48 © Silverstein Properties and the World Trade Center Design Team

p 50 © Illustration by Don Foley

p 51 © National Institute of Standards and Technology, US Department of Commerce

pp 78, 203-213 Courtesy of Avery Architectural and Fine Arts Library, Columbia University

DIGITAL
MODELLING